CORRUPTIBLE

"Passionate, insightful, and occasionally jaw-dropping, *Corruptible* sets out the story of the intoxicating lure of power—and how it has shaped the modern world."

—Peter Frankopan, internationally bestselling author of
The Silk Roads: A New History of the World

"We know power corrupts, but how exactly? Is it a quick moral collapse or a slow rot? Dangerous as a drug addiction, power changes both those who have it and those who just want a quick fix. Klaas gives us a new, insightful, and seditious road map to this primal urge to dominate, which, thankfully, not all of us share equally."

—Richard Engel, chief foreign correspondent of NBC News

"The power-hungry don't ask why, they only ask why not. . . . Keeping such people far from the levers of power is at least half the battle, as Brian Klaas explains so well in *Corruptible*—a GPS system for navigating a world increasingly full of illiberal democracies, modernized dictatorships, and populists who care only for power."

—Garry Kasparov, chairman of both the Renew Democracy Initiative
and the Human Rights Foundation and former world chess champion

"A brilliant exploration . . . This book builds Brian Klaas's reputation, offering an essential guide through our world of democratic decay, corruption, and cronyism."

—Dan Snow, bestselling author of *On This Day in History*

CORRUPTIBLE

Who Gets Power and How It Changes Us

Brian Klaas

Scribner

New York   London   Toronto   Sydney   New Delhi

Scribner
An Imprint of Simon & Schuster, Inc.
1230 Avenue of the Americas
New York, NY 10020

Copyright © 2021 by Brian Klaas

First Scribner hardcover edition November 2021

SCRIBNER and design are registered trademarks of The Gale Group, Inc., used under license by Simon & Schuster, Inc., the publisher of this work.

For information about special discounts for bulk purchases, please contact Simon & Schuster Special Sales at 1-866-506-1949 or business@simonandschuster.com.

The Simon & Schuster Speakers Bureau can bring authors to your live event. For more information or to book an event, contact the Simon & Schuster Speakers Bureau at 1-866-248-3049 or visit our website at www.simonspeakers.com.

Interior design by Wendy Blum

Printed in Italy

1   3   5   7   9   10   8   6   4   2

Library of Congress Cataloging-in-Publication Data
Names: Klaas, Brian P. (Brian Paul), 1986– author.
Title: Corruptible: who gets power and how it changes us / by Brian Klaas.
Identifiers: LCCN 2021014213 | ISBN 9781982154097 (hardcover) |
ISBN 9781982154103 (paperback) | ISBN 9781982154110 (ebook)
Subjects: LCSH: Power (Social sciences) | Leadership. | Dictators.
Classification: LCC HN49.P6 .K57 2021 | DDC 303.3—dc23
LC record available at https://lccn.loc.gov/2021014213

ISBN 978-1-9821-5409-7
ISBN 978-1-9821-5411-0 (ebook)

To all the nice, non-psychopaths out there
who should be in power but aren't

CONTENTS

I

INTRODUCTION

Does power corrupt, or are corrupt people drawn to power? Are entrepreneurs who embezzle and cops who kill the outgrowths of bad systems, or are they just bad people? Are tyrants made or born? If *you* were thrust into a position of power, would new temptations to line your pockets or torture your enemies gnaw away at you until you gave in? Somewhat unexpectedly, we can start to find an answer to those questions on two forgotten, faraway islands.

Far off the western coast of Australia, a little speck of land called Beacon Island barely rises above the surrounding sea. Scrubby green grass covers its surface, skirted by beige sand on its triangular coastline. You could just about throw a baseball from one side and hit the ocean on the other. It seems unremarkable, an uninhabited blip of an island with a bit of coral peppering the shallows offshore. But Beacon Island holds a secret.

On October 28, 1628, a 160-foot-long spice ship called the *Batavia* set sail from the Netherlands. The trading vessel was part of a fleet owned by the Dutch East India Company, a corporate empire that dominated global trade. The *Batavia* carried a small fortune in silver coins, ready to be exchanged for spices and the exotic riches that awaited in Java, part of modern-day Indonesia. It carried 340 people. Some were passengers. Most were crew. One was a psychopathic pharmacist.

The ship was organized into a strict hierarchy, "in which the accommodation got more spartan as one moved toward the bow." In the stern, the captain held court in the great cabin, chewing on salted meat as he barked orders to his officers. Two decks below, soldiers were crammed into an unventilated, rat-infested crawl space that would be used to hold spices on the return journey. All on *Batavia* knew their rank.

A few rungs below the captain was a junior merchant named Jeronimus Cornelisz, a down-and-out former apothecary. He'd signed up to sail in desperation after losing everything through a series of personal calamities. Shortly after the sails were first unfurled, he set in motion a plan to reverse his misfortunes. In conjunction with a senior officer, Cornelisz plotted a mutiny. He steered the ship off course in preparation for seizing control in isolated waters. If all went according to plan, he'd take control of the *Batavia* and start a lavish new life, bought with the silver coins in the hold.

It didn't go according to plan.

On June 4, 1629, the wooden hull of the *Batavia* splintered as it crashed full speed into a coral reef in the low-lying Abrolhos Islands off the Australian coast. There'd been no warning, no call to change course. In an instant, it was clear that the boat was doomed. Most of the passengers and crew tried to swim ashore. Dozens drowned. Others tried to cling to what was left of the *Batavia*.

Realizing that nobody would survive unless they were rescued, the captain took control of the emergency longboat and most of the salvaged supplies. With forty-seven others, including the entire senior leadership of the crew, he set off for Java. He promised that they'd soon return with a rescue party. Hundreds were abandoned, with little food, almost no water, and only a faint hope that, someday, someone would return. Nothing grew or lived on the barren island. It was obvious: the survivors were running out of time.

Cornelisz, the would-be mutineer, was among those left behind. There was no longer a seaworthy ship to take over. But he didn't know how to swim, so standing on what remained of the sinking *Batavia* seemed preferable to plunging into the water and frantically splashing his way to the island. For nine days, seventy men, including Cornelisz, occupied a shrinking territory of dry wood. They drank as they contemplated the inevitable.

On June 12, the ship finally broke apart. The surf bashed some of the remaining men against the sharp coral, giving them a quicker end than others who flailed for a few minutes before drowning. Cornelisz somehow survived. He eventually "floated to the island in a mass of driftwood, the last man to escape *Batavia* alive."

When he reached the refuge of soggy sand on what is now Beacon Island, the anarchy and chaos of survival instincts reverted to the established order of hierarchy and status. Though Cornelisz washed ashore ragged and weak, he was still an officer. That meant he was in charge. "The *Batavia* was a highly hierarchical society," the historian Mike Dash says, "and that survived on the island as well." The hundreds marooned on the sparse grasslands of the pitiful island rushed to help their superior. They'd live to regret it. Or at least some would.

Once recovered and replenished, Cornelisz did some quick calculations. The situation was dire. The food, water, and wine that had survived the wreck wouldn't last. The supply wasn't going to expand, he figured, so it was necessary to reduce the demand. The survivors needed fewer stomachs to fill.

Cornelisz started to consolidate power by eliminating potential rivals. Some were sent on foolhardy missions in small boats and then pushed overboard to drown. Others were accused of crimes, a pretext used to sentence them to death. Those grisly executions asserted Cornelisz's authority. But they also provided a useful loyalty test. Men who would kill on his orders were useful. Men who refused were a threat. One by one, the threats were eliminated. Soon, the pretexts disappeared, too. A boy was decapitated to test whether a sword was still sharp. Children were murdered for no reason. The killings were done on Cornelisz's orders, but he didn't murder anyone himself. Instead, he displayed his dominance by dressing himself in fine garb from the ship: "silk stockings, garters with gold laces, and . . . suchlike adornments." The others wore soiled rags as they waited their turn to be murdered.

By the time the *Batavia*'s captain returned with a rescue mission months later, more than a hundred people had been killed. Cornelisz finally got a taste of his own island justice: He was sentenced to death. His hands were cut off. He was hanged. But the gruesome episode raises a disturbing question about humanity: If Cornelisz hadn't been on board, would the massacres have been avoided? Or would they just have been led by someone else?

Four thousand miles east of Beacon Island, on the other side of Australia, lies another deserted island, in the Tongan archipelago, called 'Ata. In 1965, six boys, ages fifteen to seventeen, ran away from their boarding school. They stole a fishing boat and started sailing north. On the first day, they only made it five miles before they decided to drop anchor and rest for the night. As they tried to sleep, a strong storm tossed around their twenty-four-foot boat, ripping away the anchor. The gale-force winds soon snapped the sail and destroyed the rudder, too. When daylight broke, the boys had no way to steer, no way to navigate, and were adrift on the mercy of ocean currents. For eight days, they coasted south, completely unaware of which direction was home.

As the six teenagers began to lose hope, they spotted a looming splash of green in the distance. It was 'Ata, a craggy island covered with dense vegetation. With limited ability to steer their damaged fishing boat, the boys waited until they drifted near the shore and abandoned ship. They swam to save their lives. It was their last hope before they were swept out to the unforgiving open ocean. At last, they made it, cut up from the rocks, but alive.

The cliffs that lined 'Ata had made it challenging to clamber ashore, but they turned out to be the young castaways' saving grace. The jagged rocks made perfect roosts for seabirds, and the boys began working together to trap them. With no fresh water to be found, they improvised and drank seabird blood. After foraging around their new home, they upgraded to coconut juice. Eventually, their meals went from raw to cooked as they started their first fire. The boys agreed to keep constant watch over the simmering flames, ensuring that it would never die out. Each boy took his turn tending the embers, twenty-four hours a day. This lifeline allowed them to cook fish, seabirds, even tortoises.

Their living standards improved further through collaboration. The boys worked together for four days to tap into the roots of one of the island's larger trees, collecting fresh water one drip at a time. They hollowed out tree trunks to collect rainwater. They made a primitive house out of palm fronds. Every task was shared. There was no leader. There was no gold lace or stockings. There were no barked orders, no plots to consolidate power, no murders. As they conquered the island, their successes—and failures—were divided evenly.

Six months into being castaways, one of the boys, Tevita Fatai Latu, slipped and fell during his daily seabird hunt and broke his leg. The other five boys rushed to help him, using the traditional Tongan method of heating coconut stalks to create a splint, immobilizing the bone back in place. For the next four months, Tevita couldn't walk, but the other boys took care of him until he could again help with daily chores.

At times, there were disputes. (Tempers will occasionally flare whenever you stick six people together 24-7 with a menu that largely consists of seabirds and turtles.) But when an argument broke out, the boys had the good sense to simply move apart. Those who were at loggerheads would isolate in different parts of the island, sometimes for up to two days, until they cooled down and could again work together to survive.

After more than a year, they began to accept that their new life wasn't temporary. So, they settled in for the long haul, passing the days by fashioning crude tennis racquets and holding competitions, arranging boxing matches, and exercising together. To avoid depleting their stocks of birds to eat, they agreed to a daily limit per person and began trying to plant wild beans.

Fifteen months after the boys were shipwrecked, an Australian named Peter Warner was puttering along in his fishing boat, searching for places to catch crayfish. As he approached an uninhabited island, he spotted something unusual. "I noticed this burnt out patch on the cliff face, which is an unusual thing in the tropics because bushfires don't start in that humid atmosphere," Warner, now eighty-nine years old, recalls. Then, something astonishing came into view, a naked boy sporting fifteen months' worth of hair. The boys whooped and waved palm leaves hoping to catch the boat's attention. When the boat got close enough, the boys jumped into the ocean and began swimming toward the rescue that they never thought would come. Unsure of what was happening, Warner wondered whether the boys had been banished to the island as prisoners, a punishment reserved for the worst of the worst in Polynesian society. "I was a little bit alarmed at the sight of these healthy-looking teenagers with no clothes on them, no haircut," he tells me. Warner loaded his rifle and waited.

When they reached the boat, the boys politely explained who they were. Warner had no idea that any boys had gone missing, so he radioed to an operator and asked them to call the boys' school in Tonga to verify their story. Twenty minutes later, the tearful operator informed Warner that the boys had been missing, assumed dead, for well over a year. "Funerals have been held," the operator said. The boys were brought back to Tonga and reunited with their families. In the aftermath of their rescue, the oldest boy, Sione Fataua, traded his anxieties about survival for his worries about returning home: "A few of us had girlfriends. Perhaps they won't remember?"

As the Dutch historian Rutger Bregman put it, "The real *Lord of the Flies* is a tale of friendship and loyalty; one that illustrates how much stronger we are if we can lean on each other." For Warner, who still regularly sails with one of the boys from the castaways, the entire episode provides "a great boost for humanity."

Two desert islands, two conflicting visions of human nature. In one, a single power-hungry individual consolidated control over others to exploit and kill them. In the other, egalitarian teamwork prevailed and cooperation reigned supreme. What accounts for the difference?

Beacon Island had structure. It had order. It had rank. It ended in tragedy. 'Ata, on the other hand, was a jagged and vertical hunk of rock, but the society carved out by those boys over fifteen months was completely flat. These conflicting desert-island tales raise difficult questions. Are we doomed to exploitation because of bad humans or because of bad hierarchies? Why does the world seem to be full of so many Cornelisz-style leaders in positions of authority and so few like the boys on 'Ata?

And, if you and your coworkers ended up stranded on a desert island, would you overthrow the boss and work together as equals to solve problems like the Tongan teenagers? Or would there be a bloody struggle for power and dominance like there was on Beacon Island? How would you behave?

This book answers four main questions.

First, do worse people get power?

Second, does power make people worse?

Third, why do we let people control us who clearly have no business being in control?

Fourth, how can we ensure that incorruptible people get into power and wield it justly?

For the past decade, I've been studying these questions across the globe, from Belarus to Britain, Côte d'Ivoire to California, Thailand to Tunisia, and Australia to Zambia. As part of my research as a political scientist, I interview people—mostly bad people who abuse their power to do bad things. I've met with cult leaders, war criminals, despots, coup plotters, torturers, mercenaries, generals, propagandists, rebels, corrupt CEOs, and convicted criminals. I try to figure out what makes them tick. Understanding them—and studying the systems they operate in—is crucial to stopping them. Many were crazy and cruel, others kind and compassionate. But all were unified by one trait: they wielded enormous power.

When you shake hands with a rebel commander who committed war crimes or have breakfast with a ruthless despot who tortured his enemies, it's startling how rarely they live up to the caricature of evil. They're often charming. They crack jokes and smile. At first glance, they don't appear to be monsters. But many were.

Year after year, I've struggled with haunting puzzles. Are the torturers and war criminals a different breed altogether, or are they just more extreme versions of the petty tyrants we occasionally encounter in our offices and neighborhood associations? Are there would-be monsters hiding among us? In the right circumstances, could *anyone* become a monster? If that's the case, then the lessons learned from bloodthirsty despots could be useful for reducing smaller-scale abuses in our own societies. It's a particularly urgent puzzle to solve because we're constantly disappointed by those in power. Tell anyone you're a political scientist and a question often follows: "Why are so many horrible people in charge?"

But another puzzle keeps demanding an answer: Were these people *turned* awful by the power they held? I've had my doubts. Another possibility has gnawed at me: that those who seemed to be made worse by power are just the tip of the iceberg. Perhaps something much bigger and more serious is lurking beneath the waves, waiting to be discovered, so we can fix it.

Let's start with the conventional wisdom. Everyone has heard the famous aphorism "Power corrupts, absolute power corrupts absolutely." It's widely believed. But is it true?

A few years ago, I was in Madagascar, a sprawling red-earthed island off the coast of Africa. Everybody knows Madagascar for its lovable ring-tailed lemurs, but it's home to an equally interesting species: corrupt politicians. The island is largely governed by crooks who cash in as they rule over 30 million of the poorest people on the planet. Buy a latte and a muffin and you've just spent a week's wages for the average person in Madagascar. To make matters worse, the rich often prey on the poor. And I was there to meet one of the richest men in Madagascar: the island's yogurt kingpin, Marc Ravalomanana.

Ravalomanana grew up destitute. At the age of five, to help his family survive, he'd load up baskets with watercress and peddle them to passengers on a dilapidated train that passed by his school. One day, he caught an unexpected break: a neighbor gave him a bicycle. Young Marc started cycling to nearby farms to ask for excess milk, which he'd turn into homemade yogurt. As he built his fledgling business, he tried to give back to his struggling community. When he wasn't volunteering at the local church or singing in its choir, he hawked the yogurt off the back of that rickety bicycle, growing his business pot by pot and year by year.

By the late 1990s, he'd become the island's dairy baron and one of Madagascar's richest men. In 2002, he became President Ravalomanana, a shrewd politician who understood the value of a rags-to-riches story in a country where just about everyone was still in rags. As president, he promised change. Initially, he delivered. His government invested in roads, cracked down on corruption, and rooted out poverty with sky-high economic growth. Madagascar became home to one of the fastest-growing economies in the world. It appeared to be a success story, an against-the-odds parable that good people from humble beginnings make wise, just rulers.

I decided to pay Ravalomanana a visit. When I arrived at his palatial house, he walked out of the front door sporting a navy blue Nike track-suit with a white stripe down the side. Beaming, he shook my hand and led me inside. He showed off his workout room, where he'd been doing calisthenics since 5:00 a.m. ("It's the only way to keep your mind sharp enough to make important decisions," he told me). Then, he pointed out his custom-made decorative shrine to Jesus, a sort of model-train version of Bethlehem with a large wooden cross overlooking the minia-turized town. We went upstairs, and at the end of a corridor, he threw open large mahogany double doors. An enormous table was behind them. Every inch was covered with food, piles of warm croissants, eggs prepared every possible way, five kinds of juices, and enough yogurt to feed his childhood village for a week. The days of poverty and watercress were long gone.

Even though Ravalomanana's chief of staff joined us, only two places were set, one for him, and one for me. I sat down, opened my notebook, and reached for my pen, only to realize I'd forgotten it.

"No problem," Ravalomanana said. "We may be poor, but we have pens."

He picked up a small bell next to his fork and shook it. Within sec-onds, two employees raced into the room, each hoping to be first to the table.

"Pen," Ravalomanana barked.

The two men hurried off. Both returned within thirty seconds, each clutching a brand-new ballpoint, competing for praise. The slower man looked dejected when he didn't get it.

That's when Ravalomanana got down to business. He was preparing to launch his bid to retake the presidency in the upcoming election. He looked intently at me.

"I saw from Google that you have experience advising campaigns," he said. "Tell me, what should I do to win mine?"

The question caught me off guard. I was there to study him, not advise his campaign. But I wanted to establish rapport, so I improvised. "Well, when I helped manage a campaign for governor back home in Minnesota, we came up with an effective sort of gimmick. We visited all eighty-seven counties in eighty-seven days, to show we cared about the whole state. There are one hundred nineteen districts in Madagascar. Why don't you do one hundred nineteen districts in one hundred nineteen days?"

He nodded, signaling that I should continue.

"You could wrap it up with your rags-to-riches image. Just ride a bicycle through each town to remind people of your childhood selling yogurt while showing that you understand what it's like to be poor."

He nodded, turned to his chief of staff, and said, "Buy one hundred nineteen bicycles."

Ravalomanana was no stranger to winning elections with unusual tactics. He had no qualms breaking the rules, either. In 2006, he was favored to win reelection, but was unwilling to leave anything to chance. He rigged the election with a novel tactic: forcing his main opponent into exile and then blocking him from returning home to register his candidacy. Every time his rival tried to return to Madagascar, Ravalomanana picked up the phone and ordered all the airports on the island closed, causing the aircraft carrying his opponent to turn back. It worked. The rival wasn't allowed to register from abroad, so he was left off the ballot. Ravalomanana won in a landslide.

In 2008, Ravalomanana—a man of humble beginnings, church choirs, and charity volunteering—got greedy. After six years in power, it seemed that something had changed inside him. In a country where the average person earned a few hundred dollars per year, he used $60 million of state funds to buy a presidential aircraft (somewhat ambitiously named Air Force Two). He tried to license the aircraft to himself, rather than to Madagascar's government. Year after year in power, his corruption seemed to grow worse and worse.

Eventually, it would prove his downfall. In 2009, an upstart radio DJ turned politician organized protests against President Ravalomanana. The former DJ took to the airwaves to egg on the peaceful protesters as they marched to the presidential palace. As they arrived, soldiers defending the yogurt kingpin opened fire. It was a bloodbath. Hundreds were shot. Dozens were killed. People were outraged. Not long after the blood was cleaned from the streets, Ravalomanana was toppled in a coup d'état, a military takeover that put the radio DJ in power.

Perhaps the conventional wisdom is right: power does corrupt. Ravalomanana the five-year-old dreamed only of upgrading from watercress to yogurt. His business played by the rules. He wasn't violent. He helped others, not himself. Taking control of the island, it seems, somehow altered him. It made him worse. But perhaps it wasn't Ravalomanana's fault. In the end, the DJ president may have become more corrupt than the dairy baron he replaced. Maybe if you, or I, were suddenly made the president of a notoriously corrupt island, we would become corrupt ourselves. It'd just be a matter of time.

Sometimes, though, the conventional wisdom has got it all wrong. What if power doesn't make us better or worse? What if power just *attracts* certain kinds of people—and those people are precisely the ones who shouldn't be in charge? Maybe those who most want power are least suited to hold it. Perhaps those who crave power are corruptible.

If you've ever read a pop psychology book or watched a documentary about prisons, odds are pretty high that you've heard of a notorious study that seemed to suggest power does indeed corrupt. There's just one problem: everything you think you know about that study is wrong.

Late in the summer of 1971, Philip Zimbardo, a researcher at Stanford University, built a fake jail in the basement of the psychology department. He recruited eighteen college students as participants in a quasi-scientific experiment aimed at determining whether social roles can transform the behavior of normal people beyond recognition. The hypothesis was simple: Human behavior is surprisingly chameleonlike. We match the role we have, or the uniform we wear.

To test whether that was true, Zimbardo randomly assigned nine of the volunteer participants to be "guards." The other nine became "prisoners." For $15 per day for two weeks, they were to live out an all-too-real criminal-justice role play. What happened next is now infamous. The guards almost immediately began abusing the prisoners. They attacked them with fire extinguishers. They took away their mattresses and forced them to sleep on the concrete floor. They stripped their peers naked just to show who was boss. Power, it seemed, had made them awful.

Deprived of control, the prisoners transformed from proud, outgoing college students into insular and submissive shadows of their former selves. In one harrowing moment, a guard who had already been abusive toward his fellow college students lined up the prisoners to humiliate them.

"In the future, you do work when you're told."

"Thank you, Mr. Correctional Officer," a prisoner replies.

"Say it again."

"Thank you, Mr. Correctional Officer."

"Say, 'Bless you, Mr. Correctional Officer.'"

"Bless you, Mr. Correctional Officer."

The study was supposed to continue for two weeks. But when Zimbardo's girlfriend visited the fake jail and saw what was happening, she was horrified. She convinced him to shut the experiment down after six days. When the findings were published, it shocked the world. Documentaries were made. Books were written. The evidence seemed clear: Demons are within all of us. Power just lets them come out.

But there was a catch. The seemingly straightforward narrative of the Stanford Prison Experiment, which had become conventional wisdom in psychology, wasn't so clear-cut. Only some of the guards were abusive. Several resisted and treated the student prisoners with respect. So even if power does corrupt, are some people more immune than others?

Plus, a few prisoners and guards now say they were just putting on a performance. They believed the researchers wanted to see a show, so they gave them one. A recently unearthed audio recording of the experiment's preliminary phase has raised questions about whether the participants were coached to be harsh toward prisoners, rather than spontaneously becoming nasty. So, the picture is a bit murkier than we were led to believe. But even with those caveats, the experiment is harrowing. Ordinary people, if put in the right conditions, can become cruel and depraved. Are we all just sadists waiting to be unmasked once we get control over others?

The answer, thankfully, is probably not. Zimbardo's conclusions didn't take into account a crucial aspect of the study: how the participants were recruited. To find prisoners and guards, researchers placed this ad in the local newspaper:

> Male college students needed for a psychological study of prison life. $15 per day for 1–2 weeks beginning August 14th. For further information and applications, contact . . .

In 2007, researchers at Western Kentucky University noticed a small, seemingly insignificant detail about that ad. It made them wonder whether it had inadvertently skewed the study. To find out, they replicated that ad, only changing $15 to $70 (to adjust for inflation since the 1970s). Every other word in the updated ad was identical. Then, they created a new ad. It was the same in every way, with one key difference: it replaced the line "for a psychological study of prison life" with the phrase "for a psychological study." In some college towns, they placed the "prison life" advertisement. In others, they placed the "psychological study" ad. The idea was to have one group that volunteered for a prison experiment and another group that volunteered for a generic psychology study. Would there be any difference between the people who responded?

Once the recruitment period closed, the researchers invited the prospective participants in for psychological screening and a thorough personality evaluation. What they found was extraordinary. Those who responded to the prison experiment advertisement scored significantly higher on measures of "aggressiveness, authoritarianism, Machiavellianism, narcissism, and social dominance and significantly lower on dispositional empathy and altruism" compared to the generic study. Just by including the word *prison* in the advertisement, they ended up with a disproportionately sadistic batch of students.

That finding could invert the conclusions of the Stanford Prison Experiment in ways that fundamentally transform our understanding of power. Instead of demonstrating that ordinary people thrust into power can become sadistic, it may demonstrate that sadistic people seek out power. Maybe we've had it backward. Maybe power is just a magnet for bad people rather than a force that turns good people bad. In that formulation, power doesn't corrupt—it attracts.

But there's still another mystery. Even if people ill-suited to power are drawn to it, why do they seem to attain it so easily? After all, in modern societies, a significant amount of control isn't taken, but *given*. CEOs don't engage in gladiator-style combat with midlevel managers to reach the corner office. Craven and corrupt politicians, at least in democracies, need to get ordinary people to support them to take charge. The recent revelations about the Stanford Prison Experiment raise the possibility that bad people are drawn to power. But what if we, as humans, are also somehow drawn to giving power to the wrong people for the wrong reasons?

In 2008, researchers in Switzerland conducted an experiment to test that hypothesis. They recruited 681 local children—all between the ages of five and thirteen. The kids were asked to play a computer simulation in which they had to make decisions about a ship that was about to embark on a voyage. Each child had to select a captain for their digital ship based on two faces that appeared on-screen. No other information was given. This was designed to force the children to decide: Who *looks* like a good captain to you? Who appears as if he or she would make an effective leader of your imaginary ship?

What the kids didn't know was that the two possible captains weren't a random assortment of people. Instead, they were politicians who had competed in recent French parliamentary elections. The pairs of faces were randomly assigned to the children, but each pair they saw contained the winner of an election and the runner-up. The results of the study were astonishing: 71 percent of the time, the children picked as their captain the candidate who'd won the election. When the researchers ran the same experiment with adults, the researchers were astonished to see nearly identical results. The findings were remarkable on two fronts. First, even children can accurately identify election winners based on faces alone, highlighting how superficial our assessments of leadership potential can be. Second, children and adults don't have radically dissimilar cognitive processing in picking people to be in charge. It gave fresh meaning to the phrase taking someone *at face value*. As further evidence that our powers of leadership selection are flawed, several other studies have shown that those who are more aggressive or rude in group discussions are perceived as being more powerful and leader-like than those who are more cooperative or meek.

Yes, this is already getting complicated. Power might corrupt good people. But it also might attract bad people. And maybe we, as humans, are somehow drawn to bad leaders for bad reasons.

Unfortunately, the complexity is just beginning. There's another wrinkle to consider. What if people in power do bad things not because they're a bad person to begin with, and not because they turn bad after taking power, but because they're stuck in a bad system? That idea makes a lot of sense. After all, playing by the rules might get you promoted in Norway, while it guarantees that you'll never attain power in Uzbekistan. That helps explain why *some* people in positions of authority are genuinely wonderful—out to help others rather than helping themselves. The allure of power and the effects of being in charge may therefore depend on the context. Thankfully, contexts and systems can be changed. That provides a bit of good news: perhaps we're not doomed to a world in which abusive Cornelisz-style leadership is inevitable. Perhaps we can fix it.

One study conducted in Bangalore, India, provides some evidence for that optimistic view. The researchers wanted to see what kinds of people were drawn toward government careers in a place where the public sector is known for graft and bribery. India's civil service provided a good testing ground, as it's infamous for rampant corruption. Everybody knows that becoming a government official in Bangalore provides opportunities to take home some off-the-books pay. In the experiment, designed by two economists, hundreds of university students were asked to roll standard dice forty-two times and record the results. As with all dice, it was just down to luck. Before they rolled the dice, however, the students were told that they'd be paid more if they had some good fortune and rolled higher numbers. More fours, fives, and sixes would lead to more cash.

But because the results were self-reported, students could lie about their dice rolls. Many did. The number six was recorded 25 percent of the time, while the number one was recorded only 10 percent of the time. With statistical analysis, the researchers could be sure that such skewed results couldn't possibly have been due to chance. A few students were even so brazen as to claim that they rolled sixes no fewer than forty-two times in a row. But there was a twist in the data: the students who cheated in the experiment had different career aspirations from those who reported scores honestly. Those who self-reported bogus high scores were much more likely than the average student to say that they aspired to join India's corrupt civil service.

When another team of researchers ran a similar experiment in Denmark—a country where the civil service is clean and transparent—the results were inverted. Students who self-reported their scores honestly were far more likely to aspire to be civil servants, while those who lied were the students who sought other professions that could make them filthy rich. A corrupt system attracted corrupt students, and an honest system attracted honest students. Perhaps it's not about power changing people, but rather about the setting. A good system can create a virtuous circle of ethical power seekers. A bad system can create a vicious cycle of people willing to lie, cheat, and steal until they reach the top. If that's the case, then our focus shouldn't be on powerful individuals—it should be on repairing our broken systems.

We're left with a series of possible solutions to our exasperatingly complex puzzles. First, power makes people worse—power corrupts. Watercress becomes a yogurt empire, and before you know it, you're rigging elections and buying airplanes with money that isn't yours. Second, it's not that power corrupts, but rather that worse people are drawn to power—power attracts the corruptible. The psychopathic pharmacists can't resist climbing a doomed ship's hierarchy, and the sadists can't resist the allure of slipping on a uniform and beating a prisoner with a baton. Third, the problem doesn't lie with the power holders or power seekers, it's that *we* are attracted to bad leaders for bad reasons, and so we tend to *give* them power. Our captains— and not just of imaginary ships—are selected for irrational reasons. When they crash us into rocky reefs, we have only ourselves to blame. And fourth, focusing on the individuals in power is a mistake because it all depends on the system. Bad systems spit out bad leaders. Create the right context and power can purify instead of corrupting.

These hypotheses are potential explanations for two of the most fundamental questions about human society: Who gets power and how does it change us? This book provides answers.

II

THE EVOLUTION OF POWER

What are we? Humans? Or animals? Or savages?

William Golding, Lord of the Flies

Of Chimps and Children

Before we dive into questions of who seeks power, who gets it, and whether it changes us, we have to zoom out a bit first. There's a more fundamental question. Why do we, as humans, set up our societies in a way that inevitably makes a small group of people powerful and a large group of people powerless?

Let's return to the tale of the two desert island shipwrecks. The juxtaposition between the doomed *Batavia* and the stranded Tongan boys of 'Ata doesn't just provide a puzzle related to human nature. It also raises a question that we rarely think about: Why do hierarchies exist? Rank and status define so much of our daily existence that we never pause and imagine the alternative. But what if relationships between people were mostly flat and equal, rather than a series of top-down arrangements of bosses and generals and coaches and presidents? Sure, it sounds a bit like the fever dream of an anarchist-Marxist collective at a bourgeois liberal arts college. But if you gaze back far enough into history, that seemingly utopian world free from hierarchy was precisely what it was like for many humans for most of the time that our species has graced the planet. To understand our present, we need to travel back in time.

Between 3.5 and 4.5 billion years ago, if you wanted to visit your ancestors for a family reunion, you would've had to travel deep into the ocean to find a steaming-hot deep-sea vent. In the scalding temperatures created by magma flowing out of the earth's crust, you could bond with a single-celled organism over its being not just your ancestor—but also the ancestor of everything currently alive on the planet. Its name is LUCA, the Last Universal Common Ancestor. And we share it with every bird, every sea urchin, every slime mold. Through LUCA, all life on earth is related. But it doesn't tell us much about ourselves.

Fast-forward a few billion years, and you could meet the somewhat more difficult-to-pronounce furry forefather of the human family, called CHLCA, or Chimpanzee-Human Last Common Ancestor. It'd certainly be easier to recognize than the single-celled LUCA—CHLCA represents the last moment in which our predecessors were indistinguishable from chimpanzees. On the branches of hominid evolution, gibbons broke off first, then orangutans, then gorillas, and finally we split from chimpanzees somewhere between 4 million and 13 million years ago.

Even after millions of years of evolution, we remain closely related to chimpanzees. Modern humans share 98.8 percent of our DNA with chimps (though that statistic does sound *slightly* less impressive when you realize that we also share 80 percent of our DNA with dogs and 50 percent with bananas). Still, there's a reason why you feel as if you recognize a spark of humanity when you watch chimpanzees playing or taking care of their young or, indeed, when you see them in displays of dominance and submission. In many ways, they're like us.

These similarities present a seductively simple hypothesis: if you want to understand how humans relate to power, status, and hierarchy, maybe you can just look at chimpanzees. If they're our closest animal relative, perhaps we can understand ourselves by understanding them. On the other hand, if chimpanzees follow a law of the jungle in which the biggest, physically strongest chimps rule and the smallest, physically weakest chimps get ruled, then we have a problem. That model doesn't take us far in explaining, for example, Angela Merkel.

Decades ago, a Dutch primatologist named Frans de Waal noticed that the social structures of chimpanzees were far more complicated than was previously known. To be in charge, a chimpanzee certainly needed to be large and physically strong. But it wasn't guaranteed that the biggest chimp would always become the most powerful chimp. Instead, aspiring leaders had to build alliances, curry favor with kingmakers, and distribute resources. Those who did climb their way into the alpha male position had no job security. Usurpers were always waiting for a moment of weakness so they could form their own coalitions and topple him. The dynamics of chimpanzee hierarchies were so sophisticated that de Waal began to see those interactions as distinctly political. He wrote his seminal work, *Chimpanzee Politics*, in 1982.

The book was controversial. It ascribed intentionality and strategic social planning to animals, something that was assumed to be unique to humans. There was plotting, scheming, and coalition building. Weak chimps could form pacts to offset the power of strong chimps. Clever chimps could outwit their rivals. De Waal even describes chimpanzee coups d'état, brewing for days, but executed with precision in an instant. Regardless of which group of chimpanzees de Waal observed, there was always a question of status. And that status was defined by some chimps relentlessly pursuing power over others. Hierarchy was inescapable. As with the *Batavia*, chimps always knew their rank.

"Chimpanzees—all chimpanzees, including females—are very much into power," de Waal tells me. "You cannot deal with a chimp without him or her trying to dominate you and trying to intimidate you, just to see how you react. They are always going to test you. They always want to see where they stand relative to you. And if they perceive some weaknesses, they're going to push you as they try to get the upper hand."

But as much as power influences the behavior of chimpanzees, it isn't their sole consideration. Just like some humans, some chimps are irresistibly drawn to power. Others try their hand at dominance, but don't mind ending up as followers. "The drive to reach the top, which is a very risky business, is not present in all of them," de Waal says. "You may have very large males who are happy with position number three, for example." This complexity seems familiar to us. Some of us seek power. Others shy away from it and move aside to let others lead. Score one point for the theory that chimps and humans are astonishingly alike when it comes to seeking, getting, and wielding power.

That is, in some ways, a disturbing prospect. After all, most chimpanzees can't seem to escape their drive to at least try to dominate others. In a 1964 study, chimps that were isolated at birth and raised outside any social structure still behaved in ways associated with displays of social dominance. Hierarchy, power, and domination seem to be just part of being a chimpanzee. Does our shared genetic code doom us to the same obsessions?

Not quite. Despite our being 98.8 percent similar genetically, that 1.2 percent of our DNA that separates us from chimps is packed full of key differences. In the billions of A's, C's, G's, and T's that make us who we are, around 15 million letters depart from the chimpanzee script. Many of those changes are meaningless, transcription errors that have had no discernible effect on our biology. That's because not all DNA base pairs are equal. Some are crucial, providing a blueprint to make sure we have two arms and that those arms are attached to our upper torso rather than sprouting out of our head. Others are just junk.

In the early 2000s, Katherine S. Pollard, a computational biologist, set out trying to figure out which of those 15 million letters that separated us from chimps mattered. To do so, she followed a simple logic: over millions of years, some aspects of our genome have changed considerably from our last common ancestor with chimpanzees; others are unchanged. Surely, if you could identify which parts of the genome have changed the most—which were the biggest outliers—you could unlock the secret to what makes us human.

But there was an evolutionary twist. Minor variations were most likely to be the result of random mutations. They were the junk, the meaningless accidents. But any major changes wouldn't be accidental. Any genetic code that was changing faster than the speed of random mutation was being "selected." In other words, those changes provided our quasi-human ancestors with a better chance of survival. Because it helped them survive, the helpfully rewritten snippet of DNA became more likely to be passed on to future generations. In that elegant way, useful genetic innovations were "sped up." If Pollard could find the snippets that had "accelerated" the most, she could see precisely how we had evolved from our primate ancestors.

In November 2004, Pollard sat down with her computer code, clicked a mouse, and pinpointed millions of years of genetic divergence: 118 bases of DNA that combined to form something now known as HAR1, the human accelerated region. HAR1 switches on during our brain development. If something goes wrong with HAR1, the brain can go haywire, even degenerate in deadly ways. Pollard had found many of the key base pairs that made us different from chimpanzees.

But it isn't enough to know *where* we differ. We need to know *how* we differ. When it comes to our behavior, what separates us from monkeys and apes? It turns out, some surprising clues suggest we have an innate preoccupation with fairness and equality that chimps simply don't. It offers a glimmer of hope that, deep down, we're more Tongan teenagers than *Batavian* murderers.

Michael Tomasello, a professor of developmental psychology at Duke University, may have found that glimmer in the eyes of toddlers. He designed a simple study. Pairs of two- and three-year-old children were randomly assigned to either be a "lucky" child or an "unlucky" child. The lucky child was given three rewards. The unlucky child received one. If an innate sense of fairness and justice is part of being human, then something should gnaw at the toddlers about the discrepancy between them. But if we're just interested in dominance over others, then the lucky child would gleefully accept its good fortune and not spare a second thought on the unlucky child.

The study had three versions. In the first, the children would walk into a room and the lucky child would find three rewards waiting for him, while the unlucky child would find one. In the second, both children would pull a rope. The lucky kid would again get three rewards, compared to one for the unlucky kid. In the third setup, the children would work together equally on a task, and at the end there would still be a three-to-one split. The idea was to see whether our instinct was toward sharing, and, crucially, whether it mattered how the rewards were allocated.

In the first version of the study, none of the children shared. In the second, some did. But the third version—in which equal, collaborative effort led to an unequal outcome—produced the most intriguing result. None of the two-year-olds shared. But an astonishing 80 percent of the lucky three-year-olds gave up one of their rewards to be on equal footing with their unlucky companion. Their instinct was toward fairness—particularly after cooperating. Seemingly random allocations didn't bother the toddlers, but unfair allocations after equal effort clearly unsettled them once they were three years old. When we stop tasting our pacifiers, we start to develop a distaste for injustice.

Unless you work with a bunch of jerks, you'd assume a similar result in adults. But that sharing impulse we usually see with colleagues could be learned rather than innate. It could also emerge as a result of social pressure. After all, who dares to risk becoming the office pariah by taking two pieces of cake and leaving a colleague with nothing? With three-year-olds, social stigma is less of a factor. But could social-justice-warrior toddlers simply be a by-product of good parenting or hours plopped in front of *Sesame Street*?

"It could be argued that these children were only blindly following a sharing rule that they learned from their parents," Tomasello says. "But if that was the case, they should have divided the rewards with the other child equally in all three conditions—unless, implausibly, the rule they were taught was to share resources only after collaboration. More plausibly, the act of collaboration engendered a sense of 'we' that led children to see their partner as equally deserving of the spoils." Tomasello and his coauthors began to wonder whether such an instinct—a cooperation instinct—had somehow evolved in humans.

But was it uniquely human? Tomasello decided to conduct a similar study with chimpanzees. When the experiments were run, sharing was rare. Crucially, the setup didn't change the outcome at all. Collaboration was irrelevant. There was no sense of "we" and no sense of fairness. For chimpanzees, dominance doesn't come with second thoughts.

This, then, is the puzzle of the human evolution of power. We started off as chimpanzees. But somewhere along the path to modern humanity, we developed a strong sense that working together should be rewarded with equal spoils. And we developed an innate desire to cooperate, not just dominate. How, and why, did that happen? To find out, we'll need to gaze back into our hunter-gatherer past and answer a seemingly unrelated question: Why can't chimps play baseball?

How Our Shoulders Shaped Society

In Africa's Kalahari Desert, there lives a group of hunter-gatherers known as the !Kung. While Botswana, Namibia, and Angola have grown into complex, modern states all around them, the !Kung have retained their prehistoric way of life. Central to that life is a hunting ritual that provides a window into the egalitarian impulse that has characterized humans for most of the time we've lived on earth.

To survive, !Kung hunters must bring back meat. It's time-consuming. They often return empty-handed. But when they do successfully kill an animal and bring it back to the village, they're neither celebrated nor cheered. Instead, they undergo a ceremonial humiliation, a ritual known by anthropologists as "insulting the meat." Even if the hunter's fresh kill could feed the village for a week, the complaints are the same: "You mean to say you have dragged us all the way out here to make us cart home your pile of bones? Oh, if I had known it was this thin, I wouldn't have come." This strange custom has a purpose: to cut the hunter down to size. Members of the !Kung band explained the logic to the Canadian anthropologist Richard Lee in the late 1970s: "When a young man kills much meat, he comes to think of himself as a chief or a big man, and he thinks of the rest of us as his servants or inferiors. We can't accept this. We refuse one who boasts, for someday his pride will make him kill somebody. So we always speak of his meat as worthless. In this way we cool his heart and make him gentle."

Just in case a headstrong hunter is too thick-skinned to be humbled by those cutting insults to his meat, another mechanism ensures that none get too big for their britches. When the !Kung hunt, they use arrows. Each arrowhead is owned by a different individual or family, regardless of who is doing the hunting. With regularity, the members of the community swap arrowheads with one another. Then, when a kill is made, the credit isn't given to the hunter, but rather to the owner of the arrowhead used to take down the animal. Because the !Kung swap the arrowheads frequently, the process is effectively randomized. With that clever bit of social engineering, every family gets approximately equal credit for feeding the band. This system ensures that prolific hunters don't emerge as leaders, but rather that the successes and failures of the !Kung are distributed. Hierarchy as we know it doesn't exist. Society is flat by design.

That doesn't mean that prehistoric humans and modern hunter-gatherers were indifferent to power or hierarchy. Instead, as the evolutionary psychologist Mark van Vugt explained to me, "It would be very strange if even in these hunter-gatherer societies there wouldn't be people who tried to dominate others. That's basically part of our primate legacy." But whenever anyone did try to seize power within the !Kung community, they'd be ostracized, ridiculed, humiliated, or, in extreme cases, killed. While !Kung rituals may seem strange to us, in human history, they're normal. We, not them, are the weird ones.

If the three-hundred-thousand-year history of our species, *Homo sapiens*, were condensed into a single year, we would mostly live in non-hierarchical, flat societies from New Year's Day until approximately Christmas. In the final six days of the year, hierarchy would become the norm, as complex civilizations took root across the planet. Only then would dominance and despotism define us. Our modern societies are an outlier. The alpha male equivalent of our chimpanzee ancestors disappeared from many prehistoric human societies. So, where did they go?

If you put the world's most powerful chimpanzee in a baseball uniform, gave him the best coaching, and made him practice throwing every day, he could still only throw a baseball about twenty miles per hour. That's about the same speed as a puny, unexceptional seven-year-old pitcher in Little League. A decent twelve-year-old can strike out a batter with a sixty-mile-per-hour fastball, triple the top speed of even the Nolan Ryan or Mariano Rivera of chimpanzees. Our primate ancestors would be more likely to hit the batter or have the ball fly sideways than throw a strike. But it's not a fair competition. "Humans are the only species that can throw objects both incredibly fast and with great accuracy," writes Neil Thomas Roach, an evolutionary biologist at Harvard University. Around 2 million years ago, our *Homo erectus* predecessors got a bit of lucky evolutionary cosmetic surgery done to their shoulders. Suddenly, they could throw objects with deadly speed and accuracy. It drastically changed the course of our species.

Four hundred thousand years ago, one of our ancestors shaped a branch of a yew tree into a point. The wood was also crafted to make it more aerodynamic. The fruit of that labor, now known as the Clacton Spear, is the oldest worked wooden object ever discovered. Sixty thousand to seventy thousand years ago, bows and arrows enter the archaeological record. But before either of those weapons was developed, our hominid ancestors could throw rocks with an accuracy that a chimp could only dream of mimicking. Our use of ranged weapons separates us from other primates. That distinction transformed our social structure.

With ranged weapons, killing became more about brains and skill than brawn and size. In the battle for power, projectiles are a brutal equalizer. Suddenly, a small hominid who made a better spear or practiced throwing it could easily kill someone much bigger and stronger. The traditional link between power and size was severed. Goliaths were no longer invincible. Davids with ranged weapons could topple them.

This shift is still on display in modern society. During the Vietnam War, for example, one of the most ruthless killers in the American military was a Green Beret named Richard Flaherty. He was awarded the Silver Star and two Bronze Stars. He was also four feet ten inches tall—six inches shorter than the average American female. But you don't even need to be trained in combat to be deadly if you have the right projectiles. You don't even need to be an adult. About once a week in the United States, someone is shot by a toddler who accidentally fires a gun. Some of those accidents are fatal. Meanwhile, the idea of a baby chimpanzee accidentally killing an adult is ludicrous. Our primate cousins can only kill with brute strength.

The development of ranged weapons therefore changed what "the fittest" meant when it came to survival of the fittest. Size was no longer as important. Evolutionary biologists have argued that this shift is a key reason why the physical size differences between males and females are narrower in humans than in any other great ape species. (If the scientists are correct, then part of the reason why men are usually inches rather than several feet taller than women is because of how our shoulders are designed.) But the biggest change that came from ranged weapons and the great leveling they made possible was the flattening of hierarchies—from chimpanzee despotism to hunter-gatherer cooperation.

Still, we shouldn't think of ourselves as an overly cuddly species. Humans, like chimps, are drawn to power. But as humans split from chimps, the *path to power* diverged, too. When taking power requires killing by physical combat, it becomes dangerous and possibly deadly to challenge a dominant member of your group. To take control, you must put yourself in harm's way. That provided some protection for those in charge because they often knew they'd win a physical fight. They were bigger and stronger. But with the development of ranged weapons, would-be leaders needed to watch their back much more. Suddenly, even the scrawniest member of the group could pose a threat. A potential rival could be hiding in the woods, ready to throw a spear at you. The rival could shoot you with a bow and arrow while you slept or could chuck a rock at your head when you least expected it.* Suddenly, it became much harder for a bigger member of a group to physically dominate the smaller members of the group against their will. Rather than accepting the rule of the physically powerful, humans now had a choice.

Chris Boehm, an anthropologist at the University of Southern California, developed a broadly accepted explanation for the subsequent flattening of hierarchies in human society. He coined the somewhat clunky term *reverse dominance hierarchy* for the phenomenon, but the idea is simple. A dominance hierarchy is a steep triangle, with the head honcho towering over everyone else from the apex. A reverse dominance hierarchy is a flat line, where everyone is more or less equal, at least formally. Boehm explains that anyone who tried to change the flat line back into a steep triangle did so at his or her own peril.

Nonetheless, hunter-gatherers often needed to fight to preserve a lack of hierarchy. In our species, many of us like having control over others. That makes sense from an evolutionary perspective. Having at least some power has tended to coincide with survival and, by extension, reproductive success. But if society is set up so that only one person can be the leader, then almost everyone who wants power won't get it. Sure, you might get lucky. But for any given individual, being dominated by some-

---

* This is also the reason we don't need to know how tall Lee Harvey Oswald was or whether he lifted weights.

one else was the most likely outcome of a hierarchical society. So, instead of accepting that primate-style arrangement, many early humans designed a different way of life, in which nobody could be in charge. Any individual who tried to seize power—what Boehm calls an upstart—would get dominated by the group, torn back down to the same level as everyone else. The upstart could face expulsion, harassment, even death. The !Kung rituals of insulting the meat and rotating arrowheads are just two mechanisms that developed to deter such upstarts. As one anthropologist put it, "All men seek to rule, but if they cannot rule they prefer to be equal." Our instinct to rule was superseded by a stronger desire to not be ruled by someone else.

As a result, Boehm argues that for several hundred thousand years— from New Year's Day to Christmas in our condensed species year— humans lived in relative equality in groups called bands. They were home to anything from a few dozen to up to around eighty members. Groups would deliberate and discuss before deciding. Leaders who were particularly skilled or knowledgeable about a given topic might have more ability to persuade others, but they wielded no formal authority.

We know this through three forms of imperfect evidence. First, archaeological digs of burial sites for ancient hunter-gatherers rarely show differentiation within graves.[*] This changed considerably when hierarchy became normal and powerful individuals were buried in larger graves, or with more possessions, or in some way that marks that they were separate from the masses (think of the Pyramids). Second, archaeological evidence rarely shows major variance in nutrition between band members. There were few fat Henry VIIIs while peasants went hungry. And third, with few exceptions, the surviving bands of modern hunter-gatherers live this way—without chiefs but with consensus-driven deliberations. Those living strands of our Stone Age societies give us a glimpse into our collective past. It's quite a big departure from our world, in which every aspect of our lives is affected by social hierarchies.

Admittedly, our understanding of nonhierarchical hunter-gatherer

---

[*] There are a few exceptions. For example, one corpse, of a young boy in Italy, was buried with ornate status symbols. Magnificent prehistoric burial chambers have also been discovered near modern-day Moscow.

society is incomplete and could be overstated. Manvir Singh, an expert in human evolutionary biology, has convincingly challenged the conventional wisdom by showing that some prehistoric, sedentary hierarchical societies *did* exist (in places such as south China, the Levant, and southern Scandinavia). He argues that there was much more diversity in the structure of prehistoric societies than is currently acknowledged. Moreover, some experts question whether the nutritional evidence is misleading or whether "egalitarianism" actually meant equality (particularly with regard to the sexes). But there's compelling evidence that for most of human history, formalized, complex hierarchies were far, far less common than they are today. At first glance, a world without overbearing bosses or incompetent politicians sounds pretty attractive. Is it time to bring back the Stone Age?

Make no mistake: these societies were certainly not utopian. More than one in four infants died in their first year of life. Nearly half of children didn't survive to puberty. When an upstart or a power-hungry abuser emerged during prehistory, conflict and tragedy often followed. Sometimes, upstarts could be dealt with through ostracism. (Social stigma is a powerful weapon if your entire world consists of eighty individuals and there are no other people to become friends with. It was like a high school clique, a prehistoric *Mean Girls*, on steroids.) In bands of hunter-gatherers, ostracism meant social death, at least for a while. But despite that powerful deterrent, people *did* break the social codes of the society. When that happened, there was no police department to turn to, no judges to determine guilt and innocence. It was a much more lawless ancient version of the Wild West. Murder was frequently used to settle disputes. According to a recent study by Spanish researchers published in *Nature*, about 2 percent of all deaths in hunter-gatherer societies were caused by homicide. That closely mirrors the rate of the primate-on-primate killings among great apes. (In our defense, we're certainly not the worst of the worst in the animal kingdom; the within-species killing rate among cheetahs is 8 percent; 12 percent for wolves; 15 percent for sea lions; and up to 17 percent for seemingly cuddly Madagascan lemurs.)

But *who* were the troublemakers in these prehistoric bands of murder-happy humans? From modern hunter-gatherer societies, we know that the demographic profile of power-hungry upstarts isn't random. "The problem personalities were males," Boehm explains. "Group leaders, shamans, proficient hunters, homicidal psychotics, or other men with unusual powers or strong tendencies toward political ambition." Such is the complexity of humanity's puzzle: when we lived more like the Tongan castaways, we still had latent elements of the *Batavia* in our societies, waiting to be unleashed.

We know that this absence of hierarchy didn't last. Look around you. Our lives are defined by status and power, from the delicate dance of watercooler politics and luxury handbag status symbols to police abuse of racial minorities and gender inequality that persists like a stubborn weed. Just as the passengers on board the *Batavia* knew their rank, we're constantly reminded of where we stand in modern society. So, what changed? How did we go from an abundance of primitive flat societies to the most complex hierarchies in the history of the world?

War and Peas

Between eleven thousand and five thousand years ago, everything changed. Bands were mostly replaced by tribes, chiefdoms, and archaic versions of states. Hierarchical societies that did exist got more hierarchical. Our world was no longer flat. Power returned with a vengeance. What happened?

One bespectacled and bearded Russian émigré decided to find out.

Peter Turchin learned a visceral aversion to supercharged hierarchies from an early age. His father, Valentin Turchin, was an early pioneer of artificial intelligence in the Soviet Union. But when he spoke out against Soviet abuses, Valentin had gone too far, upsetting his superiors. Valentin became a dissident, fleeing to the United States, and taking his twenty-year-old son, Peter, with him. Decades later, the younger Turchin is a polymath and professor at the University of Connecticut, one of the smartest thinkers you've probably never heard of. Turchin looks the part of a professor who spends his waking hours pondering grand theories and hypotheses. He's got the professorial glasses, salt-and-pepper hair that matches his beard, and is more comfortable in a polo shirt than a suit and tie. He speaks eloquent academic English with a lingering Russian accent. His hands move enthusiastically as he explains each of his big, sweeping ideas to a fresh potential convert—not to a cause, but to his way of seeing the world.

Turchin is obsessed with two questions. First, how have societies evolved to create grotesque levels of inequality and bad governance? And second, can we answer such historical puzzles using math and data? To tackle those questions, Turchin has pioneered a field he calls clio-dynamics, after Clio—the muse of history—and dynamics, the study of change. With his novel approach, he set out to unlock the secret origins of human hierarchies.

Central to his thinking is a concept called multilevel selection. It's complicated, but can be illustrated with a simple example from Turchin's latest book, *Ultrasociety*. Let's start with the most basic parts of Darwinian natural selection. At the individual level, if a trait makes you better at surviving and producing offspring, it's more likely to be passed on to the next generation. Your kids will have that trait, and perhaps they'll pass it on to their own children. That trait is "selected." Conversely, traits that make you more likely to die and therefore fail to have children are culled from the gene pool over time.

Now, consider how those dynamics would affect warriors. The traits that make warriors good at fighting also make them more likely to die. The best warriors eagerly throw themselves into deadly battles. Many die in those battles, thereby eliminating themselves from the gene pool. Cowards who run away don't die. Surely, then, bravery in combat wouldn't get selected because it makes us less likely to survive long enough to have many children. So why are we still blessed with a plentiful supply of brave people?

The explanation to that seeming paradox may not lie at the individual level, but rather at the group level. If you have an army full of brave warriors and you find yourself on a battlefield pitted against an army full of cowardly warriors, it doesn't take a genius such as Peter Turchin to predict who will win. One brave soldier in an army of cowards will die, but an army of brave soldiers working together has a better chance of surviving. And if the warfare is brutal, in which the losing side gets slaughtered, then the cowardly warriors who run away and get killed (sometimes along with their relatives) are the ones removed from the gene pool. In an age of warfare, a society full of brave warriors is more likely to survive—and produce lots of children—than a society of cowards. Groups matter.

Of course, the real world is more complicated. At the individual level, brave warriors might be more likely to die in combat, but those who survive to tell the tale sometimes have their pick of sexual partners. The returning hero may have better luck at the prehistoric equivalent of a cocktail bar than the surviving coward. And sometimes, one society can defeat another on the battlefield, but both societies nonetheless survive and continue to thrive, creating no difference in the genetics that are passed to the next generation. This complicated interplay between individual-level selection (an individual warrior's prospects for survival in our example) and group-level dynamics (the prospects that the society as a whole will survive and thrive) is the core conundrum that multilevel selection seeks to explain. Understanding those dynamics is crucial because our modern world is the by-product of lots of little social experiments, generation after generation. Some ways of life that were tailor-made for survival spread, while other ways of life died out because those who practiced them were wiped off the map. (Another way to think about this concept is to imagine one society that believed that having children was forbidden by God and another that believed that it was God's will to have ten children per couple. The antichildren society would last one generation. The society obsessed with divine procreation would proliferate. In that way, traits, beliefs, and social systems have an effect on which ideas, customs, and people survive into the next generation.)

But what does all of this have to do with the rise of hierarchy?

Around 500 BC, the Greek philosopher Heracleitus said, "War is the father of all things." He was onto something. And again, our story—guided by Turchin's theories—returns to ranged weapons. Let's imagine two equally skilled armies. The larger army has a thousand soldiers and the smaller army has five hundred soldiers. If the armies march toward each other to fight with fists or swords, then the larger army has roughly a two-to-one advantage. Each soldier typically fights only one other soldier at a time, so slowly, but steadily, the smaller army will run out of soldiers and will be forced to retreat, or they'll all be killed. The advantage is real, but it isn't insurmountable. Smaller armies facing two-to-one odds sometimes win.

Now, let's imagine that the armies have archers instead of swordsmen. Everything changes because it doesn't have to be one-on-one combat any longer. It's like dodgeball, in which a two-on-one advantage is likely to end badly for the sole survivor being pummeled from two angles at once. Similarly, two archers can fire at the same enemy soldier. The math of ranged combat is different. Let's see how. (Bear with me for the only bit of math in the book.)

The two armies—one with five hundred archers, the other with one thousand archers—unleash their arrows at once. For simplicity, let's say that 30 percent of the archers hit their target. Three hundred archers from the smaller army are wounded or killed (30 percent of 1,000 arrows fired equals 300). But only 150 archers from the larger army are hit (thirty percent of 500 arrows equals 150). After one exchange of fire, it's now a battle of 850 versus 200. The two-to-one advantage has quickly shifted to a more than four-to-one advantage. After one more volley, everyone in the smaller army will be wounded or killed. The bigger army will still have 790 archers left.

Battlefields don't always follow the logic of math on blackboards. Tactics, terrain, the element of surprise, and the quality of weapons or soldiers all are incredibly important variables. But the key point is this: mathematical logic shows that the advantage of having a larger army is much greater for armies using ranged weapons than those engaged in close combat. (And smaller armies using ranged weapons can sometimes win resounding victories even against much larger armies equipped with swords and spears, as Henry V was delighted to find out in the Battle of Agincourt.)

But why does this all matter? Why is the math of arrows and swords relevant to understanding why you might have a boss, a boss's boss, and a boss's boss's boss at work? For a simple reason: as ranged weapons became more common, the dynamics of warfare started to dramatically favor societies with more soldiers. If a few hundred people got together and formed an army under the rule of a single chief, egalitarian bands of twenty to eighty members just couldn't compete. And when humans get together in larger groups, flat societies become impossible. Put enough people together, and hierarchy and dominance *always* emerge. It's an ironclad rule of history.

Some people had to learn this the hard way. Bands that stubbornly stuck to the old ways of flat society started to get wiped out by those who joined together and embraced chiefs. Plus, on the battlefield itself, having leaders (generals) with formal power over their soldiers was much more effective than a ragtag bunch of soldiers making their own decisions. It was the opposite of the !Kung hunting rituals. To win a war, you didn't want to insult your best and bravest. You needed to elevate your best fighters, not cut them down to size.

Those battlefield dynamics didn't stay on the battlefield. Once people become a general, they tend to get a taste for power. "The people that were put in charge—the military leaders—gradually usurped more power for themselves and set themselves up as chiefs," Turchin says. Bands became tribes and tribes became chiefdoms. But if Turchin is right that warfare triggered this social shift, why didn't it happen sooner? Why was there a sudden rise in hierarchy in a narrow band of human history? The answer lies not with weapons, but with food.

Around eleven thousand years ago, humans changed how we fed ourselves. The First Agricultural Revolution (or Neolithic Revolution) was ushered in with the domestication of a few "pioneer crops," including peas, chickpeas, lentils, and flax. Barley, figs, oats, and others soon followed. Farming began. It was disastrous for our nutrition. Our food supply became more reliable, but it shifted humans from a varied diet to one that only offered a narrow slice of nutrients. Before farming, the average height of a hunter-gatherer was five foot ten for men and five foot six for women. Virtually overnight, the average height for men shrank down to five foot five and down to five foot one for women. Even today, our average height has not fully recovered. But aside from reducing our size, the agricultural revolution also seems to have ushered in a new era of inequality. We became a bunch of greedy short people.

The traditional explanation for that abrupt shift, popularized by Jared Diamond in *Guns, Germs, and Steel* goes like this: Agriculture made it easier to have excess food. Once there was more food to go around, some people hoarded it. Those surpluses made inequality possible. They also made it possible to support a larger group of people, because growing peas was scalable in a way that hunting gazelles wasn't. As surpluses and population sizes grew, societies became both more complex and more hierarchical. And with surpluses and hierarchy came more conflict, as individuals and groups fought to establish their primacy in a rapidly changing system.

Others have proposed more nuanced explanations. Manvir Singh points out that some people were already able to get a steady supply of food prior to the agricultural revolution, through fishing, for example. And Robert Carneiro, writing in 1970, developed a theory called environmental circumscription. The idea is elegant. He argues that the rise of agriculture put a premium on controlling land in a way that was simply absent for hunter-gatherers. What's the point of controlling a patch of dirt if the gazelles you're hunting are just going to move somewhere else? With farming, your survival was linked to the soil you occupied. More soil meant more productive capacity. Controlling land became much more important.

But there was a twist: If you lived in, say, the Amazon Basin, then good farmland stretched in every direction. Getting forced off your land isn't as big of a deal when equally good farmland is everywhere. That's not true if you live in, say, coastal Peru, where your back is to the sea. In Carneiro's terminology, the land in Peru is "circumscribed" in a way that the land in Amazonia isn't. As a result, if wars were fought in Amazonia, the losing group would just retreat, setting up shop in another fertile section of land elsewhere. In coastal Peru, however, there was nowhere else to go. The losing group would be conquered. Being conquered meant that you would either be killed or, more likely, subsumed as part of the winning society.

In that way, Carneiro argued, warfare in circumscribed areas created larger populations, which ultimately created more complex societies. These eventually became proto-states, the earliest versions of what we would recognize as countries. Amazonia, to this day, still has plenty of hunter-gatherers. Coastal Peru became home to a series of complex societies, culminating in the Incan Empire—an empire defined by hierarchy. Perhaps the evolution of human society from egalitarian bands to top-down empires, then, can be explained by flukes of geography.

So, which theory is correct? Was it war, or was it the rise of agriculture? Our world is too complex for one unifying theory that explains everything. Most scholars, however, agree that both warfare and agriculture—"war and peas," if you will—played a significant role in generating large, complex hierarchical societies. This shift happened with astonishing speed. According to Turchin's data, groups of tens of people in bands were around for hundreds of thousands of years. Then, groups of hundreds formed farming villages around 8000 BC. Groups of thousands emerged as simple chiefdoms in 5500 BC. Groups of tens of thousands, known as complex chiefdoms, followed suit by 5000 BC. The first archaic states, comprising hundreds of thousands of individuals, rose around 3000 BC. By 2500 BC, there were macrostates with millions of subjects. And by 500 BC, mega-empires topped out in the tens of millions. In a comparative blink, we went from many smaller, flatter societies to enormous, hierarchical behemoths defined by inequality and dominance.

The rest, quite literally, is history.

As hierarchies became more widespread, struggles for power increased. Upstarts who would've previously faced ostracism, humiliation, or death now had a real prospect of becoming genuinely powerful. Power begets conflict, so violence increased. The 2 percent murder rate of the hunter-gatherer societies increased substantially, approaching 10 percent in some of our darkest eras (from the Iron Age to about five hundred years ago). At first glance, then, hierarchy seems pretty bad. After all, the *Batavia* hierarchy allowed a psychopath to murder more than a hundred people simply because he had power over others. More people were murdered under chiefs and despots than under egalitarian bands. But if hierarchy is to blame, how can we explain the reassuring fact that just 0.7 percent of humans on the planet today meet their end through homicide—a rate around a third of what we would expect from our primate ancestry? More reassuring still, if you look at the best-governed complex societies on the planet—such as Japan, Norway, or Germany—between 0.05 and 0.09 percent of their citizens die at the hands of another human being. That's up to forty times lower than the rate for hunter-gatherer societies. Modern states are the most hierarchical social structures ever conceived and developed. They're also the safest.*

The obvious conclusion is that hierarchy and power are neither good nor bad. They provide a tool—a tool that can be used to facilitate cooperation and community or to exploit people and kill them. Turchin agrees: "Hierarchy is like fire. It can be used to cook food or to burn people." But without it, all of the marvels of civilization would be impossible. "We are not ants," Turchin explains. "We don't have a pheromones system. So hierarchy is the only way that humans can cooperate and coordinate in large-scale societies." Plus, because hierarchy can breed competition, it can also spark innovation. Competition for status in more meritocratic societies can sometimes produce much better outcomes than if everyone just rested on their laurels as equals.

The story of the Tongan castaways is heartwarming. The story of the *Batavia* is heart-wrenching. But the Tongan castaways don't offer us a model for our modern societies. Flat societies are deeply limiting for humans. Our choice is either to live in tiny cooperative groups or to embrace hierarchy. That's why power and status are here to stay.

So, if we're stuck with hierarchy—if we need bosses and generals and presidents and prison guards—then why are so many of those people dreadful? To find out, we need to figure out why corruptible people tend to seek power. Improbably, the solution to that puzzle lies with a statistician from World War II, the daughter of a cannibal emperor, some hyenas, and a power-hungry, flamingo-obsessed president of a homeowners' association in Arizona.

---

* Part of the reason for this is that, unlike egalitarian hunter-gatherer bands, modern criminal justice systems provide a mechanism to both deter social deviance and eliminate the need for deadly vigilante justice when it happens.

III

MOTHS TO A FLAME

It is a well-known fact that those people who most want to rule people are, ipso facto, those least suited to do it. . . . Anyone who is capable of getting themselves made president should on no account be allowed to do the job.

—*Douglas Adams*, The Restaurant at the End of the Universe

Airplanes and Cavemen

Abraham Wald was a survivor. In the late 1930s, Wald saw himself for what he was: a statistician from Cluj, Romania, who was working at the Austrian Institute of Economic Research. But when the Nazis invaded Austria in 1938, they saw Wald as something else: the grandson of a rabbi and the son of a kosher baker. Wald moved to the United States to escape persecution from Hitler. He eventually landed a professorship at Columbia University.

On July 1, 1942, a secret group of statisticians known as the Statistical Research Group (SRG) was formed at Columbia. Their office was a nondescript building on a quiet road in the West Harlem neighborhood of Manhattan, just opposite Morningside Park. There, eighteen of the best statistical minds in the United States—including Wald—worked for the next three years. Their task was straightforward: to help win World War II. Their weapons weren't guns or bombs, but probabilities. They were asked to use statistical methods to identify possible improvements to the Allied fighting machine—the kinds of improvements that generals, presidents, and prime ministers might otherwise overlook.

The military would bring them a problem. The math whizzes would puzzle over it for a bit and agree on a solution. "When we made recommendations," one member of the SRG later recalled, "frequently things happened." Machine guns on fighter planes were loaded differently. Quality-control checks on wartime production lines became more aggressive. Fuses on artillery shells were tweaked to become more reliably destructive. Math could prove a decisive weapon. Every calculation the statisticians made, every equation they solved, could save lives or cost lives.

At that stage of the war, large numbers of Allied fighters and bombers were being shot down in combat over Europe. To reduce those losses, the generals already knew how to make the pilots better—with more training in the cockpit. But to make the planes better, they realized that they needed some help from the nerds of West Harlem.

See if you can solve the problem they presented to Wald.

Airplanes returning from the skies over Germany are riddled with bullet holes. You systematically evaluate them, mapping out the areas that have been ripped apart by enemy fire. The planes you analyze have holes peppered across the wings, tail, and fuselage (or body) of the plane. The question from the generals was, Where should they put extra armor on the plane to reinforce the areas that were getting shot?

The statisticians had to get it right. Any excess armor in the wrong spots would slow the planes down, making them sitting ducks for Nazi machine guns. Failing to reinforce vulnerable areas could lead to more dead pilots. Take a look at the diagram below showing the distribution of bullet holes on the planes returning from Europe. Put yourself in Wald's shoes. Lives hang in the balance. Where would you tell the generals to reinforce: wings, tail, fuselage, or all of the above?

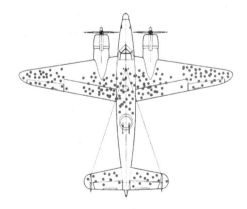

If you answered wings, tail, fuselage, or all of the above, congratulations, you would've accidentally killed many American airmen.

Wald saw something in his mind that the generals hadn't: the invisible planes. When Allied airplanes were shot in the wings, tail, or fuselage, they mostly managed to limp home, smoking but safe. They survived. When planes were shot elsewhere—specifically when the engine near the nose was hit—they weren't included in the military study. Why not? Because they were flaming wrecks in Germany. They didn't make it back.

Wald realized that the planes in Germany—the ones that the military couldn't study because they no longer existed—were the only ones that mattered. Had it not been for Wald, the military would've reinforced only the bits of the plane that were least vulnerable to enemy fire while making the planes heavier and slower. Instead, he told them to reinforce the places that *didn't* have bullet holes. The military followed his advice. They reinforced the armor over the engines. It saved lives. Wald helped the Allies win the war.

Wald understood something called survivorship bias, a subset of the statistical concept of selection bias. The idea is simple: you need to study all possible cases, not just the cases that "survive." Take another example that's much older than World War II. Did cavemen really live in caves? We have plenty of evidence that they did. After all, there are hundreds of cave paintings throughout the world. That seems pretty conclusive. But how would we know if there were actually way more prehistoric Picassos living in grasslands and painting on trees? The trees—and any art brushed into their bark—are long gone. It may be that cavemen rarely ventured into caves to paint, but when they did, only that artwork was preserved. That's why survivorship bias is sometimes referred to as the caveman effect. Our understanding of the world is often badly skewed not just by the evidence we have, but by the evidence we don't have.

Wald's story is a great example of the real-world perils of ignoring survivorship bias. But Wald's insights were also a far more literal form of survivorship bias. Eight other members of his family might have provided fascinating contributions in their lives, too. We don't know, because they were killed by the Nazis. And Abraham Wald, who took revenge by ensuring that fewer Allied planes would crash during missions over Germany, was himself killed in a plane crash in the Nilgiri Mountains of southern India while on a mathematical lecture tour in 1950.

To understand why corruptible people are drawn to power, you don't need to study airplanes or correct the record about cavemen. But Wald's insights about survivorship bias are important to understanding who seeks power, who gets power, and who stays in power. It's not random. And if you only focus on the evidence in front of you, you'll badly misunderstand how the world actually works.

Let's apply Wald's logic to your boss, or the president or prime minister of your country, or that football coach in junior high who made you run laps until you threw up (or so I have heard). Why is that person in charge? To answer that question, three levels of survivorship bias need to be explored. First, who seeks power? Who wants to be the boss, the leader, or the coach? In answering that question, identifying the people who *don't* want to be in power is just as important at identifying those who do. Only those who try to gain power are the "survivors." The rest are removed from consideration.

Second, who gets power? With the possible exception of the junior high school coach, most positions of authority involve competition. It's not always a fair fight. Systems can be biased. And even if they aren't, some people are just better at climbing the ladder than others. The "survivors" in this round make it into power. Those who try, but fail, don't.

Then there's the third level of surviving: Who stays in power? Plenty of people are a bit like Icarus: they soar too high, only to get burned and plummet back to earth. The leaders we focus on—good and bad—tend to be people who hang on to power for enough time to wield it with impact. Ever heard of Pedro Lascuráin? I hadn't either. That makes sense because he holds the dubious title of the shortest-reigning president in history, ruling Mexico for roughly fifteen minutes during a 1913 coup d'état. Those who get power but lose it or leave it are like the paintings done by cavemen on trees. They disappear.

We tend to focus on people who hit the trifecta: they seek power; they get power; and they hold on to power. Those who make it through all three levels are the survivors in survivorship bias. They're the individuals we consider to be powerful. Everyone else is comparatively invisible, like the charred, crashed planes in Germany. But unless you include the hidden evidence, as Abraham Wald did, we'll end up misunderstanding the problem. And if you don't understand a problem, you can't solve it.

As history has so cruelly demonstrated, not everyone who ends up in power is a great person. Right now, we have a mix. Some great people are in positions of leadership: kind coaches, bosses who empower, politicians who genuinely try to make life a little bit better for others. But many, many authority figures are nothing like that. They lie and cheat and steal, serving themselves while they exploit and abuse others. They are, in a word, corruptible. And they do a lot of damage.

In an ideal alternate reality, we wouldn't have a mix. Instead, *only* the good people—let's refer to them for simplicity as incorruptibles—would be our leaders, our bosses, our police officers. Meanwhile, the people you wouldn't want to have in charge—let's call them corruptibles—would have no power at all. To build that ideal world, you have to think about all three levels. You would want to make sure that incorruptibles seek power, get it, and hold on to it. Meanwhile, you would want to throw up roadblocks everywhere to deter those pesky corruptibles at all three levels. That is easier said than done. Much of the world is dominated by systems that attract and promote corruptible people. As future chapters will show, systems that are made can be unmade. But to start, we need to focus on who *seeks* power.

The Cannibal Emperor and Hyena Hierarchies

Who pursues power is not random. Certain types of people crave it and try to seize it for themselves. That produces a form of "self-selection bias." We recognize self-selection bias easily in other aspects of our lives. For example, tall kids are more likely to try out for the high school basketball team than short kids. That's why basketball teams are never a random, representative sample of the population. The same is true for those who seek power. Certain traits cause some people to want power more than others. Too much attention is paid to the notion that power corrupts. Not enough attention is paid to why corruptible people seek power.

So, what causes some people to want to lead? Why are others content to follow? Are leaders born, or made? And is a thirst for power just a genetic trait, like blue eyes or curly hair?

On a chilly autumn day in 2019, I met Marie-France Bokassa at a bistro near the Gare Saint-Lazare in Paris. When I arrived, she was there waiting, smoking a cigarette, sipping on a small glass of white wine, and flicking through her phone. She was smartly but not extravagantly dressed, with designer glasses and bright red lipstick. She smiled as I sat down. The only hint that she might have a story to tell was around her neck—an oversize diamond that didn't look like the kind of thing a normal person might have. And that's because Marie-France isn't a normal person.

She's the daughter of a monster.

In September 1979, French troops arrived in Bangui, the capital of the Central African Empire—a destitute country you've probably never heard of that was ruled by a ruthless tyrant you've probably never heard of. That tyrant was Marie-France's father: Jean-Bédel Bokassa. When Bokassa took power, he wasn't just sworn in. He was coronated. It was to be modeled on Napoléon's crowning as emperor in 1804. And in that same tradition, he was to be known as Emperor Bokassa I. At the coronation in 1977, there was a strict dress code. Children wore white. Midlevel officials wore blue. Top officials wore black. Bokassa, the star of the imperial show, was clad in an ermine cloak stitched by France's finest tailors. He wore a glittering crown with an eighty-carat diamond at the front, made by the most exclusive jeweler in France. Bokassa stood with a custom-made golden scepter in front of a bespoke twelve-foot-tall bronze statue of an eagle. The throne cost the government $3 million dollars, a bargain compared with the $5 million paid for the crown and scepter. In total, the ceremony cost $22 million, about a quarter of the government's entire annual budget.

At the time, the average person in the country made $282 per year.

By 1979, the French—the former colonial power—decided that Bokassa was a dangerous megalomaniac (who could've possibly seen that coming?) and that it was time for him to go. A small deployment of French troops deposed the dictator and replaced him with France's chosen successor. When soldiers arrived at Bokassa's favorite palace, the Villa Kolongo, they found a world of obscene luxury. There were chests of diamonds, gold overflowing from cupboards, enough high-tech cameras to supply the world's paparazzi. As they cataloged the nauseating wealth that Bokassa had stolen from his people, they realized that the pond next to the palace was stocked with Nile crocodiles. To remove them, they drained the pond. As the water receded, bits of discolored white came into view, sticking out of the black mud. The French soldiers realized with horror that these were the decaying bones of some thirty victims—all that was left of those who had dared to defy Bokassa. Some had reportedly protested when he insisted on sleeping with their wives. They met their end as a dish for Bokassa's pet crocodiles.

But the crocodiles weren't the only ones eating Bokassa's enemies. When French troops opened the refrigerator at Villa Kolongo, they found two carved-up bodies. One was unidentifiable. The other was the body of a math teacher. Their corpses were being kept fresh, as human meat was allegedly on the menu for special occasions. Some have claimed that Bokassa served it to visiting dignitaries. "You never noticed, but you ate human flesh," Bokassa reportedly told a visiting French diplomat. (Bokassa denied being a cannibal up until his death.)

The emperor was an ogre. He had an unquenchable thirst for power. But was that a thirst that developed over time, or was he born with it? Was Bokassa's desire to control, abuse, and kill other people written into disturbing snippets of his DNA?

Bokassa died in 1996, making him rather difficult to interview. I needed to speak to the next-best thing: someone who shared his genetic code. I had many options to choose from. Bokassa had at least fifty-seven children, born to seventeen official wives (and probably many more from unofficial ones). Most of the Bokassa kids now live in France. Some have made out better than others. Two have been jailed for fraud or drug abuse. Three have been arrested for shoplifting. And one son—Charlemagne— was rather unlike his French namesake. He ruled over nothing more than a Paris metro station, where he lived and begged to survive. He was found dead in that station at the age of thirty-one.

Marie-France Bokassa has done better than most. I met her near the Gare Saint-Lazare because that was the most convenient location for her train in from Hardricourt, a suburb outside Paris. Like many of the Bokassa children, Marie-France spent much of her childhood there in one of her father's palaces. She still lives in the shadow of his former residence. But I wondered, Does she live in his genetic shadow, too? Is she doomed to the same thirst for power that made him become a dictator?

"My only family identity was shaped by my father," she told me, pausing to sip her wine. "I didn't know my mother. And my father put a mark on me, like I was part of the Bokassa brand."

For most people, being tied to a brand that evokes human-fed crocodiles and cannibalism would make you want to rush down to the local government office to get your hands on the nearest name-change form. But that wasn't Marie-France's reaction. She is proud to be a Bokassa.

"Bokassa—it's a name that is powerful," she told me with a mischievous grin. "I wouldn't want to change it."

Every discussion of human behavior eventually returns to the age-old nature-versus-nurture debate. So, in the interest of politeness, I gave Marie-France an easy out: I suggested that her father's behavior had been shaped by a traumatic upbringing. Perhaps the ogre was made, not born. After all, when he was a young boy, Bokassa's father was beaten to death by a French colonial officer. Bokassa's mother committed suicide the following week, leaving him orphaned. That's enough to ruin a childhood, but was it enough to make him depraved?

Marie-France paused to think. "His childhood taught him that you have to be hard. You have to be strong." Marie-France swirled her chardonnay in its glass. "But I saw the underlying fragility that was created in him by a catastrophic childhood. And Central Africa saw the consequences of that childhood, too."

Marie-France suffers, seemingly, from a variant of Stockholm syndrome when it comes to her father. She told me that most of her family still functions as a bit of a cult, with their deceased father as the cult leader. They all view Bokassa I as a hero, not a tyrant. Marie-France told me that, until recently, she had a large portrait of her father in her house, which she'd speak to every day to reassure him that he'd be proud of the woman she has become. That approval was something she'd long sought and seldom received.

"My father changed his mood constantly," she explained. "One minute he was jovial, relaxed. The next, he was in a fit of rage. He was always mercurial, unpredictable. And he never went a full day in the same kind of mood. He was volatile, explosive." Once when one of Marie-France's sisters forgot to serve her father his daily whiskey, he burned her clothes as punishment.

In writing a memoir about her childhood, Marie-France began to come to terms with her father's brutality—brutality that she only glimpsed from those mood swings when she was a little girl. But even as she's started to accept his true legacy, she rejected the notion that power corrupted him. "I don't think power changed him," she insisted. "He was always the same man. I didn't see any changes myself. And I certainly didn't see any change from when he took power to when he left it. He always had the same personality. The same positive traits and the same flaws." But even if she's right that power didn't corrupt Bokassa, there's no denying that he couldn't resist its magnetism. Something within him caused him to crave control over others. Power attracted him.

I wondered whether Marie-France had inherited that thirst for authority. I asked her if she believed that Emperor Bokassa had given her more than just his brand. Had he stamped his personality onto her, or just his name onto her birth certificate?

She thought for a second. "On the plus side, I inherited his generosity, his authenticity, his joviality, and his intelligence."

She took a long pause, her voice breaking when I asked her the obvious follow-up: "What about on the other side?"

"I . . . also inherited his temper . . . his authoritarian personality, and his severe mood swings," she said, sighing.

Marie-France now runs a *salon de thé*—a tearoom—near the former Bokassa palace outside Paris. Over a glass of wine, she was lovely and charming. But it was impossible not to consider a disturbing possibility. Under the right circumstances, could she become someone who wouldn't serve people tea, but would instead serve people with tea?

Before she returned to Hardricourt, Marie-France told me that she believes that a Bokassa should once again rule over the Central African Republic. When I asked whether that Bokassa could be her, she did what every aspiring politician does when faced with that question. She smiled and said she couldn't rule it out.

In a way, I'm being unfair to Marie-France. We aren't our parents. Genes aren't our destiny. But the chemical cocktail within us does shape our behavior. The question, then, is how much genes make a difference in who seeks power—and how much is left up to us.

In a study from the University of Minnesota (known as the Minnesota Twin study, not to be confused with the Minnesota Twins baseball team), researchers compared identical twins with fraternal twins. Identical twins start out as the same fertilized egg, which splits in two, meaning that both twins share 100 percent of their genetic code. Fraternal twins are just siblings that occupy the mother's womb at the same time. By comparing identical twins to fraternal twins that are raised in the same environment, you can isolate how much genes make a difference. That's precisely what the scientists in Minnesota did. They mapped the genomes of hundreds of twins and then had each individual list any leadership posts they'd ever held within companies or community organizations. What they found was extraordinary: when it came to predicting leadership, 30 percent of the variation between individuals could be explained by genes. That may not sound like a lot, but given the mind-boggling complexity of the thousands of factors that drive human behavior, it's an eye-popping number.

That finding also raised an intriguing possibility: Could some fragment of DNA determine whether we're born to lead or born to follow? Jan-Emmanuel De Neve (then at University College London and now at Oxford University) decided to find out. He led a team that tried to find snippets of genetic code associated with people taking charge. They sequenced the genomes of four thousand people, mapping out every little chemical in our DNA blueprint. Simultaneously, they charted the life histories of each person in the study, identifying which people had held leadership positions and which hadn't. In 2013, De Neve's team announced the discovery of what they called a "leadership gene." They'd identified rs4950 as a bit of genetic code that's strongly correlated with ending up in positions of authority later in life. In technical terms, the study estimated that having an additional A allele rather than a G allele on that part of our genetic code increases the odds of having a leadership position by roughly 25 percent.

We have roughly twenty-one thousand identified genes in our DNA.

If De Neve and his team were right, and they'd pinpointed a leadership gene, could we make leaders just by inserting an extra little bit of genetic code? Are we on the cusp of being able to pay a little extra cash for an ultra-ambitious designer baby who will crawl straight to the corner office on the top floor?

Not so fast. All of these findings are overstated and misleading.

If you tried to find statistical correlations between genes and current leaders in, say, the United States, the two most prominent genetic factors would be having a Y chromosome (being a man) and being white. It's not that white men are somehow better leaders (as we'll soon make emphatically clear), but rather that white men currently *get into* power more often than other types of people. That's a different puzzle from who *seeks* power.

Of course, De Neve's research team adjusted the data to take demographic characteristics such as race, age, and gender into account. They still found that the rs4950 snippet is correlated with holding a leadership position. But that could be for all sorts of reasons. It could be tied to traits that make you better at getting into power within modern society, such as being ambitious or confident or affable or extroverted or tall. All of those traits do have genetic roots, but that doesn't necessarily mean that those traits make you *desire* power more. Plus, not all routes to power are equal. Perhaps extreme thirst for power—a trait embodied in Emperor Bokassa—is passed down genetically, but the same is not true for the children of midlevel managers at insurance companies. We don't know. We're back to square one.

Even if we can find genes that are associated with current leaders, there are still confounding factors. It's extremely difficult to tell whether a person's behavior is driven by their genes or by their environment, having supportive parents, past experiences, wealth, or even randomness. Perhaps you were born to be a dictator, but your environment just didn't foster it. You grew up in a democracy and your parents didn't encourage you enough when you plotted revenge against your childhood enemies. You could've made it to the palace had you been born into an abusive family in Uzbekistan. Bad luck.

Despite these caveats, there's a good reason to believe that genes play an important role in human dominance: evidence from the animal kingdom. After all, we are animals, and genes play a role in determining leadership in other species. For example, spotted hyenas seem to inherit their place in the hierarchy of the pack from their mother. If the mom hyena was top dog (all right, fine, hyenas aren't technically members of the canine family but rather have their own special one called Hyaenidae), then the baby hyena is virtually assured to rise to be leader of the pack, too. Moreover, researchers have used selective breeding to mate submissive rats with other submissive rats and dominant rats with other dominant rats. Sure enough, the behaviors became ever more pronounced with each generation. The selectively bred rat grandchildren were supersubmissive or superdominant. In mice, one study genetically altered mice to remove a gene of interest, known as SLC6A4. Those mice who had that gene "knocked out" became submissive, regardless of whether their parents were dominant or submissive. In zebra fish—a striped little fish native to South Asia that's often found in home aquariums—a series of experiments demonstrated that social dominance is indeed inherited from the social status of the father. But that seems to come partly from genes being passed from father to son and partly from the father teaching his offspring how to achieve status within the aquarium hierarchy. The world is complex. Genes clearly matter. But they aren't the only thing that matters. (We can't conduct similar experiments on humans because of a pesky thing called ethics.)

So, here's what we're left with: Genes *definitely* affect who gets power because certain traits make you better at obtaining authority over others (more on this in the next chapter). But we still aren't sure how or whether genes affect who wants power in the first place.

What we do know is that some humans don't want power at all. In a recent corporate survey in the United States, just 34 percent of respondents said they aspired to a leadership position in their company. Only 7 percent wanted a top-level leadership position. Power, it seems, isn't universally coveted. Plus, the motives of that hard-charging 7 percent vary. Some want to serve their community or company. Others crave recognition or prestige. And some are hungry to dominate or abuse others for gratification. How can you tell which is which?

That question is far older than genomic research. The ancient Greeks spoke of *thymos*, which has many potential meanings, but is often translated as a need for recognition. Such recognition was usually secured by becoming a leader, whether in battle, oratory, or politics. Fast-forward a few thousand years, and the late Harvard psychologist David McClelland developed a measure called nPow, which stands for "need for power." It's correlated with a desire to control other people and achieve recognition through that control. Others have proposed different measures, such as something called Social Dominance Orientation (SDO), which measures our individual propensity to want to dominate others—and our affinity for hierarchies that put some people above others. Reliable measures of SDO can even be taken in children. (Most of us want enough power to feel as if we're in control of our own lives—but not much more.)

Still, we don't have all the answers. Clearly, humans exist on a spectrum. Some of us are addicted to power. Some of us avoid it altogether. But whether that variation is driven more by nature or nurture is still a somewhat open question waiting to be resolved. We just don't know.

But let's put these genetic uncertainties aside for a moment and think about another question: Can we, as humans, make it more or less likely that good people will seek power? Can we tweak recruitment policies or change perceptions of what kinds of people should be in control to ensure that gentler, kinder people start to self-select and throw their hats into the ring?

From Maori Teens to M113s

After the horrific murder of George Floyd in the spring of 2020, police reform has taken center stage in the United States and around the world. The problem is that most of the reform efforts are making the same kind of analytical error that the World War II generals were making before Abraham Wald set them straight. Departments are thinking too much about how to change the behavior of police officers they already have while thinking too little about the invisible would-be police officers they don't have. To fix policing, we need to focus less on those who are already in uniform, and more on those who've never considered putting one on.

Doraville is a small town of just over ten thousand people in northwest Georgia. Its top attraction on Tripadvisor is the Buford Highway Farmers Market (narrowly edging out Treat Your Feet massage). About twenty miles northeast of Atlanta, Doraville's crime rate is slightly higher than that of many small towns in America, but it's hardly a war zone. Most years, there are zero murders.

Nonetheless, Doraville's police department owns an M113 armored personnel carrier—a "close-combat battlefield vehicle" that has been used in fighting the Vietcong, insurgents in Fallujah, and terrorists in Afghanistan. If anything goes down at the local Home Depot, the police are ready.

A few years ago, anyone considering putting on a badge with the Doraville PD was greeted with a recruitment video on the department's website. For fifteen seconds, a logo flashes on-screen, a menacing skull set against a black background. It's a reference to the Punisher, a comic book vigilante who uses murder, kidnapping, and torture to punish criminals. Then, the armored battle cruiser emblazoned with SWAT: DORAVILLE POLICE DEPARTMENT screams into view at top speed, its treads kicking up dirt. A hatch opens. A shadowy figure tosses a smoke grenade out. Six men dressed like soldiers emerge from the vehicle. They're wearing camouflage, ready to blend in should they be deployed to the concrete jungle next to the Shaking Crawfish restaurant or if they need to impose martial law at Marshalls. Their assault weapons are drawn. The Punisher logo flashes again, followed by the image of an eagle carrying a lightning bolt in one talon and a gun in the other—the insignia of SWAT operators. Mission accomplished, the soldier cops return to their combat vehicle. The M113 drives off. The whole spectacle is set to the dulcet tones of "Die Motherf**er Die" by Dope.

Most people watch that video from a small-town police department and think, "This is insane." But others watch it and think, "Sign me up!" Whether you fall into one category or the other isn't random. After watching that video, people drawn to acting like a soldier in an occupying army are more likely to submit an application. People drawn to being a community support officer who helps elderly residents cross a busy street probably won't. And women, or minorities, who weren't depicted in the Doraville recruitment video at all, would understandably wonder whether they'd be welcome in the department. When you recruit into positions of power, it's not just about who gets the job and who doesn't. It's also about who applies in the first place.

In 1997, the US government created something called the 1033 Program to deal with surplus military equipment. The idea was to send it to police departments rather than to the junkyard. Win-win. Or so it seemed. Over two decades, more than $7 billion in military hardware—helicopters, military-grade ammunition, bayonets, mine detectors, mine-resistant vehicles, you name it—has been transferred to police departments large and small. A two-man department in Thetford Township, Michigan (population 6,800), acquired a million dollars' worth of army gear, including mine detectors and Humvees. The sheriff's office of Boone County, Indiana (population 67,000), has a heavily armored amphibious assault boat. No matter that the largest body of water in the entire county is a small pond near an isolated farmhouse. The police department in Lebanon, Tennessee (population 36,000), has a tank.

Why have toys if you can't use them? Or to put it in the form of an aphorism, when you have a hammer, everything looks like a nail. When you have a police tank, even Walmart looks like a battlefield. And that changes who tries to put on the uniform.

Let's be clear: A huge number of police officers have admirable motives for serving their community. But some don't. "If you're a bully, a bigot, or a sexual predator, policing is a really attractive career choice," says Helen King, who served as assistant commissioner of the Metropolitan Police in London. She's right. There's considerable evidence, for example, that domestic abuse by police officers is a significant problem. Some argue that such abuse is correlated with an intense, high-stress job. But other intense, high-stress jobs don't seem to have similar levels of domestic abuse. There's a more convincing explanation. Perhaps some abusive people are drawn to a powerful occupation, such as being a police officer, where it's easier to get away with abusing others. Who do you call if your abuser *is* the police? "The challenge for the establishment is to try and weed those people out in the recruitment process," King told me.

To get the right people in the uniform, the image of the police department matters enormously. The presence of tanks and assault vehicles skews who are drawn to the uniform and how they behave once in it. To request an assault vehicle from the 1033 Program, local police departments need to justify it by filling out a form that includes this prompt: "Provide estimated usage/mission requirements for the requested armored vehicles." When local police officers start seeing their job as military missions, they're going to hire more soldiers to complete them.

That's precisely what happened. Six percent of Americans have served in the military, but 19 percent of American cops are ex-soldiers, according to the Marshall Project. Government programs—and lots of funding incentives—encourage that transition for retiring soldiers. Some government grants are only given to police departments that hire veterans. That can be a great idea, in moderation. The traits for being an effective SWAT team captain do overlap significantly with those for being an effective marine captain. Military personnel are often disciplined. They're often drawn to service. And like police officers, they're willing to make the ultimate sacrifice. But policing the streets of Boston or Kansas City isn't the same as patrolling Baghdad or Kabul. Yet, Kabul and Baghdad are often what today's soldiers turned cops are used to. The jobs of soldier and beat cop shouldn't be the same, and conflating two distinct skill sets too much can be disastrous. Should we be surprised if some former soldiers revert to their earlier training to use deadly force while in the police Humvee instead of the army Humvee?

But here's the kicker: this effect is most pronounced in the departments that make policing *feel* like an army. Even after controlling for confounding variables such as crime rate or population size, researchers have found that police departments that bought the most surplus military gear killed more civilians to begin with *and* saw the numbers of civilians that they killed in a given year rise significantly *after* the military equipment arrived. Departments that kill more civilians want to become more militarized. Adding military gear makes them even deadlier.

Nonetheless, so much of the debate about police reform in the United States is focused on changing police tactics: de-escalation training, body cameras, banning choke holds, better oversight when force is deployed. All are worthwhile reforms. But they're all aimed at changing what the police *do*. Too little attention has been paid to a more fundamental cause:

who the police *are*. What's likely to be more effective, spending millions trying to retrain the small group of overly aggressive people who view themselves as soldiers and see policing as a war, or attracting less aggressive people to the profession in the first place? America's police chiefs need their modern version of Abraham Wald to explain that they need to start thinking more about who *isn't* in their force.

New Zealand is doing precisely that.

An Asian woman wearing a police vest sprints up a hill, following an unseen suspect. She turns to the camera. "New Zealand police are looking for new recruits who can make a real difference!" There's a quick cut to an indigenous Maori police officer in hot pursuit of the same suspect. "Those who care about others and their communities!" The Maori officer sprints past an elderly man with a walker slowly traversing a zebra crossing. The officer does a double take and returns to help the old man safely cross the street. For more than two minutes, the chase continues. Finally, a female officer catches up to the perpetrator. "Drop it!" she shouts at the suspect. A dog barks, revealing itself as a canine criminal. It opens its mouth and relinquishes the stolen handbag from its teeth. The entire hot pursuit has been of a fluffy border collie. "Do you care enough to be a cop?" flashes on-screen.

This scene is from a playful police-recruitment campaign launched by the New Zealand police in 2017. The contrast with the Doraville, Georgia, advertisement is so stark it's almost comical. No weapons are shown. The stated goals of policing are directly linked to helping the community. Throughout, the series of amusing gags helped the videos spread like wildfire across social media (this video has 1.7 million views on YouTube in a country of 4.8 million people). "We take policing seriously, but not ourselves," says Kaye Ryan, deputy chief executive for people with the New Zealand police.

In another video called "Hungry Boy," the police department conducted an experiment. They sent a child who looked severely malnourished to rummage through garbage cans looking for food in the center of a city. Secret cameras videotaped the reactions of those who encountered him. Some people walked by. Others stopped, asked if he was hungry, and tried to help. The compassionate people are highlighted in the recruitment advertisement. "They cared enough," it says on-screen. "Would you?" The ad ends with the "Do you care enough to be a cop?" logo. The implication was that the people who would stop and help a child should be in uniform. The others who walked past need not apply. If you had compassion for the vulnerable, New Zealand's police wanted you in their ranks.

Rather than the Punisher, New Zealand's police wanted the Helper. Camouflaged combat gear and "Die Motherf**er Die" are nowhere to be seen. Any Kiwis who think police officers should act like a militarized occupying army aren't likely to fire off an application after seeing the videos of helping a malnourished child or the chasing of a mischievous dog. But does it matter? Did New Zealand's police recruitment strategy actually change who became a cop?

In the last few years, New Zealand's police force recruited eighteen hundred new officers. The recruitment videos deliberately highlight women as well as ethnic minorities, particularly Maori officers and Asians and Pacific Islanders. "It's not that we don't want the white men," Ryan told me. "It's just that they come anyway."

Whoever comes to apply—from older white men to teenage Maori women—has to spend twenty to forty hours out on the beat with a police officer for an assessment before the actual vetting process even begins. "If they take quite a military-style or adversarial approach in dealing with the community, it doesn't work out for them," Ryan explains. "Our own cops say, 'Hang on, they're coming in for the wrong reasons.'" Rather than equipping their community cops like soldiers and emphasizing recruitment from the army, the New Zealand police guarantee that behaving like a soldier on the streets of Wellington means you won't get to put on a police uniform in the first place. They recruit and screen in a way that tries to entice those who *aren't* naturally drawn to policing.

It worked. Total applications are up 24 percent. That's a big deal, because as we'll see shortly, increased competition is crucial to getting better people into power. The number of female applicants rose 29 percent, while Maori applicants are up 32 percent. Today, roughly one in four police officers in New Zealand are women, compared to just over one in ten in the United States. The force is also close to being representative of New Zealand's ethnic breakdown. Compare that to America, where hundreds of major police departments are, on average, 30 percent whiter than the communities they patrol. (In 2014, when riots broke out in Ferguson, Missouri, after an unarmed black man was killed by police, two in three residents of the local community were black. Meanwhile more than eight in ten of Ferguson's police officers were white.) Beyond the obvious issues that creates, the perception of racial bias in policing creates a vicious cycle. If people believe that the police abuse racial minorities, then people who want to abuse racial minorities will be more likely to sign up. That's one of the difficulties of police reform. To fix policing, you need better recruits—and to get better recruits, you need to fix policing.

New Zealand tackled that problem head-on. They focused on the equivalent of the invisible planes in Germany—the invisible desirables who weren't applying for the job. As a result, New Zealand has one of the most effective and least abusive police forces on the planet. Only twenty-one New Zealanders were killed by police between 1990 and 2015, an average of 0.8 deaths per year. If you scaled that rate up to adjust for the much larger US population, you'd expect American cops to kill about 50 people per year. Instead, in 2015 alone, police officers in the United States killed 1,146 civilians. Perhaps America could learn a thing or two from New Zealand.

What the police do matters. But who the police are may matter even more. And if you don't design recruitment policies properly, you'll end up attracting all the wrong moths to the flame of power.

Sometimes, the problem can be even worse. From Doraville to Wellington, there are usually a lot of people who want to be cops. But what happens when a position of authority isn't particularly attractive? Without competition, self-selection is the *only* thing that matters. If only one person applies for a powerful job, then any power-hungry cretin can waltz right into authority. That's like rolling out the red carpet to the worst kinds of control freaks. And they, too often, are precisely who run our neighborhoods.

Arizona Autocrat

Roger Torres (not his real name) is a fighter. Not just a fighter in the metaphorical sense. Someone who actually used to compete in mixed martial arts. His record was impressive: twelve wins—including four knockouts, he tells me, with a link to an official website to back it up. "My nickname was the Cannon because I hit hard," Torres boasts. But when Roger and his wife bought a property in a sunny Arizona community, he didn't realize that he was entering a showdown in an arena he wouldn't be able to escape for years.

In 1970, only about a million Americans lived in communities governed by bodies called homeowners' associations (HOAs). Today, around 40 million do. Add in condominium boards and it's another 30 million. Together, these hyperlocal quasi-governments collect roughly $90 billion per year in dues to pay for utilities, maintenance, repairs, and the communal costs of upkeep. That's about twice as much money as the total state tax revenues for Florida.

The HOAs usually establish elaborate rules, too. Some of the revenue that fills rainy-day funds for repairs or improvements comes from fines imposed on rule breakers. The more you enforce the rules, the more your rainy-day fund grows. But unlike government tax collectors, HOA enforcers aren't faraway bureaucrats in Washington. They're your neighbors.

Here's the problem: Who wants to be the person who patrols the neighborhood and imposes hefty penalties when Susan down the street puts her trash bins two feet away from the curb instead of the requisite one foot or less? It's not exactly dripping with the glory of *thymos*.

In Roger Torres's small Arizona community, there wasn't much competition to rule the HOA. "The apathy was rampant," he says. "Nobody paid any attention. Often they couldn't fill the board because nobody wanted to do the job." Those who served were roped into it because *someone* had to. That is, until Martin McFife (also not his real name) came along. For him, the homeowners' association wasn't a burden. It was a calling.

Because the HOA was basically begging people to take on the responsibility, the board snapped up McFife when he volunteered. He ran in the election unopposed. But there was a problem after he won. "He was such a disagreeable a-hole," Torres says, "that nobody wanted to work with him." Torres suspects this wasn't an accident. Instead, it seemed McFife was deliberately ruffling the feathers of those on the board so that they'd just figure it wasn't worth it anymore. And that's precisely what happened: when the incumbents who didn't want to be on the board in the first place were up for reelection, they retired instead. McFife handpicked their replacements. The planes that survived were *his* planes. He'd consolidated power with the efficiency of an autocrat.

McFife ruled over the small community like one, too. One Sunday, Torres was heading out of his house. The next day was trash day, but the HOA had strict rules: no trash bins could be on the street before noon on Sunday. Torres was in a hurry. He glanced at the clock. It was 11:55 a.m. He put his trash bins out. Five minutes later, at precisely noon, an HOA enforcer rolled by. Torres was fined.

Every time he disputed a fine, more fines would follow, a punishment for daring to challenge McFife's cabal. Roger's palm trees were suddenly deemed to be in violation of the rules. Fine. A frond looked as if it *might* be dying. Fine. "He wanted the trees aggressively trimmed back yearly so that they perpetually looked like a carrot because that was what he preferred," Torres explains.

Eventually, Torres couldn't take it any longer without fighting back. He formally complained that the rules were being arbitrarily applied. Shortly after that complaint, a letter arrived in the mail. It was an entirely new rule book, filled with fresh regulations. Some of the guidelines were incredibly specific. "Gravel now had to be indigenous to Arizona," Torres recalls. "We even had rules made just for us, so I felt honored." The Torreses had installed a security camera on their property because teenagers were doing drugs near their yard. The new rule book forbade security cameras. "We had some decorative rocks that McFife didn't like," Roger says. "So, the rule book now specified that decorative rocks larger than a softball had to be buried up to one-third their height." When that rule change didn't prompt the Torreses to remove the offending rocks, they started going missing

In protest, they did something they knew would drive their local HOA tyrant crazy: they put a pink flamingo in their yard as a sign of resistance. Soon, their neighbors did the same. Pink flamingos popped up everywhere. McFife was furious. And while he couldn't be sure, he stewed over whether some out-of-state gravel had survived his purge.

It was time for decisive action. In a special "Important Homeowner Update," all the area residents received a document trashing the Torreses. "Still refusing to trim their dead palm tree fronds, they have now added a flock of pink flamingos. . . . Are the Torreses *really* your 'good friends' and considerate, helpful neighbors?" These newsletters targeting the Torreses by name—and there were several—are laced with shouty capital letters and lines such as "This feels like a 'set-up.' We've seen this play before and it ends with Neighborhood Decline!" One concludes with "The stakes are high. . . . Time is of the essence." To be fair to McFife, he'd counted seven lightbulbs that needed to be replaced. The fate of the community hung in the balance. Time to redeploy the M113 from Home Depot and bring in the amphibious assault vehicle! (In all seriousness, the HOA meetings grew so contentious that the board did pay for a police officer to attend them.)

Then, the Torreses did something McFife hadn't anticipated: they used his rule book against him. They invoked a little-known bylaw to force a recall election. The board was wiped out. "McFife lost his mind once he got booted," Torres explains. "He started patrolling the neighborhood on a daily basis, taking pictures of all the things he didn't like." I've seen the subsequent newsletters he produced. They're filled with photos of allegedly out-of-place cacti and an oleander plant that hadn't been watered recently enough for his liking. It's all a bit nutty. In the next election, McFife had his chance to rise, phoenixlike, from the ashes of defeat. He received three votes.

Roger sold his house and has vowed to never again live in a property managed by a homeowners' association. "From what I gather from talking to our old neighbors," Torres says, "the people that bought our house aren't trimming back the palm trees to McFife's personal preference either, I'm sure to his great displeasure."

There are hundreds of stories like these. There are even entire organizations and internet subcultures dedicated to documenting abuses by HOAs (many involve embezzlement, too). These experiences showcase a valuable lesson. There is *always* self-selection bias with power. Whether it's trigger-happy police officers or power-hungry tyrants in homeowners' associations, power tends to draw in people who want to control others for the sake of it.

Thankfully, once you recognize that tendency of power, you can counteract it. As the New Zealand police realized, you can try to attract different moths to the flame. Businesses can conduct reviews to ensure that their recruitment, retention, and promotion mechanisms draw in people who may not seek power but would wield it effectively. Political parties can approach people in the community who could become good leaders rather than waiting for people to put themselves forward. And if homeowners' associations want to avoid being governed by the neighborhood despot, then they should consider creating incentives (including decent pay) to recruit people who want to do the job for better reasons than to harass the people down the block. Finally, it's not just about attracting different types of moths, but also attracting more of them. The more you have fluttering around power, the more you can zap the corruptibles and still be left with incorruptibles. But when there's no competition—when whoever reaches the flame first gets to control others—well, then you're more likely to be stuck with a power-hungry tyrant obsessed with palm fronds and haunted by flamingos.

IV

THE POWER DELUSION

Why Our Stone Age Brains Cause Us to Give Power to
All the Wrong People

White Guy in a Tie

Mitch Moxley isn't a backup dancer, but he's danced in music videos. He's not a model, but he's appeared as one of "China's 100 Hottest Bachelors" in a Valentine's Day issue of the Chinese edition of *Cosmopolitan* magazine. With China's population at 1.3 billion, there were several hundred million bachelors to choose from. The editors picked Moxley. Never mind that they hadn't even seen a photo of him before he was selected.

The editors got lucky. Moxley fit right into the magazine. His hair looks as if it has carefully been prepared by someone who knows what he or she is doing with a pair of scissors and some expensive product. Moxley wouldn't look out of place in a fancy hotel bar with a sturdy whiskey glass in his hand while regaling you with bizarre tales from his reporting junkets in Mongolia and North Korea. But none of that was what set Moxley apart. Instead, he stood out for one reason: he was a white guy living in China.

One day, while Moxley was scraping together a living as a freelance journalist in Beijing, a friend called with a job offer in Dongying, a small, unremarkable coastal city in northeast China. Dongying's only claim to fame was that it was allegedly the birthplace of Sun Tzu, who wisely counseled, "Secret operations are essential in war; upon them the army relies to make its every move." Moxley was about to be part of a secret operation. But it wasn't on a battlefield. It was in a factory.

"I didn't really know too much about it other than that they wanted to get a group of foreigners together for some kind of ceremony," Moxley tells me. The gig was to pay $1,000 for a week's work. "My friend asked me if I wanted to come, and I was like, 'Yes, definitely.'" There was some vague talk of quality control. Moxley figured he should come clean and play it straight. "Just so you know," he told his friend, "I have no experience in quality control or in business whatsoever." Moxley's friend replied, "Not a problem. Bring a suit."

The following Thursday at 7:45 a.m., Moxley, along with two other Americans, two Canadians, and an Australian, hopped on a flight to Dongying. They were completely in the dark about the job they'd been hired to do. All that seemed clear was that it was important that they *appear* to be businessmen at a new factory. With a fresh haircut, a shiny pair of new shoes, and a cheap, ill-fitting suit, Moxley had prepared for his part reasonably well.

When the six arrived in Dongying, they reported to the factory for their first day on the job. They were enthusiastically greeted and shown to their offices. Each man had a desk. "On each desk were a hard hat with a company decal and an orange safety vest with an oversized zipper that read "D&G—DOLOE & GOB8ANA," Moxley later recalled in his book, *Apologies to My Censor.* But the vests weren't the only fakes. Moxley and his fellow white male conscripts were the fakes, sent to pretend that they were from a nonexistent Californian parent company that was involved in the factory's long-awaited launch. If they'd looked Chinese, nobody would've taken notice. But big shots from California coming to Dongying? That stood out.

"We sat in this office reading magazines and talking," Moxley says. "Then, once a day we had to do a tour of this factory. We would pretend to take notes and look at things." When the tour ended, it was back to the magazines. That was the job. One of his friends referred to it as renting a "white guy in a tie."

After a few days of posing as interested investors and businessmen, it came time for the grand opening. The mayor was there. Women in ceremonial dresses smiled on the red carpet. One of Moxley's fake colleagues, a guy named Ernie, stood up and read a speech he'd been handed. "They picked him because he looked the oldest," Moxley explains. He watched the surreal event while sporting his trendy DOLOE & GOB8ANA safety vest. When the speech concluded, there were fireworks. Chinese pop music was pumped through speakers in celebration. "The factory was only halfway done," Moxley remembers. "So I still don't know what the ribbon-cutting ceremony was for."

Moxley's experience wasn't unique. Instead, it's part of a bizarre industry in China in which foreigners are used as props to lend credibility to an operation. Sometimes, white women are hired to add sex appeal to a new bar. In one instance, a film director named David Borenstein was hired to go onstage in rural Chengdu. He, along with his fake band, were introduced to the crowd as "America's top country music band called Traveller." They didn't exactly fit the part. Borenstein played the clarinet, but nobody seemed to know that a clarinet isn't a staple of country music, so it didn't matter. The lead singer was "a Spanish woman who didn't speak English and couldn't really sing."

These stories sound exotic and bizarre. But they're just reflections of a fundamental truth about human society: we're often more obsessed with how something or someone *appears* than with who they are or what they can do. Power is no different. If you look like a leader, it's easier to become a leader. Whether it's in Dongying or Denver, we give authority to all sorts of people for precisely the wrong reasons. In the Chinese factory, credibility flowed from Mitch Moxley *because* he is a white guy. But is it *so* different in Western societies? Why do we seem to give so much control to such a small slice of people?

Of the 500 largest corporations in the United States, 468 are run by a man. That leaves just 6 percent with a woman at the helm. Of those same 500 corporations, 461 are led by a white person, leaving just 8 percent for nonwhite CEOs, even though 40 percent of Americans are nonwhite.

In the United States, white men comprise roughly 30 percent of the total population. Yet, 431 of the 500 Fortune 500 CEOs are white men, representing 86 percent of the overall total. In fact, the number of white male Fortune 500 CEOs named John or Jon (27) equals the number of Asian CEOs (16) and Latino CEOs (11) combined. Only four black CEOs are on the list. None of the Latino or Black CEOs are women. In the table below, you'll see the difference between the reality of Fortune 500 CEO representation and that respective demographic within the US population.

Demographic	Approximate Percentage of US Population	Percentage of Fortune 500 CEOs
Men	50	94
White men + women	60	92
White men	30	86
White women	30	6
Black men	6.5	0.8
Black women	6.5	0
Latino men	9	2
Latino women	9	0
Asian men	3	3
Asian women	3	0.4

These numbers aren't much better elsewhere. In the United Kingdom, for example, as of the summer of 2020, only five of one hundred top companies (the FTSE 100) were led by women. More CEOs named Steve were on that list than female CEOs.

That distortion shows up in public recognition, or lack thereof, too. Try to name a male leader from the tech sector. If you're like most people, the names Steve Jobs, Mark Zuckerberg, Elon Musk, and Bill Gates spring to mind immediately. Now, try to name a female tech leader. A recent survey of one thousand Americans asked that precise question. Ninety-two percent of respondents admitted they couldn't name a single female tech leader. Eight percent said they could. But when those people were pressed to actually name one, most couldn't. Among those who actually produced a name, guess what two of the most common replies were. Alexa and Siri.

In addition to reflecting societal racism and sexism, these disparities matter because they can deter extraordinarily talented women and ethnic minorities from joining major corporations that are dominated by white men. Trevor Phillips, a former politician who has worked extensively on power imbalances in British business, refers to the lopsided demographics in senior management as the Snowy Peaks and Vanilla Boys problems. When ethnic minorities or women look to the top of the corporate hierarchy and only see snowy peaks or vanilla boys, some, he argues, will search for a company that has a more diverse senior leadership team. That can compound the problem in major corporations, Phillips argues, because talented women and ethnic minorities sometimes move to smaller start-ups where there's a greater chance of rising through the ranks quickly. "They think that they're not going to get anywhere or that they're just window dressing," he told BBC News.

It's not just business, either. As of 2020, just 16 of the 193 member countries of the United Nations were led by a woman—a little over 8 percent of the total. And only 58 countries (30 percent of the total) have *ever* had a female leader. The United States is, of course, on the wrong side of that split.

There has been progress, but it's too slow. In 2000, roughly one in every seven elected officials in national congresses and parliaments were women. Today, it's up to one in four. Better, but still abysmal. And if you zoom in on rich, developed democracies that are supposed to be world leaders on issues such as gender equality, well, they don't live up to their rhetoric or stated ideals. In 1990, women comprised less than 2 percent of Japan's parliament. Today, it's still a mere 10 percent. In the United States, the proportion has tripled, from 7 percent in 1990 to 23 percent today. But think about that: when it comes to the proportion of women in political power, the United States is still below the world average of around 25 percent.

Even the seeming success stories are often worse than they seem. The world leader in women's representation in national government is tiny Rwanda, in central Africa, with women comprising 61 percent of parliament. But that's because the male dictator, Paul Kagame, has skillfully and cynically packed the parliament with women who rubber-stamp his agenda, so that he can elicit more foreign aid from Western donors *because* he has largely powerless women rubber-stamping his despotic rule rather than men. He often uses women as symbolic props, not as leaders. How depressing is that?

We also—let's face it—end up with a lot of cruel, incompetent people in positions of authority. At first glance, that's a bit perplexing, because power is relational. In other words, individuals can't be powerful alone. To become powerful, you need people to control. Power is therefore given, not taken. Or, as primate expert Frans de Waal put it, "You cannot be a leader if you have no followers." So, it raises the obvious question: Why do we let awful, incompetent, even murderous people control us? And why are so many white guys in ties?

The answer is partly because of the flawed evolution of our brains, dating back to prehistoric times. To see how this happened, we need to take a closer look at signaling and status symbols.

Honest Springbok, Dishonest Crab

If you were a springbok, your main worry in life would be turning into someone else's lunch. Specifically, you'd be worried about being a particularly delicious course on the tasting menu of a lion, a cheetah, or a pack of wild dogs. So, how would you behave if you spotted a nearby lion, a cheetah, or a pack of wild dogs salivating in your general direction?

Surely your instinct wouldn't be to leap into the air, making sure that the predator saw you. Yet that's precisely what springboks do. In a particularly springlike fashion, they launch themselves as high as they can, with their legs held as stiff and unmoving as possible, as though they're being judged for style points by an unforgiving Russian at the Olympics. When they crash back to the ground, they can feel confident that the predator has seen them. Mission accomplished. But why do that? Anyone who's ever gone grocery shopping while hungry knows it's not a good idea to show a glimpse of something delicious to a ravenous creature.

This ritual is known as stotting or pronking—take your pick of whichever silly word you prefer—and evolutionary biologists have hypothesized that its purpose is to show the predator how wonderfully agile the springbok feels at the moment. Should the cheetah be looking for a quick lunch, it should look elsewhere, for the pronking springbok has made clear that she or he wouldn't be an easy catch.

These types of behaviors exist throughout the animal kingdom. They're examples in "signaling theory," which argues that species have evolved to quickly convey information that can save everyone a lot of trouble. Without stotting and pronking, the only way a cheetah might find out which springboks are like Usain Bolt would be to chase them and find out. That's bad for the cheetah *and* bad for the springbok, because both end up wasting valuable energy in a pointless chase. The springboks evolve to pronk, and the cheetahs learn to avoid those individuals who would score a perfect ten even from the most curmudgeonly Olympic judge. Because pronking ability accurately conveys a springbok's agility and speed, it's known as an honest signal. Honest signals are everywhere. Picture a brightly colored frog that will poison you with toxic venom if you ignore the signal and eat it. You'd only have yourself to blame. It tried to warn you.

But not all animals are so honorable. Some snakes have coloring that suggests they're poisonous when, in fact, they're perfectly harmless. Then there's the fiddler crab, which has a comically oversize claw to warn off rival males who might try to compete for a mate. It looks the animal kingdom's equivalent of those oversize foam "We're number one!" fingers sold at baseball stadiums, except it's supposed to be menacing. When a fiddler crab loses a fight, its intimidating claw is often torn off, too. It grows back, but the replacement is weaker than the original and virtually guarantees that the crab will lose any future showdowns. Luckily, the other fiddler crabs can't tell the difference between regrown or original claws, so they still avoid picking fights. The ostentatious but useless new claw does the trick. It's the animal equivalent of a criminal brandishing a realistic-looking toy gun to rob a bank. This is known as a dishonest signal.

Signaling theory has another key dimension, which is whether a display is costly or not. Is there a downside to signaling? If so, it's costly. Peacocks provide a great example of a costly honest signal, where their plumes do accurately signal their mating desirability, but also slow them down and make them more vulnerable to predators. (Pronking is modestly costly because the springbok has to use precious energy to leap into the air.) By contrast, some signals cost nothing. Frogs with red stripes don't have to spend anything to send their signal. It's just always there.

These dimensions (honest versus dishonest, costly versus costless) are useful for analyzing human behavior when it comes to power, too. We're constantly exhibiting honest and dishonest signals about whether we are dominant and powerful or weak and submissive. Sometimes, we don't even realize we're doing it. Other times, it's deliberate—such as when you see someone drive by in a flashy car that costs as much as a house. But signaling theory raises an intriguing hypothesis: Are powerful people just better at *appearing* powerful?

To find out, I met Professor Dana Carney on a sunny January afternoon in Berkeley, California. She's a psychologist and a professor in the Berkeley business school, too, where she studies everything to do with power. In 2010, Carney's work became world-famous. She, along with Amy Cuddy and Andy Yap, authored a research paper showing something astonishing. By adopting what they called the power pose—in which people adopt a posture that takes up more space and projects an aura of strength and confidence—they found that people instantly felt and behaved like someone much more powerful than they actually were. They also discovered that standing that way caused a spike in hormones that helps you feel more in command of a situation. With that simple technique, they argued that anyone could "instantly become more powerful," a finding that they claimed had "real-world, actionable implications." Carney's coauthor Amy Cuddy gave a TED talk about their work. To this day, it's the second-most-downloaded TED talk ever, watched by 60 million people.

There was just one problem: when other researchers tried to replicate these findings, they couldn't. When others conducted the same experiment with the same pose, there seemed to be no effect whatsoever. Carney responded with integrity. She later publicly distanced herself from the research, saying that she does "not believe that 'power pose' effects are real." (Cuddy continues to insist that the research is valid, despite growing evidence to the contrary. This controversy helped launch something called the replication crisis in psychology, which caused substantial changes in how research is produced, vetted, and published.)

But even though power poses probably don't change much about how you feel, it's absolutely the case that the way we present ourselves affects how others perceive us. (Anyone who's shown up underdressed to a formal event knows what I'm talking about.) Carney's other research is laced with examples of how quickly we size up others in trying to determine how to act toward someone. It's instantaneous. Our brains are remarkably effective at creating a composite assessment of someone from tiny, seemingly insignificant cues that add up to a complete picture and a verdict: high status, low status, or somewhere in between.

We are, at times, consciously aware of how to signal status. Big houses, Rolex watches, and designer clothes are all examples of deliberate (and costly) signaling to show excess wealth. However, not all rich people want to show off. This divide is often captured by the classification between "old money" and "new money." You're far more likely to see a twenty-five-year-old start-up billionaire in a yellow, diamond-encrusted Ferrari compared with, say, the Kennedys or the queen of England. Signals of excess wealth are particularly likely among those who have come from deprived backgrounds. It's a mechanism to show the world that they've made it and now inhabit a new status. The signaling is most effective when it's frivolous, because it shows you're so rich that you're willing to effectively light money on fire for no practical benefit. (This is one possible reason why ornate, expensive hubcaps with no practical function often grace the cars of drug dealers who rose from poverty.) In indigenous societies in northwest Canada and the United States, "potlatch" ceremonies even involve high-status individuals or families deliberately *destroying* wealth to show that they can. In some instances, rivals compete to show how much they can destroy. If someone eventually bows out because the cost is too great, the person loses face and often suffers a corresponding loss of power and status in the community.

Such ostentatious displays of wealth as a mechanism to attain status were deemed "conspicuous consumption" in the late nineteenth century by the economist Thorstein Veblen.[*] The French sociologist Pierre Bourdieu later argued that, contrary to earlier belief, such displays are com-

---

[*] Veblen graduated from the small liberal arts school Carleton College, in Northfield, Minnesota—a town with the motto "Cows, colleges, and contentment." It's also my alma mater, and I'm therefore obliged to report this completely superfluous fact.

pletely rational because they simply represent the conversion of money into social capital. For example, philanthropists often end up being perceived as leaders in society simply by waving around big checks for good causes. Bill Gates seems to have figured that out more than Jeff Bezos.

Researchers have even established that humans instinctively use displays of wealth to attempt to signal status. We don't even think about it, in much the same way that pronking springboks probably don't consciously decide to leap into the air to show their fitness to a cheetah. In one experiment, men were asked to donate to a charity. Who agreed to donate and how much they agreed to give varied substantially—based on how rich they were, their generosity, all the kinds of factors you'd expect. But then, the researchers ran the experiment with a twist, by introducing an attractive member of the opposite sex. When charitable donations were solicited in the presence of a moderately attractive woman, men gave more. When they were solicited in the presence of an extremely attractive woman, men were even more likely to empty their pockets. Men clearly believed—either consciously or subconsciously—that flashing some cash was a surefire way to signal status in front of attractive women. (Women, interestingly, didn't change their donating patterns even when an attractive man was in the picture.)

Signaling is an important shortcut for status displays because we don't walk around with our bank account balances or our job titles taped to our foreheads. You can often tell when someone is destitute, but it's much harder to differentiate the rich and powerful just by looking at them. Even billionaires wear blue jeans. And, as with animals, plenty of humans try to use *dishonest* signals to their advantage. The sidewalk stands selling cheap knockoff Rolexes or Ray·Ban sunglasses are there to help you channel your inner fiddler crab. That's why the most effective signals of status are genuinely costly. If they weren't costly, they'd no longer be as effective.

In seventeenth-century France, for example, lace was a status symbol because it was so expensive to produce. Elite ladies of the day would devote huge resources to making sure that their lace stood out as the most intricate. Then it became possible to machine-stitch lace. The masses could have it. Almost overnight, lace became meaningless.

Status symbols can even invert themselves. In the past, tanned skin was a clear indication of low status. It meant that you were toiling in the fields under the hot sun, unable to afford a life of leisure indoors. By the 1930s, though, that signal had completely flipped. Tanned skin now meant that you were affluent enough to afford sunny holidays away from the dark recesses of an office or factory floor. Darker hues became a showpiece for the rich and powerful. Then, tanning beds made it possible to look as if you had been to Mexico when you had just gone to the discount salon next to the Mexican restaurant. As soon as it became possible to use tanning as a less costly, dishonest signal, its potency diminished. (Today, tanning-bed usage signals something else: a willingness to get skin cancer.)

As a species, we obsess over these arbitrary signals. We do so because we understand that appearances do help you rise—or fall—on the ladder of life. They matter. But these forms of signaling do little to help us understand the "white guy in a tie" problem that Mitch Moxley experienced. After all, women and aspiring leaders from ethnic minorities can buy Rolexes and Ray·Bans and drive fancy cars. Communities that are underrepresented in the pantheon of modern leadership can do the human equivalent of pronking endlessly. Still, the power gap persists. So why do we consistently make such badly skewed decisions about the people we put in charge? Yet again, we need to travel back in time and understand the origins of our species.

Stone Age Mismatch

Next time you try, but fail, to maintain a diet, don't blame yourself. Blame your Stone Age ancestors. Over the last several million years, our brains grew and grew, tripling in size from those of our chimpanzee cousins. But for the last two hundred thousand years or so, our brains have stayed the same size. This has led evolutionary psychologists—people who focus on how the human psyche has changed over vast time scales—to conclude that "our modern skulls house a Stone Age mind." For example, to survive in the past, our minds were wired to have strong, positive reactions to sugar. Two hundred thousand years ago, sugar came from nutritionally beneficial foods, such as yams or fruit. But fruit wasn't overly sweet back then because there was no selective breeding. Most Stone Age fruits consumed by our hunter-gatherer ancestors were about as sweet as a carrot, according to evolutionary biologist Daniel Lieberman. Our brains are set up for mildly sweet fruit, not Froot Loops. Similarly, we evolved to immediately gobble up any shreds of fat we could get our hands on because fat used to be so scarce in our diets. Today, we pipe processed sugar and fat straight into our bloodstream at a rate that had previously been impossible. The corresponding spikes in diabetes and obesity in the modern era are examples of "evolutionary mismatch," where our bodies and brains evolved for a lifestyle that no longer exists. (Similarly, evolutionary psychologists have shown a mismatch in how we remain instinctively terrified of snakes and spiders even though they pose virtually no threat to the overwhelming majority of humans on the planet today. But they used to be a major cause of death for hunter-gatherers.)

These mismatches occur because of how abruptly human society changed. In the past, those who followed the brain's cravings for sugar and fat were more likely to survive. Today, those who follow our Stone Age instincts are more likely to become obese or develop diabetes or even die. Similarly, we should now be afraid of automobiles, not spiders. But there simply hasn't been time for our brains to catch up and adapt to all the sudden, fundamental changes of how we live our lives.

So, if our Stone Age minds have created a mismatch with our diet and our fears, then it seems logical to wonder whether we also have a corresponding mismatch in selecting leaders. Are we hardwired to favor traits in leaders that our Stone Age ancestors would've found most desirable? It seems reasonable to wonder, for example, whether the traits that would've made someone good at fending off saber-toothed tigers or hunting gazelles are the same traits that make someone good at midlevel management of, say, a paper-supply company.

There's plenty of evidence that we use physical appearance as a shortcut when choosing leaders. That isn't new. Plato spoke of it in *The Republic*, when he described a ship of fools led by a captain who was incompetent, but was taller and stronger than the others. Plato had a point.

The science seems to show that when we pick people to lead, our Stone Age brains and the evolutionary history of our species have caused us to prioritize men over women, tall men over short men, and people who look most like ourselves over those who don't.

For the last several decades, Mark van Vugt, professor of evolutionary psychology at the Vrije Universiteit in Amsterdam, has been studying these skewed preferences and the mismatches that created them. In his book *Selected: Why Some People Lead, Why Others Follow, and Why It Matters*, he shows that while these preferences have a stronger pull in some situations than others, they're always present. But—and this is a crucial point—just because these cognitive biases exist doesn't mean that they're inevitable, acceptable, or "natural." It *is* possible (and essential) to override these idiotic impulses. But we can't fix that broken Stone Age way of thinking until we acknowledge that it exists within many of us.

As we saw in chapter 2, hunter-gatherer societies were flatter than modern ones. But those societies still had informal leaders who would organize, say, a hunting expedition, or who might develop a bit more gravitas in group decision-making. Such informal leadership lent itself to a certain type of person. As van Vugt explains, "Leadership in ancestral humans was often a physical activity such as in hunting or warfare. Leaders led by example and often from the front, and so there would have been selection on cues of health, stamina, and an imposing physique."

It wasn't just a preference for bigger and stronger individuals. They were actively selected during evolutionary processes. Van Vugt argues that bands of humans who picked physically weak leaders during hunts or battles with rival bands were more likely to die, culling those who made that mistake from the human gene pool. Bands who picked physically strong leaders in moments of life and death were more likely to live, reinforcing that choice.

Think about it this way: There've been roughly 8,000 generations of humans in the last two hundred thousand years. Of those, something like 7,980 generations have lived in societies in which size and strength were major advantages for survival. That's about 99.8 percent of the history of our species. That realization has given rise to something known as evolutionary leadership theory. Our social world has changed, but our brains haven't. Humans have learned to pick leaders for reasons that no longer reflect modern realities. It's time to unlearn those outdated instincts.

Gender and Giants

About a decade ago, a group of scientists at prestigious universities were asked to rate student applicants for a job as a laboratory manager. They were sent a series of CVs. In their evaluations, they had to rate the applicant and suggest a starting salary based on the person's qualifications and experience. "The cover story was that we were interested in creating a new mentoring program to help undergraduate students move forward in science careers," Professor Corinne Moss-Racusin of Skidmore College tells me. "We just asked faculty to give their honest feedback about each lab-manager application."

What the faculty members didn't know was that the CVs were fake. The quality of the applicants varied—some more qualified, others less—but the crucial manipulation was at the top of the page. Each fabricated CV was randomly assigned a name, either from a list of female names or male names. The same exact CV would look as if it came from a Sarah or an Alexander, a David or an Ann, a James or a Kelsey. That was the only difference between them. Otherwise, the applicant quality was evenly split. In a just world, names would make no difference to evaluations. But we don't live in a just world.

The faculty evaluations consistently rated male applicants higher and assigned them a higher potential starting salary. It didn't matter whether the faculty member doing the evaluation was male or female. They all showed a bias against women. Society is slowly waking up to such long-standing gender discrimination. But a crucial question is still unanswered: Is that bias only culturally learned, or is our misogyny also rooted in our prehistoric past?

As long as we've been recording history, women have been written out of it. Professor Mary Beard of the University of Cambridge, in her book *Women & Power*, showcases countless examples of sexism from antiquity to modernity. It wasn't just that women didn't get power in the ancient world, but rather that the very idea of granting power to women was often viewed as an absurd concept. As Beard explains, in the fourth century BC, "Aristophanes devoted a whole comedy to the 'hilarious' fantasy that women might take over running the state. Part of the joke was that women couldn't speak properly in public." As Beard highlights, when women were elevated into positions of power, one of three things tended to happen to them. First, they would be described as manly, suggesting that only women that mimicked men as much as possible could aspire to power. Second, they were depicted as animals "barking" or "yapping" when they spoke—physically incapable of the manly gift of human speech. And third, they were depicted as conniving and manipulative, usurpers who abused power when they managed to, somehow, wriggle into it.

Fast-forward two thousand years or so, and those sexist tropes persist. So much so that in 1915 the feminist author Charlotte Perkins Gilman felt compelled to write a novel called *Herland*. It's set in a fantasy world in which women give birth exclusively to girls. Men don't exist. Women rule. Gilman's imagined utopia is free from war and domination of others.

Herland seems a *bit* extreme, mind you, but mountains of evidence suggest that elevating more women to leadership positions wouldn't only be just, it would also be wise. It's important to avoid being a gender essentialist (suggesting that men and women are fundamentally and irreconcilably good at some things and bad at others—a view that has been used to maintain the oppression of women for centuries). But substantial research has demonstrated that, on average, women are less prone to despotism than men and more eager to rule by democratic means. It's also true that women either perform the same or better than men on just about every leadership metric you could imagine. (A potential confounding effect here comes, ironically, from how difficult it is for women to get into top-level roles in modern, male-dominated society. Because women face more barriers to rise to the top, women who make it may be more exceptional than some mediocre men who manage to fail upward. That difference in difficulty at reaching the top could skew the data, because a small number of exceptional women are being compared to at least some unexceptional men.)

The bottom line is, clearly there's no male gender advantage in wielding power. Yet, society acts as if one certainly exists. Take a moment to reflect on how bizarre gender politics are when it comes to political leaders. With clocklike regularity, Vladimir Putin releases photos of himself shirtless on a horse, practicing judo, or doing some other warrior show of strength. Those signals can be effective because our Stone Age brains still link some perceptions of leadership to physical size. But it's absurd. Imagine if you were going in for surgery and your surgeon spontaneously did twenty push-ups to show you his physical prowess. You'd find another surgeon and probably call the medical licensing board. But when it comes to political leaders, modern societies often reward masculine shows of strength. Due to evolutionary mismatch, such signals are now utterly irrelevant. After all, Angela Merkel and Jacinda Ardern have been two of the most effective politicians in recent memory. Should anyone care how much they can bench-press?

If you're skeptical that sexism in leadership is tied to our Stone Age brains—which is understandable, as evolutionary psychology theories are contested—it's harder to ignore another set of research findings that go beyond cultural misogyny.* Modern computer-imaging technology allows researchers to manipulate pictures of faces with pinpoint accuracy. With a click, a face can be made to appear more or less stereotypically masculine. Some scientists wondered, If you take a picture of a person but enhance its perceived masculinity slightly, how does that change our feelings toward that face? The relationship isn't as straightforward as you might think. As you'd expect, male faces are chosen in leadership experiments more often than female ones. But something interesting happens when participants in leadership-selection experiments are told to choose a leader against a security threat (the risk of conflict or an ongoing war). In those experiments, the effect of masculinity is magnified. The experiment suggests that we're subconsciously more likely to favor leaders who look more manly during times of crisis. It's absurd, but the data show that the effect is real.

Van Vugt calls this notion—that we tend to pick modern leaders who share physical characteristics with men who would've made good warriors or hunters in the Stone Age—the savanna hypothesis. He explains, "Evolution has burned into our brains a set of templates for selecting those who lead us, and these templates are activated whenever we encounter a

---

* One of the main criticisms of evolutionary psychology is that it's impossible to test and verify its core claims. We can't go back and conduct experiments on people who lived two hundred thousand years ago. Therefore, there's good reason to be cautious with any sweeping conclusions.

specific problem requiring coordination (such as in times of war)." It's one of the reasons that authoritarian-style *strongmen* (the term is no accident) gin up fear or provoke conflicts to consolidate power. They're activating our hunter-gatherer instincts to turn to someone who seems strong when we perceive a threat. We can either pretend these biased, sexist leadership templates don't exist within us (or at least many of us), or we can accept that they do and work to overcome them. Even then, that's only part of the battle. We still have to overcome the internalized misogyny that's learned or exacerbated by our sexist culture.

The savanna hypothesis isn't just about a bias in favor of male leaders. If the hypothesis is accurate, we would be drawn not just toward men but toward large, physically imposing men. And that's precisely the case. In securing power, it's good to be tall—and it has been for some time.

More than two thousand years ago, Alexander the Great granted an audience to the captured Persian queen Sisygambis. Alexander was accompanied by his best friend, Hephaestion, who was taller. Immediately, Sisygambis knelt before Hephaestion to plead for her life, mistakenly assuming that the taller aide was the king. It was a grave, if understandable, insult. (Alexander spared her anyway.) Still, the implication was clear. Height was believed to be a pretty good predictor of status.

A few millennia later, in 1675, the Prussian army created an infantry unit known as the Potsdam Giants. The sole distinguishing feature of the regiment was that the soldiers were tall. To be considered for the elite regiment, you had to be at least six feet two, an exceptional height for the era. The Prussian king Friedrich Wilhelm I, who was apparently stranger than the usual monarch, would make the tall soldiers march before him when he was in his sickbed to cheer him up. When he showed the Potsdam Giants to the visiting French ambassador, he said, "The most beautiful girl or woman in the world would be a matter of indifference to me, but tall soldiers—they are my weakness." His obsessions grew so great that he reportedly began kidnapping tall people across Europe to turn them into soldiers—at one point even paying £1,000 (an enormous sum in those days) for an operation to seize an Irish giant on the streets of London. When those kidnapping plots became too expensive, he tried to breed tall people, forcing tall men to marry tall women and marking long babies with red scarves to identify them as future recruits. When Friedrich Wilhelm rode in his carriage, he is said to have required tall soldiers to walk on either side of him and hold hands over the carriage, showing off their long arm span.

Setting the king's bizarre proclivities aside, all of this fixation on height was pointless. By the time Friedrich Wilhelm I was ruling, height had effectively been neutralized as a distinguishing feature in modern combat. Having a gun and an itchy trigger finger was all you needed. To prove the point with a poetry that only history can produce, the Potsdam Giants were disbanded when the lofty Prussians were defeated at the Battle of Jena-Auerstedt by the not-so-giant Napoléon Bonaparte.

Whether these tall Prussians were beautiful, as the king believed, is debatable. But they're certainly a beautiful illustration of evolutionary mismatch. Friedrich Wilhelm selected them based on a trait that no longer conferred a major advantage. The Potsdam Sharpshooters would've been a better choice, but he was fixated on height. It seems bizarre and irrational. Yet the more closely you examine our choices in the modern era, the more it seems that we have plenty in common with the height-obsessed eighteenth-century king of Prussia.

American presidents are consistently taller than the men of their time. Even after accounting for a variety of other factors, researchers who crunched the numbers found that candidates who are taller usually win more votes than their shorter opponent(s). Taller presidents also have a higher chance of being reelected. Lest you think this is just a historical fluke, researchers conducted experiments in which they showed participants identical images in which the background was digitally manipulated to make the person in a photograph seem taller or shorter than average. Participants were then randomly assigned whether they'd see a tall man and tall woman or short man and short woman. Taller men were perceived as more leader-like. It had a major impact. But for women, the role of height in shaping perceptions of leadership was much smaller. That conforms nicely to the Stone Age brain hypothesis, as height would be of greater significance for a male hunter or warrior. (Nevertheless, this nuance was apparently lost on an aspiring female Australian politician named Hajnal Ban, who had her legs broken and stretched in 2002 so she could grow by three inches before her election bid. She won.)

It's not just politicians, either. Studies from eighteenth-century Germany to modern-day America and Britain show that tall people earn more money throughout their careers. One study found that several extra inches of height correlate with, on average, roughly $200,000 in additional lifetime earnings. There's no rational reason for it, yet it persists, as a modern mismatch.

So, we give power to men more than women, and to taller men more than shorter men. Part of the reason we do that is rooted in our outdated minds. But that's only part of the puzzle. What about race?

Baby Faces and Bigotry

In your daily life, you likely encounter dozens, if not hundreds or thousands, of strangers. Even in places you frequent, such as the grocery store or your office building, you'll cross paths with people who are completely unknown to you. If you're a frequent flier, or if you live in a major metropolis, encountering people who speak a different language, wear different clothes, or come from different cultures is routine.

But for our hunter-gatherer ancestors, such encounters were exceedingly rare. Because of territoriality, venturing into unknown land was akin to playing Russian roulette. The biologist and author Jared Diamond, in his book *The World Until Yesterday*, argues that hunter-gatherers classify everyone into three groups: friends, enemies, or strangers. Friends are those dozens of families that make up your band, or who are from bands you're on good terms with. Enemies are people you recognize, but are from a rival band that lives in the same area. The third camp—strangers—are rare. But, to be safe, you must automatically assume they're potential enemies. In the prehistoric past, hunter-gatherers would never meet someone who was from halfway across the world, meaning that encounters with people from different races were effectively close to zero. As a result, racism couldn't have been reinforced by psychological evolution over hundreds of thousands of years the same way that biases for height and gender were. Plus, given the origins of our species, most Stone Age hunter-gatherers didn't look remotely like modern Europeans or Americans. So, is all racism culturally learned?

Unfortunately, our Stone Age brains produce serious biases about people who look different. For survival, our social species has evolved to quickly use cues to identify whether someone is like us, and a friend, or unlike us, and a potential foe. This impulse gives rise to what social scientists call sorting between "in-group" and "out-group" individuals. In-group individuals are to be embraced, while out-group individuals are to be shunned, driven off, or even killed. Crucially, those from an out-group are more likely to be people that we see as potential threats—a point that we'll return to momentarily.

Today, many people still rely on these arcane, bigoted sorting mechanisms as a cognitive shortcut, even though it's completely irrational. In one experiment, researchers in Britain recruited football (soccer) fans for a psychology experiment. Everyone who wasn't a Manchester United fan was screened out of the participant pool, but participants didn't know that's why they'd been selected. Then, the participants had to complete two unrelated tasks. They were told that the second task would take place in a nearby building. The real experiment happened as participants moved from the first building to the second. Each person would encounter someone (an undercover member of the research team) who was visibly injured and needed assistance. In every instance, the encounter was the same, with just one randomized difference. A third of the time, the supposedly injured person was wearing a Manchester United jersey. A third of the time, the person was wearing the jersey from Liverpool, a rival team. And a third of the time, the injured person was wearing a neutral shirt. The participants stopped to help those wearing Manchester United jerseys a whopping 92 percent of the time, compared to 35 percent for someone in a neutral shirt and just 30 percent for those wearing a rival-team shirt. The rates of assistance tripled, based only on a logo.

In another experiment, college students participated in a team-based game in which cooperation and trust were crucial to success. When given the chance to choose a leader, they had two options. They could pick someone with a losing record who happened to be from their university, or someone with a winning record who was from another university. Consistently, the students picked the worse leader, who was from their own school. Why do we do that? Our prehistoric templates for determining in-groups and out-groups shift our behavior, even when it's irrational and damaging to our best interests. We trust those whom we identify with. But we're suspicious of those who don't seem to be "one of us."

In the modern world, those templates from ancestral brains intersect with centuries of explicit and implicit culturally learned racism to create even more biased assessments of those who are from a different, particularly minority, ethnic group. That's demonstrated with some depressing research that shows white Westerners sometimes behave as though black people are "strangers" who are potential threats—a phenomenon that further compounds the systemic institutional racism that plagues modern societies.

All human faces can be scored by how baby-faced they appear (the technical term is babyfaceness). Countless experiments have demonstrated that we instinctively pay attention to this trait when assessing others—and judge them based upon it. In the criminal justice system, there's evidence that judges and juries treat baby-faced defendants as less responsible or culpable for their actions than less baby-faced defendants, even if they're the same age. We seem to automatically believe that babyfaceness is a proxy for innocence. As a result, those who are more baby-faced are often perceived as less threatening than those with more hardened, adult facial features.

But there's a disheartening twist.

Studies have found that whether babyfaceness helps or hurts you gain power is dependent on race. Here's what the research seems to show: Black people are more likely to be viewed by white people as threatening. That's partly because of the "strangers" template in our Stone Age brains and partly due to a long, grotesque history of learned and internalized racism. No surprise there. But just as white people are more prone to viewing black people as threats, they're less prone to viewing *baby-faced* black people that way, according to experiments. Further research has shown that, in a white-dominated society, baby-faced black people are therefore more able to attain power than less baby-faced black people. White people view black people with more adult faces as a threat, leading to reduced career advancement. According to this research, this relationship is inverted for white people. In similar studies, baby-faced white CEOs were perceived to be weak rather than threatening. In a white-dominated society, it seems that having a baby face helps you if you're black and hurts you if you're white. It's horrifyingly bonkers. But it seems, on aggregate, to make a difference that compounds preexisting racial biases in society.

The point is this: irrational evaluations of faces based on archaic threat instincts still seem to be entrenching inequality in our modern world. This could partially explain (but never excuse) why highly qualified people from ethnic minorities often get passed over for leadership positions in favor of less qualified white people. But it goes beyond faces. When researchers sent out fake CVs for job openings that used names such as Emily or Greg, those applications got far more callbacks than identical CVs that seemed to come from people named Lakisha or Jamal. The black-sounding names were discriminated against relative to their objective qualifications.

There is, however, some good news. In-group and out-group affiliations need not be defined by race. As the Manchester United study shows, we can identify with other human beings for all sorts of reasons. While racism isn't going to be overcome with quick fixes or football jerseys, forging broader forms of shared identity is one crucial first step (of many) to ensuring that leadership is populated with the best and brightest, and not just the West and whitest.

So, what can be done? First, any group that has a hierarchy should be producing data about the demographic composition of its leadership. One of the reasons why the Fortune 500 CEO list above is so glaring is because the data are readily available. The racist and sexist rot is plain to see. But for most organizations, serious skews by race or gender aren't easily quantified by those who work in the company. To fix the problem, we have to see that it exists.

Second, while it won't fix everything, blind recruitment and promotion should be used whenever possible. In many instances, it won't be feasible. After all, in a small business, you're going to be able to identify Barbara's or DeAndre's CV whether or not the name is listed at the top—and you can hardly create a blind review of presidential candidates. But in larger organizations or for first-time recruits, anonymizing applicants without names will lead to fairer decisions.

Third, hiring and recruitment panels should be as diverse as possible. Given that humans are seemingly hardwired to have biases toward those who look most like us, better decisions will get made when that myopia is eliminated.

Fourth, and finally, these kinds of interventions need to be made much, much earlier in life. It may sound silly, but anonymizing school assignments and exams whenever possible would help cut down on serious inequalities emerging during childhood due to teacher bias. (In Britain, where I teach at University College London, all essays that I grade are anonymized. It produces a fairer system.) None of these measures will destroy systemic inequalities that have deep roots in our psyche, our culture, and our racist and sexist history. But they'll each make a meaningful dent. Those dents can eventually puncture our learned and archaic biases toward people who look different from ourselves.

We've already discovered why hierarchies exist in humans and why corruptible people are more likely to try to rise to the top of them. Now, we also know why our Stone Age brains cause us to *give* power to certain types of people over others. But there's another question to tackle: Why are corrupt or corruptible people so effective at manipulating their way into power? To put it bluntly, why do so many of society's leaders seem to be narcissistic psychopaths?

V

PETTY TYRANTS AND PSYCHOPATHS

Sentiment is a chemical aberration found on the losing side.

—*Sherlock Holmes*

The Maintenance Man of Schenectady

Rich Agnello didn't have particularly unusual preferences when it came to heating his classroom. He had plenty of other things to worry about as he taught special education in Schenectady, New York. That is, until one winter day in late 2005. His classroom was frigid. The cast-iron radiator was cold to the touch. It wasn't safe to teach. "I actually went to a friend who taught science and borrowed a little thermometer to tape on the wall, so I could talk to my union about the working conditions," Agnello told me. He complained repeatedly, but the temperature never improved. Finally, he took matters into his own hands and brought in two space heaters from home.

The next day, when Agnello was unlocking the door to his classroom, he realized someone was lurking behind him. "So I turn around and there's Steve Raucci, just looking like I committed a crime against humanity," Angello recalls. "He starts yelling at me and pointing at the space heaters and saying, 'Those are illegal, you can't have those in here.'" A decade ago, speaking to journalist Sarah Koenig of *This American Life*, Agnello described Raucci's rage in that moment as "eyes bulging, and veins on his head throbbing." Agnello figured he'd just stay calm and explain the situation. He pointed at the thermometer in defense of his rogue space heaters. Raucci wasn't convinced. He stormed off.

Raucci was a school maintenance official in the Schenectady school district. He'd been given a clear mission from the higher-ups in the district: reduce the district's energy bill. Raucci got the message loud and clear. Saving money on electricity and heating was a surefire way to make the bosses happy. If he succeeded, a promotion might even be waiting for him.

"There were teachers I know of," Agnello told me, "who, if they left their computers on overnight, or if they had, God forbid, highly illegal coffee makers or something in their rooms, he would direct the custodial staff to go through with shears and clip the electrical cords of any outlawed machines." Agnello's space heaters didn't get snipped. But they did disappear.

"The next day, as I was coming into work, I'm walking up, and a man I recognized as our district electrician is running down the stairs with my two little space heaters tucked under his arms," Agnello says. When Agnello protested, the electrician just sheepishly said, "Talk to the central maintenance office," before getting into his van and speeding off. "I just started laughing, like, 'What the heck is going on?'" Agnello still laughs when he remembers his brush with Steve Raucci. Others weren't so lucky.

Raucci was far from the top of the district pecking order. He made $42,000 a year, not bad money for a school maintenance official, but nothing special. Then, he spotted a way to rapidly rise. One of his colleagues, Lou Semione, had just been made the district's energy-saving czar. The post came with a big pay bump and a pathway to more advancement. Raucci wanted the job for himself. So, as he often did, Raucci hatched a scheme. Nobody was going to give him power. He'd have to take it for himself.

Raucci came up with a plot to destroy his rival. To help Semione save money for the district, the bosses had splashed out on a new software system that could help track energy usage. It pinpointed waste and allowed centralized control to turn lights on and off. But the new software seemed daunting to Semione, so Raucci volunteered to manage it. He showed Semione regular updates and promised that everything was running smoothly. But when Semione wasn't around, Raucci started secretly manipulating the software. If Raucci could increase energy usage, maybe

Semione would get fired and the district would look for a new czar. Once, Raucci made sure that the football stadium's lights—one of the district's most power-hungry energy sucks—was switched on for the entirety of Columbus Day when everybody was away from campus. Other times, he'd make sure entire buildings were lit up over weekends. It worked. Semione was removed from the job. Raucci convinced the bosses to give him a shot instead. It may have been a small kingdom, but Raucci had made himself king.

"Hey, Lou," Raucci said in his last encounter with Semione. "I want to tell you we were fu**ing with you." As with so many conniving power seekers, Raucci couldn't just beat a rival. He had to humiliate him, too. But there's no question that Raucci got what he wanted. After being put in charge of the energy saving for the district, his paycheck rose into six figures. And once it was his turn to save money on energy usage, he became the district's electricity Scrooge. Rich Agnello's space heater couldn't be tolerated—not even as the holidays approached.

But unlike Scrooge, Raucci had no moral awakening. Instead, his behavior got progressively worse. He sexually harassed subordinates. Anyone who challenged him faced threats. When his secretary casually remarked during watercooler banter that Raucci wasn't "her type," he transferred her to a worse office. Then, in his annual Christmas speech—at an event that normally would involve a toast from the boss and good tidings to all employees—Raucci warned that nobody should cross him, lest he have to "eliminate" them. "Only I will be the fixer," Raucci hissed. If there had been a modern-day Tiny Tim, Raucci would probably have snipped the cord on Tiny Tim's electric wheelchair while it was charging.

As Raucci grew more powerful in his job, he sought a new kingdom to conquer: the school district's union. But when he launched his campaign into union politics, someone decided to blow the whistle on him. The person wrote an anonymous letter, detailing Raucci's abuses as president of the maintenance unit. He wasn't fit for union leadership, the letter claimed.

Raucci went ballistic. Someone had double-crossed him. Raucci thought he knew who it was: Hal and Deborah Gray. Hal worked under Raucci in the maintenance office. Deborah worked for the union. On

May 1, 2005, the Grays got up early to catch a flight for a vacation to Vegas. Hal went outside and saw red spray paint everywhere; RAT was written in big letters across their house. Paint had been splashed on every possible surface to make the repair as expensive as possible. The Grays were devastated. Even a Vegas jackpot wasn't likely to cover the repair bill.

When news spread of the vandalism, Raucci organized a pilgrimage for his subordinates to admire the handiwork of the "unknown" perpetrator for themselves. They clambered into school district vehicles (while on the clock) and drove twenty minutes each way to see it. Each staff member had to show Raucci that he or she was pleased that the Grays had gotten what they deserved.

A district employee, Gary DiNola, complained about Raucci's behavior to the district superintendent in 2006. Raucci found out. When DiNola came out to his car one day, his tires had been slashed. An unlit explosive device was held in place by one of his windshield wipers. It was hard to miss the message.

Vandalism and explosives soon became Raucci's language for intimidating those who dared to cross him. Ron Kriss, who had previously been harassed by Raucci, found his truck severely damaged when he tried to speak out against his boss. Raucci boasted to others about the incident. "Ron Kriss is a guy I got rid of here," Raucci bragged. "He used to park his truck, nice new little trucky truck, over by Home Depot. Parked it right in the center—to make sure nothing happened to it." If Raucci sounds like a Mafia boss to you, that's not an accident. He hung a photo of Don Corleone from *The Godfather* in his office. "For five-plus years, we lived in fear," Kriss told me.

While Raucci's underlings were terrorized, his bosses were thrilled. His aggressive energy cost cutting had saved the district millions of dollars. Raucci had made it. To solidify his grip on power, Raucci tried to build an empire of allies to insulate him from whistleblowers coming after him from below. When one school board member found himself in dire financial straits, Raucci gave him a loan. The maintenance man turned godfather was there to help with envelopes of cash.

But everyone—even a meticulous planner such as Raucci—makes mistakes. In one incident in which he attempted to use explosives to intimidate a potential rival, Raucci left behind a cigarette that he'd planned to use as a fuse. Traces of DNA were on the cigarette. The investigation team had long suspected Raucci's involvement, but here was a chance to prove it. One morning, Raucci ate breakfast at one of his favorite diners, the Peter Pause, an all-American joint in Schenectady that serves stacks of pancakes and oversize omelets. The police waited until he was done eating. Then, as he left, they collected his fork and sent it to the lab. It was a match. Raucci's DNA was on the unlit cigarette fuse.

This was still not enough proof to tie Raucci to his other crimes. So, the police recruited one of Raucci's friends—a former cop turned drug addict—to wear a wire and record Raucci. When you listen to the audio, you can hear a deranged and deluded mind at work. Or as Ron Kriss put it to me, they show that Raucci was a "narcissistic liar" with a "sick ego."

On one tape, Raucci shows delusions of grandeur atypical for a school maintenance official. "When I'm dead, they'll always be talking about what Steve did and what I could do," Raucci boasted, drifting between third and first person in the same sentence. Raucci laments that he is one of a "dying breed," and that "I'm everybody's hero . . . everybody's lucky 'cause they got a Steve." To underscore his modesty, Raucci concludes by wishing that his mother had given birth to twins because then "I could have had a Steve to go to."

In another recorded encounter, Raucci showed the undercover informant a homemade explosive device. After showing it off, Raucci carefully tucked it out of view behind a plant. This was in Raucci's office, inside a middle school. Once investigators heard that tape, they moved quickly. Kids were at risk. They put Raucci in cuffs. In addition to finding the explosive, the police also found night-vision goggles—an accessory that isn't necessary to polish floors in a high school gymnasium, but that would come in handy for vandalizing homes in the dead of night. In 2010, Raucci was sentenced to twenty-three years to life in prison.

Raucci is an extreme example, but abusive supervisors are as common to workplaces as watercoolers. They exist on a spectrum, from the relatively harmless overconfident, self-important blowhards to something much more sinister. In this chapter, we're going to look at why corrupt and corruptible individuals are so effective at rising through the ranks. How do they do it? We'll also grapple with a disturbing question: Are psychopaths better leaders?

Let's start by looking at the outliers such as Raucci—the psychopaths and narcissistic schemers. They're rare. Odds are low that your boss or coach or the police officer who pulls you over is a bona fide psychopath. But because such people can be so destructive once in positions of authority, they warrant special consideration. Once we've got a grip on what makes people such as Raucci tick, we'll move on to the more run-of-the-mill bad bosses and try to explore why overconfidence and arrogance are common traits in powerful people.

Steve Raucci exhibits classic signs of something called the dark triad. As its name suggests, the dark triad has three components: Machiavellianism, narcissism, and psychopathy. Machiavellianism comes from the reductive caricature of a single idea from Italian political philosopher Niccolò Machiavelli—that the end justifies the means. Machiavellianism therefore refers to a personality trait marked by scheming, interpersonal manipulation, and moral indifference to others. Narcissism, named after Narcissus from Greek mythology (who is destroyed because he falls utterly in love with himself), refers to personality traits that often manifest as arrogance, self-absorption, grandiosity, and a need for recognition from others. And psychopathy—the darkest trait of the dark triad—often shows up as someone who lacks the ability to feel empathy and is impulsive, reckless, manipulative, and aggressive. Each of the three traits exists on a continuum. You may even have small amounts of each trait percolating unnoticed through your veins (and a small number of you reading this sentence will be undiagnosed narcissistic Machiavellian psychopaths). For most of us, though, these traits come in tiny, harmless doses. When the three occur at extreme levels in the same person, well, then you've got a problem—and so do the people around you.

Measuring the dark triad is, like all psychological and psychiatric profiling, somewhat subjective. The gold standard of diagnoses used to be a lengthy questionnaire. Then, in 2010, two researchers realized that they could get effectively the same results with just twelve questions. These questions have become known as the Dirty Dozen—a quick, rough measure of whether someone has a mind that plays host to the dark triad. The questions include such items as "I tend to manipulate others to get my way" or "I tend to lack remorse" or "I tend to seek prestige and status." Many people will answer yes to some of these, but those who score high across all twelve are more likely to have elevated levels of dark triad traits.

Of course, a Machiavellian psychopath isn't always going to fess up to their less than perfect behavior on a self-reported questionnaire. To detect fakers, more robust measures are needed. For clinical psychopathy diagnoses, for example, the subject is put through lengthy questioning that feels more like an interrogation. When diagnosing violent offenders, what the person says during the interrogation is corroborated using witness statements and case files to make sure the subject isn't lying. But plenty of psychopaths with dark triad traits have made an art out of fooling others into thinking they're kind and compassionate and should be in control. And outside prison, there are no case files or witness statements. We're on our own in trying to identify the Rauccis that lurk among us. So how can we spot them—and ensure they don't become our leaders?

Ants, Spiders, and Snakes in Suits

In east-central Africa, around the shores of Lake Victoria, there lives an arachnid known as *Myrmarachne melanotarsa*, the dark-footed ant spider. While other spider species have round bodies, these spiders have long ones, specifically designed to appear as though they have three parts—head, thorax, and abdomen—much like an ant. Instead of walking with all eight legs like other arachnids, the dark-footed ant spider only uses its rear three pairs, allowing its front leg pair to be lifted aloft, mimicking the antennae of ants. They move like ants, too. Recent studies have even found that they live communally in "silken apartments," as though the spiders have formed their own Potemkin village of an ant colony. It is, as one researcher put it, an "Oscar-worthy performance."

This complex charade exists for a reason—or, more accurately, for two reasons. First, the dark-footed ant spiders don't get eaten by predators because the ant they mimic is fearsome prey. Second, the spiders disguised as ants can more easily feast on spider eggs. Spiders don't normally worry about ants because they get trapped in the spider's web if they try to eat spider eggs. The spiders let their guard down. That allows the ant-like spider to sneak in undetected, gallivant over the silk unimpeded, and munch down on a feast of spider eggs. As Ed Yong of *National Geographic* put it, "It is, essentially, a spider that looks like an ant to avoid being eaten by spiders so that it itself can eat spiders." It's a master class in deadly deception.

Psychopaths have much in common with dark-footed ant spiders. While they don't eat spider eggs or thrust their arms into the air like antennae while living in silken apartments, they do often try to mimic something they're not: people with normally functioning brains. And often, once in disguise, they prey on those people.

A little over two hundred years ago, a French physician named Philippe Pinel watched on in horror as a man kicked a dog to death. The man did it methodically, without remorse. He treated it as though he were accomplishing a mundane task, like hammering a nail or taking the trash out. Pinel developed a new typology for this type of behavior, something he called *manie sans delire*, sometimes translated as "moral insanity," though the more direct translation is "madness without delirium."

Show a normal person a series of violent images—helpless animals or children exhibiting extreme distress, for example—and brain regions that are associated with emotion light up like fireworks. While neuroscientists are still trying to understand the biology of empathy, it seems to operate through two systems, one "bottom-up" and another "top-down." The top-down system comes from something called a theory of mind, or mentalizing. This is where we try to understand what other people are feeling and what their intentions might be. The bottom-up system is believed to be associated with the "mirror neuron system," in which our brain activity mirrors the brain activity of someone we're witnessing. For example, brain scans have shown that if you see someone making a disgusted face—as though they'd just smelled something awful—the same parts of your brain are activated as if *you* had just smelled something awful. Neuroscientists have proposed that this is one possible mechanism for the phenomenon of "emotional contagion," in which you feel happier when you see other happy people and sadder when you see other sad people. For most of us, watching someone in severe pain or emotional distress is deeply unpleasant.

But not all of us are the same. Some of us react more than others to suffering. Using fMRI machines, scientists can quantify the change in brain activity from our baseline to a reaction to seeing someone else in pain. Empathy is incredibly complex, but this method gives scientists a rough proxy to measure it.

Valeria Gazzola and Christian Keysers took that insight and measured empathy in psychopaths. In their study, twenty-one clinically diagnosed violent psychopaths were transported to their lab to be scanned. Once inside the scanner, the psychopaths viewed someone getting hurt by another person. As the researchers expected, the neuron fireworks never went off in the way they do in the rest of us. The sections of the brain that are normally associated with emotion were dull and distant for the psychopaths. The pain of others didn't bother them.

But there was still a puzzle. Open any book about psychopathy and the phrase *superficial charm* is probably on the first page. Psychopaths are smooth talkers. They're often incredibly likable, albeit in a glib way. They seem exciting to be around. A key to their success is manipulating others, but doing so requires making others let their guard down. How could people who didn't feel for others make us like them so effectively? To find out, Gazzola and Keysers decided to re-scan the violent psychopaths. But this time, Professor Gazzola had an idea. She explicitly told them to *try* to feel for the other people—to empathize with them while watching them suffer. In that experiment, the results were completely different. The psychopaths showed neurological signs of empathy that mimicked those of normal people. This led the scientists to conclude something surprising: psychopaths *can* feel empathy toward others. It just doesn't happen naturally. Their regulation of their top-down and bottom-up processing is different from that of the rest of us.

If psychopaths can be coached to mimic ordinary people, can our normal brains be made to think like those of psychopaths? Sort of. "If people know they must fire someone, they downregulate their empathy to allow them to do what must be done," Gazzola explains. "If we want to be a charming date, we upregulate our empathy and pay full attention to the most minute signs of our date's emotion." "Normal" brains tend to have empathy switched on more often by default, whereas psychopaths' brains seem to have it switched off by default.

We can also use technology, including magnetic stimulation of our brains, to partially switch empathy off. Using "noninvasive brain stimulation," researchers have been able to get normal people to feel less empathy temporarily. Use the stimulation in the right areas and you won't be nearly as affected by horrific images as you would normally be. For brief moments, we can get inside the mindset of an unfeeling psychopath. Psychopaths, it seems, don't need any technology to override their natural state and switch empathy "on." They can flip that mental switch on as needed. Perhaps they deploy emotion like a targeted weapon, but only when it suits them.

However, just because psychopaths don't naturally feel for others doesn't mean that they're unemotional. In fact, one emotion comes extremely naturally to psychopaths: anger. If their brains tend to be a desert of compassion, they're a rain forest for aggression. The question, then, is whether these abnormal brains can confer advantages on psychopathic individuals that may make them better at taking control.

When you think of psychopaths, notorious names come to mind: serial killers such as Ted Bundy. Bundy used a classic psychopathic trait—superficial charm—to lure in his victims. But when you talk to experts who study psychopaths, they all make the same point: the psychopaths who ended up in jail are the *unsuccessful* ones. Steve Raucci, for example, wasn't good at hiding his psychopathic traits. He couldn't resist the temptation to boast when he terrorized someone or spray-painted the person's house. He couldn't control his rage. And his vindictive Christmas speeches didn't exactly go unnoticed. Raucci couldn't blend in like the dark-footed ant spiders. When he needed to raise his proverbial legs and pretend to have antennae, he planted an explosive instead. Raucci didn't have the discipline necessary to pass as something he wasn't.

But many psychopaths *can* blend in. The successful psychopaths are in boardrooms. They're signing legislation. They manage hedge funds. They are, to borrow the phrase from psychopathy expert Robert Hare, "snakes in suits." When those snakes try to slither their way into positions of power, the dark triad can, at times, help them get there.

Consider how we hire and promote people. Success relies on charm, charisma, and likability. Job interviews are performances. You may have gotten there with your CV, a good cover letter, and a strong recommendation. But once you're in the room, it's all about making the people there like you—while creating the perception that you're qualified for the job. If you seem nervous, timid, or shy, you're less likely to be hired. But if you seem confident and polished and always have an answer to whatever question is thrown at you, you're more likely to be selected. For narcissistic, Machiavellian psychopaths, the standard job interview is the perfect format. They love to talk about themselves. They strategize about how to get what they want. The end justifies the means—even if it means manufacturing lies about themselves or inventing false credentials. And they're naturally gifted at showcasing superficial charm and charisma. The way we hire disproportionately rewards the dark triad.

Scientists have tracked this by evaluating job interview performances and "impression management." Every time you try to present yourself in the best possible light to someone else, you're doing impression management. There's nothing wrong with that. We all do it. It's normal. But just like the fiddler crabs with useless oversize claws, we sometimes give off dishonest signals during impression management. Some of us even lie to make ourselves look better to others. However, when psychopaths and Machiavellians are measured in job interviews, they differ from the rest of us in intriguing ways. As you might expect, people who score high on Machiavellianism fabricate, inflate, and lie more during job interviews. But psychopaths also fabricate, inflate, and lie *according* to the interview that they're doing. Whereas some dishonest people might pad their CV a bit to get a leg up, psychopaths move chameleonlike through job interviews, completely changing themselves to match what they believe the interviewer is looking for in a new recruit. Rather than adding a tenth of a point to their college GPA on their CV across all applications, psychopaths might invent a fake economics degree in a banking interview and then fabricate a legal internship when being grilled by a law firm. Some will happily invent entirely false personas. If they're intelligent psychopaths (as many are), they get away with it.

In another study, researchers evaluated just under a thousand corporate employees for dark triad traits. They found that narcissists made more money and Machiavellians were better at climbing the corporate ladder. Psychopathy, on the other hand, damaged the career prospects of employees who scored high on it, probably skewed by the "unsuccessful" or undisciplined psychopaths who were unable to blend in. There's certainly evidence that psychopaths who are unable to manage their impulsive, aggressive, even violent behavior are going to face consequences at work. Screaming at your boss or punching a watercooler isn't exactly a surefire pathway to a promotion. And, of course, some psychopaths just aren't very smart. But the dark triad traits often don't exist in isolation. When they work in harmony, some of the most destructive elements of psychopathy can not only be blunted, but turned into advantages. The psychopaths who are in the boardrooms are the intelligent ones who figured out a way to control themselves as they sought to control others.

Paul Babiak, Craig Neumann, and Robert Hare (three of the world's foremost experts on psychopathy in the workplace) therefore wondered whether the dark triad was more or less represented in the top levels of company hierarchies. They studied more than two hundred corporate professionals from seven companies. What tied their subjects together was that all had been selected by the companies for management development—training programs to launch them into the higher echelons of the company hierarchy.

Some of what the researchers found wasn't surprising: the overwhelming majority of subjects scored a zero, one, or two on the psychopathy checklist, a measure that goes up to forty. (Ted Bundy is a thirty-nine.) With these checklists, researchers have two thresholds that are commonly used in psychopathy research. Score around twenty-two or above and the researcher will consider you a "possible" or "potential" psychopath. Score above thirty and you're definitely one.

Of the two hundred managers being groomed for the top, twelve, or about 6 percent, hit the first threshold. But an astonishing eight of the participants in the study—4 percent—rated above thirty. One person scored a thirty-three, another a thirty-four. The average score for male criminals in prisons? Twenty-two.

Admittedly, this single snapshot of two hundred people isn't necessarily representative of the corporate world (and all of the subjects were American, which introduces cultural skews). But as a glimpse of leadership in the private sector, it's disturbing. When psychopathy is sampled in society as a whole, about one in every five hundred people scores above the psychopath threshold of thirty. In the study of aspiring corporate managers, it was one in every twenty-five. Those results could be an outlier, but that study suggests that there are about twenty times more psychopaths in corporate leadership than in the general population. (Other studies have suggested that one in a hundred people are psychopaths, suggesting a fourfold overrepresentation in corporate leadership.) Most intriguing of all, of the nine subjects who scored above a twenty-five, "two were vice-presidents, two were directors, two were managers or supervisors, and one held some other management position." The psychopaths in the sample weren't just trying to make it to the top. They'd already made it.

This probably isn't just a coincidence. Dark triad traits may have a double effect: they make such corruptible people crave power, but can also make them more effective at getting it. And that may come down to an ability to focus laser-like on ruthless self-interest.

In one study, Japanese researchers set up a simple task called the ultimatum game. The rules are simple. One hundred yen is up for grabs. One player is randomly assigned to be the proposer. The other player is assigned as the responder. The proposer suggests some split for the one hundred yen. If participants are fair-minded, the proposal will be fifty yen for each player. If they're selfish, they might propose an 80/20 split, or a 90/10 split. But there's a catch. If the responder refuses the offer, neither player gets anything. The game is designed to pit our innate human desire for fairness against our economic self-interest. For example, if your selfish partner proposes a 95/5 split, you might want to smack the proposer, but it's objectively in your economic interest to accept the offer. You get five yen that you wouldn't otherwise have. But our instinctive desire to punish selfish behavior often overrides that self-interest. When the experiment is carried out, people tend to find their breaking point at 70/30. Anything more uneven than that and the proposer and responder usually leave with nothing.

What, the researchers wondered, would happen if the people playing the game were evaluated for psychopathic traits? Would psychopaths be more rational and less affected by unfairness—so long as it was in their own interest? Do they have cold, calculating lizard brains that can detach them from questions of right and wrong, just and unjust, fair and unfair? That's precisely what they found. The more psychopathic you were, the more you were willing to accept unfair offers that nonetheless benefited you. To put a finer point on it, the researchers also measured "skin conductance response." Bizarrely, our skin becomes a better conductor of electricity when we're in "emotional arousal." Scientists can therefore measure skin conductance as a rough proxy for emotional responses. In the Japanese study, those without psychopathic traits who got a fair offer didn't experience much change. But if they got an unfair offer from a snake trying to take advantage of them, their emotions went into overdrive. They got agitated. For people with more psychopathic traits, fair and unfair offers made no discernible difference in their skin conductance. It didn't seem to affect them much.

Another study conducted the same ultimatum game but did so while scanning the brains of those involved in an MRI machine. In that study, there wasn't much of a difference between the more and the less psychopathic players—they both rejected similar numbers of unfair proposed splits. But different parts of their brains lit up while they made that decision. In normal people, brain regions that are associated with normative decision-making—what is right and what is wrong—were most active when they were deciding to accept or reject an unfair offer. The decision was a moral one, tied to emotional cues about how the world *should* be. But for those who scored higher in psychopathy, those brain regions stayed comparatively dark. Instead, areas of the brain that excel in psychopaths—the areas associated with anger—were activated in the face of an 80/20 split. It wasn't that they were upset this wasn't how the world *should* be, but rather that they viewed it as a personal affront that they didn't get the outcome they believed they deserved. This may seem like a subtle difference, but it's an important one. Unsuccessful psychopaths, such as Raucci, can't control their anger, and they may turn to violence. If someone offered him an 80/20 split, he'd probably reject the offer and burn the person's house down. But successful psychopaths can manage the anger while not being swayed by compassion. Many use that combination as they rise through a hierarchy. Without much second thought, they'll throw a colleague under the bus to get ahead. That unfeeling reptile brain helps them become snakes in suits.

Because of these traits, there's a sorting effect with dark triad careers. Power-hungry, narcissistic, Machiavellian psychopaths aren't usually drawn to, say, charity work (unless it's to go unnoticed among the vulnerable, like the dark-footed ant spider). According to Kevin Dutton, a research psychologist at Oxford and the author of *The Wisdom of Psychopaths*, the ten professions with the most psychopaths are CEOs, lawyers, TV/radio personalities, salespeople, surgeons, journalists, police officers, members of the clergy, chefs, and civil servants. Another study found that those with dark triad traits are strongly drawn to positions that give them an opportunity for dominant leadership—leadership that involves controlling others—and particularly so in finance, sales, and law. While Dutton doesn't mention politicians on his list (probably because there's a reasonably small sample size), one study found that Washington, DC, has by far the most psychopaths per capita of any region in the United States.[*] The areas where the dark triad is most overrepresented are many of the most influential areas of society. A small number of destructive people can make a big difference.

Here's the emerging picture: Psychopaths are rare, but they're more drawn to power and are better at getting it. They're therefore overrepresented in positions of authority. So, what do they do with that authority? If they're not worried about others in their ascent upward, are they more prone to hurting people once they have more power?

Anyone who took Introduction to Philosophy in college has pondered the following scenario: Everyone in your village is hiding from guerrilla extremists. The guerillas have come to murder every man, woman, and child that they can find. Just as a glimmer of hope emerges that you won't be found and everyone will survive, a lone baby starts crying. De-

---

[*] Maine ranked second, for some reason, and North Carolina and Tennessee had the lowest rates, but some of that is probably statistical noise.

spite every attempt to calm the baby, nothing works. If the crying doesn't stop, everyone in the village will be slaughtered. Do you smother the baby to save everyone else?

This agonizing choice again pits our rationality against our deepest moral instincts. If you don't smother the baby, the baby will still die—just at the hands of the guerrillas instead. If you kill the baby, everyone else survives, but *you* made the choice that ended the baby's life. This excruciating scenario fiercely divides us. Some would smother the infant; others couldn't fathom such depravity. But psychopaths are less torn. Studies show that they tend to be more detached and utilitarian, choosing the depraved but self-interested action. When it comes to doing something monstrous to save themselves, psychopaths hesitate less.

That finding suggests a disturbing conclusion. Perhaps it's a benefit in modern society to be immune from moral self-reflection. Some people are horrified at the prospect of an amoral CEO, president, or prime minister. Others find it reassuring that someone who constantly faces unbearable moral choices is able to disregard compassion and focus on hard-nosed costs and benefits. (The question is whether psychopathic leaders only factor in costs and benefits to themselves or consider other people as well.) Fortunately, we can test these questions. Do cold, calculating brains perform better than the rest? Is it a gift to be released from the shackles of empathy?

As Leanne ten Brinke, a professor at the University of British Columbia told me, the evidence suggests otherwise: "Psychopaths seem to be charming and charismatic, so they climb up the ladder. But they tend to be less effective than those with fewer psychopathic traits."

Ten Brinke conducted a study with elected officials. What she found was striking. Those farther along the dark triad spectrum were better at getting reelected than their more normal-brained peers, but worse at passing legislation. They convinced people to give them power but didn't wield it effectively. For society, then, the dark triad seems to be the worst of both worlds: it helps abusive people rise to the top but makes them underperform once there.

Ten Brinke also led a study of 101 hedge fund managers, a profession in which professional effectiveness is easily measured with financial returns. To make sure that the study wasn't just capturing people who were lucky during a single period of economic growth, they studied performance over a decade, from 2005 to 2015. They found that as psychopathy increased, performance decreased. One explanation for this is tied to elevated levels of impulsivity and reckless risk-taking in those with dark triad traits. Psychopaths think they're cleverer than the rest of the population. They see risk just as we do, but figure that they can outsmart consequences. Consequences, they think, are for chumps. So, psychopathic hedge fund managers threw caution to the wind. They rolled the dice—and sometimes lost big.

When ten Brinke told me that psychopaths systematically disregard risks, it got me thinking: this explains a lot about dictators. Over the last decade, I've studied—and interviewed—several former despots. They're all a bit different. Some are charming. Others are strange and detached. They all have big egos. But they also share a common risk. Being a dictator is dangerous. Saddam Hussein, Mu'ammar Gaddhafi, and Nicolae Ceauşescu found that out the hard way. In the United States, Japan, or France, leaders who lose power end up on book tours. They become elder statesmen. They die of old age, rich and respected. That's not true for dictators. Most leave office in one of three ways: with a one-way plane ticket out of the country in the dead of night, in handcuffs, or in a casket. When I crunched the numbers, I found that nearly half of African despots who lose power end up in exile or rotting in a jail cell or executed. It's close to a coin flip. In Haiti, the odds are even worse, with two out of every three presidents meeting such grim fates. (In one bloodthirsty period, Haitian presidents ended their reigns sequentially as "exiled, exiled, bombed and blown up, imprisoned, exiled, executed, exiled, and, particularly gruesome, 'dragged from the French legation by an angry mob and impaled on the iron fence surrounding the legation and torn to pieces.'")

So, here's the question: Who looks at that job and thinks, "I want to try that!" The answer, unfortunately, is those with dark triad traits. They're convinced that they're special, so the risks of their predecessors don't apply to them. "*They* got torn to pieces because they were fools, but that would never happen to *me*." Plus, being a dictator is the dream job for those at the pinnacle of the dark triad. They get to scheme like

Machiavellians until they have total control. Their psychopath within can abuse—even torture—anyone they choose. As an added bonus for their narcissistic side, everyone praises them while they do it. "You were in particularly fine form with that toenail removal today, boss," their underlings might fawn.

Thankfully, few of us have to suffer the abuses of a dictator. But the dark triad traits that propel dictators to power might also help some of the people we encounter in our daily lives. Perhaps some professions require a certain level of Machiavellianism or psychopathy or narcissism. That's the argument in Dutton's *Wisdom of Psychopaths*. He argues that while dark triad traits in high doses make people dysfunctional monsters, plenty of "functional psychopaths" have figured out how to harness their brain abnormalities to their advantage. This idea isn't new. In the 1980s, sociologist John Ray suggested that low and high levels of psychopathy are bad for us, but that a modest, controlled amount helps us perform well under stress and avoid making bad decisions based on irrational emotions.

Dutton and Ray may have a point. In some jobs, being cold and unaffected by stress or emotion are hugely useful. Dutton highlights a few, such as being a surgeon or a Special Forces soldier. Both are at their best when they blunt their emotions the most. Functional psychopaths might also make excellent bomb-disposal technicians who never crack under pressure. In previous research, elite troops and bomb-disposal technicians didn't experience massive spikes in their heart rates during intense stress. Some were actually *more* relaxed in highly stressful situations. That physiological abnormality allows them to carry out intense tasks without getting overwhelmed. Perhaps there's a way to channel the dark triad to make society a little brighter.

But here's the rub: How can you tell whether a psychopath is functional? Manipulative superficial charm comes naturally to them. They're often masters of deception. What if you get it wrong? Do you want a dysfunctional psychopath cloaked as a functional one in a Special Forces unit? Screening tests and psychological evaluations are useful, but they're not foolproof. Even if you could correctly discern that someone is a "functional" psychopath, would you go into surgery knowing one is about to slice you open?

Thankfully, most bosses aren't off the charts with the dark triad. Unless you're unlucky, odds are pretty good that your supervisor isn't a full-blown psychopath. That's comforting in one way and disturbing in another. If the overwhelming majority of people in positions of authority *aren't* psychopaths, then what accounts for all the neurologically normal petty tyrants in our world? To put it differently, all psychopaths are overconfident, but many overconfident people aren't psychopaths—and they're all around us. If we're lucky enough to avoid a dark triad manipulator, why are we so often unlucky enough to have overconfident fools control so many aspects of our lives?

The Determined Meerkat

Meerkats may provide an unexpected insight to the mystery of why you have an overconfident boss. Meerkats are foragers who move in loose packs. They drift through the Kalahari Desert in search of their next meal. But how do they decide where to go? Scientists have discovered that they can vocalize a "move call." When they make that call, the message is clear: it's time to go. Sometimes, the move calls are ignored. Other times, they're followed. What makes the difference? In a series of experiments, scientists discovered something odd: It didn't matter *who* made the call. Social rank was irrelevant. Rather, it mattered how *certain* the individual making the move call seemed. Confidence doesn't just matter for job interviews. It also matters for meerkats.

African wild dogs don't have a move call. Instead, when one member of the pack wants to go for a hunt, it sneezes. Unlike with meerkats, the status of the sneezer matters. If a dominant wild dog sneezes, then the pack will go on a hunt if just one or two other dogs sneeze in agreement. But for a subordinate dog to get its way, a chorus of around ten dogs must sneeze along.

Humans are effectively a mix of the two. Rank matters, but so does confidence. We follow those who are above us in the hierarchy, but we're more prone to following people who are confident—even overconfident— of the path we should follow. Show us certainty in the face of uncertainty and we're sold.

A recent paper in the top science journal *Nature* argues that overconfidence exists because it used to help humans survive. In the distant past, when survival was a daily struggle, fortune favored the bold. The math behind this finding is complex, but at an individual level, overconfidence made it more likely that you would get a scarce resource, such as food. For example, if you were in a showdown with a rival, showing a bit of swagger, even aggressive overconfidence, would sometimes lead to your getting a meal you wouldn't otherwise get simply because your bluff worked. A rival—even a stronger rival—could be scared off by the right display of overconfidence and bluster. Of course, you always risk that the rival will see through it and you'll get beat up instead or even killed. But in an era in which the alternative was starvation, taking that gamble was rational.

Similarly, on a societal level, complacency and cautiousness could also mean starvation. As a result, it was often better to try *something*— even a long shot—in the battle to survive. Therefore, groups learned to follow leaders who displayed a bit of overconfidence. "It's theoretically possible there's a water hole across that stretch of savanna, but I have no idea" is less of a convincing human version of the meerkat move call than "There's definitely a water hole over there. Follow me!" If you're already dying of thirst, inaction is usually at least as bad as following someone with a false sense of certainty.

Nowadays, most humans aren't at risk of dying because they didn't manage to catch a meal or find an oasis, so following people who are often wrong but never uncertain is a risk without much reward. Chalk this up as one more example of an evolutionary mismatch, where an adaptive behavior in the past—overconfidence—is now "maladaptive" because our world has changed. Yet, overconfidence continues to thrive. In a series of studies carried out by Professors Cameron Anderson and Sebastien Brion, they found that incompetent but overconfident individuals quickly obtained social status in experimental groups. Even when competence was easily measured and plain for all to see, being overconfident made other people perceive you as more competent than you were. In that way, we're a bit too much like meerkats.

Similarly, a 2019 review of research grant applications to the Bill & Melinda Gates Foundation discovered that applications that used broader, sweeping language about the potential impact of the proposed studies got more funding than applications that used narrower, more technical language. After the research proposals were carried out, though, the research quality between those that boasted broad claims and those that made more technical claims was the same. And here's the depressing twist: there was a massive gender skew as well. Women usually wrote in straightforward, cautious language that they could back up. Men often wrote as if they could promise the moon. Because of our predisposition to overconfidence, the men got more funding. Often wrong, never uncertain remains a winning strategy in too much of our world.

From psychopathic janitors who climb the ladder to overconfident fools who pull it out from under their more competent colleagues, we have plenty of people in positions of authority who shouldn't be there. But so far, we've focused on corruptible *individuals* who seek and obtain power. Certain people, such as Raucci, or McFife in the Arizona homeowners' association, or Emperor Bokassa in the Central African Republic, are drawn to power more than the rest of us. Some of those power-hungry people are overconfident psychopaths, narcissists, or Machiavellians who are good at rising in the ranks through manipulation and intimidation.

But it's not just corruptible individuals that we need to worry about.

As a social scientist, I study the interplay between people and systems. We can't let the *systems* we operate within off the hook just yet. Steve Raucci was destructive in Schenectady. Could his worst impulses have been constrained in a school district with better oversight? Does culture matter? Would he have been more or less destructive if he were a maintenance man in Nanjing instead of New York? To answer those kinds of questions, we need to think a bit about rice, explore how the rise of bicycles facilitated some of the worst atrocities committed by our species, take a ski lesson with a man who inherited a dictatorship, and explore the structure of a beehive.

VI

BAD SYSTEMS OR BAD PEOPLE?

Give me a dozen healthy infants, well-formed, and my own specified world to bring them up in and I'll guarantee to take any one
at random and train him to become any type of specialist I might
select—doctor, lawyer, artist, merchant-chief and, yes, even beggar-
man and thief, regardless of his talents, penchants, tendencies,
abilities, vocations, and race of his ancestors.

—*John Watson, founder of behaviorism, writing in 1925*

Crops to Cappuccinos

What can you learn about humanity by watching how people behave while
sipping coffee at Starbucks? Quite a lot, it turns out.

In six Chinese cities, researchers observed approximately nine thousand people sitting at various Starbucks locations. While posing as normal
people just having their morning coffee, the researchers recorded data for
two studies. In the first study, they measured how many people were sitting alone and how many were with others. Then, in the second study,
they conducted an experiment they called "the chair test." The researchers moved a chair that would normally be neatly tucked under a table
and placed it into the aisle. It looked out of place, but more important, it
was in the way for anyone moving around the Starbucks. The researchers
then sat and watched. How many people moved the chair back to where it
should have been, and how many people just accepted that the chair was
there and moved themselves around it?

Here's what they found: In two of the six Chinese cities, many more people sat alone than in the other four cities, where patrons overwhelmingly sat with at least one other person. So why were some Starbucks locations home to more solo sippers than others? As the researchers further analyzed the data, there was another puzzle. In the same two cities that had more solo sippers, a much greater share of people moved the chair out of the way. The differences in behavior were so large that they couldn't be down to random chance.

The researchers had a hunch. So, they replicated the chair test at Starbucks locations in Japan and the United States. Twice as many Americans moved the chair out of the way. Again, this was unlikely to be due to randomness in the data. What was going on?

If you plotted the six Chinese cities on a map, you'd see a pattern. The solo-sipping chair movers were in the north. The chair accepters who sat with friends were in the south. Could something about geography explain how people behaved in their local Starbucks?

These studies were designed to test something called rice theory. For thousands of years much of southern China has been cultivating rice, a crop that requires cooperation. No single family can produce the irrigation infrastructure necessary for a successful harvest. Moreover, neighbors must rely on one another. If one family floods their rice paddy early, it could ruin the output from other families. If you don't coordinate, you're all more likely to starve.

Conversely, on the northern side of the Yangtze River, many Chinese communities have long relied on wheat. Unlike rice, wheat requires little coordination or collaboration. Plant it in your field and you're good to go. Families can act independently without affecting anyone else's crop. Scientists began to wonder: Over hundreds of generations, does crop choice have an impact on culture? Rice theory was born. Thomas Talhelm of the University of Chicago has championed the theory. Its central premise is simple: areas that have relied on rice for thousands of years become more communal, while regions full of wheat are more individualistic.

Extensive research has already proven that our behavior is subconsciously affected by the culture we grow up in or the one we live in. In individualistic cultures, people are more willing to go it alone. They'll do more on their own, but will also be more likely to take the initiative to change their environment when it doesn't suit them. In contrast, those in communal cultures are less likely to go out without other people and are less likely to personally take the initiative to change their environment. They tend to accept external environments as they are and adapt themselves to their surroundings.

That's precisely the divide that the Starbucks researchers found: the solo-sipping chair movers from the more wheat-focused areas behaved more like individualistic Americans. The group-sipping chair accepters from rice-dominated areas behaved more like communal rice-eating Japanese people. Few, if any, of the patrons being observed in these cafés had any personal links to farming. Still, the way that their ancestors fed themselves seems to have had an effect, even on something so mundane as how people act in Starbucks. (I, for one, am often a Starbucks solo sipper—which is a shame because I never have anyone to share my amusement with when I tell the barista that my name is "Brian with an *i*" and am handed a cup that says *Briani* on it.)

It's not just our behavior that's affected by our culture. We think differently, too. Consider this list of three words: *train, bus, tracks*. Now, pause and pick two that belong in the same category.

If you picked *train* and *bus* together, you're more likely to be an "analytical" thinker. They go together because both are modes of transportation. If you picked *train* and *tracks* together, you're more likely to be a "holistic" thinker. They go together because they relate to each other. Trains need tracks. Japanese people tend, on average, to be holistic thinkers. Americans tend, on average, to be analytical thinkers. And in China— a generally more communal society—the rice-versus-wheat divide shows up yet again. Chinese people from wheat regions put *train* and *bus* together much more frequently than Chinese people from rice regions.

Next time you sit alone in a Starbucks or move a chair or categorize anything in your head, you'll have to wonder, Would you have behaved the same way if you had grown up eating more rice? Such neat, overarching grand theories are always oversimplified and overstated. No matter what any fancy statistical analysis suggests, our destiny isn't written in the fields our ancestors plowed thousands of years ago. But rice theory does offer at least a partial explanation. If our behavior and our thoughts can even marginally be affected by something so invisible and seemingly distant as the crops our ancestors grew, imagine how those in power are conditioned to behave depending on differences in work culture, pressure from their bosses, or learning bad behavior from bad apples around them.

The lesson is clear: systems matter.

The question is how much. We've all encountered abusive or awful people in positions of authority. That boss who treats subordinates as though their worth is a number on their pay stub. The high school coach who relishes humiliating teenage athletes when they drop a pass. The jaded drone behind the counter at the Department of Motor Vehicles who treats you like an idiot because you don't immediately know the difference between forms PS2067A and PS2067B. We've now seen plenty of examples of how horrible people get higher up on the pecking order. But when we encounter such apparent ogres, sometimes they aren't ogres at all. How can we tell whether someone abusing power is a bad person or just the by-product of a bad system?

This is a crucial question if we want to improve the world. When those in authority act like abusive monsters, we tend to interpret their behavior as *solely* the product of individual choice or personality defects. Sometimes, as we've already seen, that's dead-on. Psychopaths and petty tyrants rarely deserve the benefit of the doubt. But sometimes when power is misused or abused, it's not because the person in charge is a "bad" person.

We, as humans, are horribly inept at deciphering the difference between awful people and awful systems. We frequently mistake unfortunate situations for malicious intent. That's because of "fundamental attribution error." Think about the last time someone took the last parking spot at the grocery store, bumped into you in the street, or cut you off while you were driving. What was your initial reaction—to assume that they're an irredeemable jerk *or* to reflect on whether it was an accident, or that they might be behaving that way because their mom just died? We systematically discount sympathetic explanations when others do the wrong thing or they make us feel like victims. The opposite is true when *we* behave badly. Next time you accidently bump into someone in an elevator or spill your coffee on someone or change lanes at the last second before an exit ramp, consider whether you see that as evidence that you are a horrible person. Unless you're into self-loathing, odds are much greater that you'll explain away your behavior with external factors: an overly crowded elevator, a clumsy accident, or the totally understandable fact that you were distracted from driving because you were thinking about, say, what a shock it would've been for the first human who heard a parrot talk.

We convict others for the same behavior we exonerate in ourselves. This kind of fundamental attribution error was systematically tested in Austria. The findings were crystal clear: motorists interpreted careless driving as malicious when someone else did it, but rationalized their own careless driving as unavoidable or justified. When others behave badly, we quickly assume it's a reflection of poor character. When we behave badly, we *know* it's not that at all.

But here's the problem: If you were put in a worse situation, or a worse system, odds are high that you'd be tempted to behave badly—even skirt the rules or harm others. You'd possibly even become the corruptible monster you love to hate. Don't believe me? I'll prove it.

Parking Tickets, Bankers, and Bees

When we say, "Nobody is above the law," that's not true. Some people are. In New York City, for example, official envoys to the United Nations and their families have diplomatic immunity. They can't be prosecuted for most crimes. Thankfully, that protection doesn't usually lead to ambassadors going on the prowl as serial killers. But the story is a bit different when it comes to serial parking violations.

For New Yorkers running late, illegal parking comes at a cost. Overstay your allotted time at a parking meter and you'll have to part with $60. Park near a fire hydrant and cough up $115. But for diplomats, their cost/benefit analysis of blocking a fire hydrant used to come without any costs. The fines would still be issued, but nobody would have to pay them. Diplomatic plates were the ultimate get-out-of-jail-free card for illegal parking. It offered quite a temptation, too. In the five years from 1997 to 2002, United Nations diplomats were cited for 150,000 parking tickets that went unpaid—more than eighty per day. Cumulatively, they racked up an outstanding bill in excess of $18 million. (Thankfully, I'm sure nobody minded because New Yorkers are internationally revered for their calm, empathic responses to people parking like assholes.)

In 2002, New York City mayor Mike Bloomberg decided to put a stop to it. Bloomberg's administration began implementing a "three strikes, you're out" rule, in which any diplomatic vehicle with more than three unpaid parking tickets would lose its diplomatic license plates. In October 2002, the Manhattan Wild West of illegal diplomatic street parking ended. To make clear that a new sheriff was in town, the city stripped thirty countries of their special license plates in one month.

This is what social scientists call a natural experiment. It's natural because it happened without the intervention of research teams. But while natural experiments don't take place in a laboratory, they follow the same logic. Just as medical experiments involve a treatment group and a control group, this natural experiment featured a control group (diplomats in the pre-enforcement period) and a treatment group (diplomats in the post-enforcement period). Everything else was mostly the same. The main difference that could explain any shifts in behavior was whether diplomats thought they could get away with parking violations.

Two economists, Ray Fisman of Boston University and Edward Miguel of the University of California at Berkeley, analyzed the data to see what patterns they could find. If you're trying to guess what they found, you probably fall into one of two camps. The first camp believes that those who park illegally are probably just inconsiderate rule breakers. You're either an illegal parker, or you're not, in the same way that you're either a narcissist, or you're not. The second camp doesn't blame the individual, but sees individual behavior as the product of culture or context. Perhaps the illegal parkers come from a society where officials are taught that the rules don't apply to them. Or perhaps people simply decide whether to break the law based on the odds that they'll face consequences.

So, what did Fisman and Miguel find?

Their evidence decisively backed up the culture-and-context explanation. There were stark differences in who parked illegally in the pre-enforcement period. Diplomats from places such as Sweden, Norway, and Japan had zero unpaid parking tickets during the five-year period. Even when they could've gotten away with it, they played by the rules. On the other end of the scale, diplomats from Kuwait averaged 249 parking violations *per diplomat*. The other nine countries rounding out the worst top ten were all bastions of corruption: Egypt, Chad, Sudan, Bulgaria, Mozambique, Albania, Angola, Senegal, and Pakistan. Clearly, cultures of corruption had a drastic effect on individual behavior.

But enforcement—the system—mattered, too. For the diplomats from corrupt countries who were parking illegally as if it were an Olympic sport, enforcement cleaned up their act overnight. Gold medalist Kuwait went from an average of nearly 250 unpaid parking violations per diplomat to an average of 0.15. Silver medalist Egypt went from 141 to 0.33. And bronze medalist Chad went from 126 to 0. Within days, diplomats from Chad were behaving the same way as diplomats from Norway, at least in how they parked their cars.

Those of you who initially had the hunch that personalities and character matter most—the first camp—are probably objecting right now. The individuals who represent corrupt regimes are more likely to be corrupt people! The pathway to representing, say, Venezuela at the United Nations is very different from the pathway to representing Norway! That's certainly true. Venezuelan diplomats can get promoted for behavior that would get Norwegian diplomats fired. But, Fisman and Miguel's analysis has an answer to that objection. In the pre-enforcement period, diplomats from squeaky-clean countries tended to park illegally more often the longer they were in New York. As they grew used to the absence of enforcement, they were increasingly tempted to mimic the behavior of diplomats from corrupt countries. Culture matters, but so do consequences.

It's not just parking. A similar effect was found in Italy, where there's a stark regional corruption divide. Southern Italy—birthplace of the Mafia—has much more corruption than northern Italy. Researchers Andrea Ichino and Giovanni Maggi wondered how much that cultural imprint affects behavior even when people move out of the area they grew up in. To figure that out, they used another clever natural experiment. They studied a national bank that has branches throughout Italy. They identified employees who transferred from one region to the other, the southern-born bankers who transferred to the north or vice versa. Their findings were similar to those of the parking study: culture mattered, but the local systems they worked in mattered enormously, too. Most employees who moved north started behaving better, while most employees who moved south started behaving worse.

We even behave differently depending on how we *believe* a system operates, rather than how it actually operates. Chile, a robust democracy in South America, has similarly low levels of corruption to Taiwan, Spain, France, and the United States. Yet, as Andres Liberman of NYU notes, Chileans routinely find themselves amused as they read stories about foreigners—often Americans—who presume that everything south of the border is hopelessly corrupt. When stopped by police, some American tourists try to bribe the Chilean cops, which is a crime. Back home in California or Connecticut, they'd never dream of bribing an officer. But in Chile, they're all too willing to give it a try. It backfires. Some end up in jail on charges of attempted bribery, all because of a false belief in how a system operates. Bad behavior clearly doesn't arise exclusively from bad character.

These insights matter enormously for understanding whether power makes people worse. If the system is to blame, then we should target our reforms at cleaning up the context. But if an individual who makes bad choices is to blame, we should target our reforms at putting better people in charge—or at least at trying to make bad people behave better.

One way to test whether systems matter more than individuals is to remove the variable of choice—at least as we understand it. That's pretty much impossible to do with humans because we're constantly making intentional choices. Instead, we need to turn to the animal kingdom. What drives "corrupt," seemingly selfish behavior in species that aren't quite as self-reflective as we are?

Few people would say that bees and wasps make individual choices. Even our language makes this pretty clear when we talk about "drones" in a colony or "hive minds." Yet, systems and consequences also radically reshape behavior in the animal kingdom. Believe it or not, some wasp and bee species have more or less corruption, and some even have dedicated workers who are supposed to act like insect cops. But whether those swarms behave badly depends much less on the individual and much more on the rules and structures around them.

Bees and wasps, like Brits and Danes, are ruled by queens. Just as with humans, there can be only one monarch at a time. Being the queen is a sweet gig. You have an entire hive devoted to you, and you get to reproduce your genetic material with gleeful abandon. In the evolutionary sweepstakes, the queen bee has won the lottery. Her genes are passed along to every bee or wasp in the hive. But worker bees and wasps have a hidden instinct: they want to pass their genes along, too. We won't go into the complicated math equations here, but dramatic evolutionary competitions are going on inside a hive. These competitions pit what is best for each individual against what is best for the hive.

All female larvae can become queens with the right diet. Give them the right baby food, and it's straight to the honeycomb version of Buckingham Palace. For each larva, then, becoming *the* queen bee is the ideal evolutionary outcome. But from the perspective of the hive, any excess queens are a waste. Queens can't carry out tasks that are normally assigned to workers. It's sort of as if we endlessly cloned Queen Elizabeth II, it probably wouldn't be particularly helpful for, say, the productivity of the British steel industry. But for bees, it's even worse. Excess queens *lower* productivity because each time a spare queen is made, it could've been a worker instead.

Bees and wasps are sophisticated social creatures, so they've evolved a policing mechanism to solve this problem. Workers become the hive's officers. They conduct search-and-seizure operations to find any rogue social climbers aspiring to join the royal family. Then they dispense a disturbing bit of Marie Antoinette–style justice. "These unfortunate creatures are beheaded or torn apart by the workers soon after they emerge from their cells in the brood comb," explain Professors Francis Ratnieks and Tom Wenseleers, two experts in the behavior of social insects. But as is the case with humans, the wasps doing the policing sometimes abuse their authority for their own gain. As Ratnieks told me, some wasps act like corrupt cops: "Some of the workers who kill eggs are also laying *their own eggs*. It's not really for the good of the colony, but for the good of yourself."

So, here's the interesting question: What causes some bee or wasp species to have more or less corrupt, opportunistic behavior compared to other species? In *Melipona* bees, for example, up to 20 percent of female larvae start developing into queens, entering a lottery that almost always ends with their heads being ripped off. In honeybees, only 0.01 percent of female larvae start developing into excess queens. That raises an intriguing question: Are *Melipona* bees just two thousand times "greedier" than honeybees? Are they the selfish jerks of the social insect world?

The answer lies with the system, not the individual. How social insect hives are built varies. Some seal eggs off, making them difficult to inspect. Others leave them open, allowing the police bees to enter (without a warrant, presumably) and make sure there's no evolutionary funny business going on. Some species have evolved to have special, larger queen cells that demarcate slots for larvae that could develop into future queens. Other species have cells that blend right in, as a future queen looks just like the future workers. When the cells are easy to inspect and the queen cells are easily differentiated from the worker ones, the policing is far more effective. Off with their heads! When the cells are closed and would-be queen larvae blend in with the worker larvae, policing is ineffective.

Just as with humans, ineffective policing creates new temptations. You'll probably get away with it, so why not try? In bees and wasps, poor policing makes it more likely that some individuals will prioritize "selfish" behaviors over behaviors that benefit the hive. "When policing is more effective," Ratnieks says, "there are fewer workers who try to lay eggs." *Melipona* bees aren't two thousand times "worse" than honeybees. They just have a system that lets them get away with selfish behavior, so they're more evolutionarily selfish. Humans, in this respect, are much like bees.

From Starbucks to beehives and banks, it's clear that systems guide behavior. But it's all still a bit murky. Wouldn't a really bad person behave badly no matter the context? And wouldn't a really good person resist the temptations of a bad system to behave honorably? To find out, we need another natural experiment—ideally one in which the *same* person ruled over two systems at precisely the same time, one bad and one good. If someone is a tyrant in one system and a visionary in another, then we can conclude that we shouldn't focus exclusively on individuals. It would provide a fresh hypothesis. Perhaps power corrupts most in bad systems. Let's find out if that's true.

Builder King / Butcher King

In 1865, as slavery was ending in America, King Leopold II ascended the throne in Belgium. Hopes were high that the thirty-year-old monarch would rule as a reformer. At first, he didn't disappoint. Leopold adopted popular, progressive initiatives, including free, compulsory elementary schools, universal male suffrage, and stricter laws against child labor. The first glimmer of weekends emerged, too, as Sundays became mandatory days off. Leopold also earned a new nickname: the Builder King. During his reign, he constructed ornate public buildings and parks. When he privately accumulated enormous plots of land and an assortment of country estates, he established the Royal Trust, so that all future Belgians could enjoy what he'd enjoyed.

Within Belgium, then, Leopold II generally improved labor rights, expanded education, and built an impressive array of public works. He developed a reputation as a benevolent reformer within his kingdom. But for him, Belgium was never the prize. *"Petit pays, petits gens,"* he once remarked with disdain. Small country, small people. He dreamed of something bigger.

One day, Leopold found himself immersed in a book called *Java, or How to Manage a Colony*. It was a sort of practical guide for colonization, a book written about the island for which that doomed ship, the *Batavia*, had set sail two centuries earlier. Leopold was hooked. The only problem was that most Belgians didn't share their king's newfound fascination. Colonization seemed too expensive for a little country such as Belgium. Leopold decided that he needed to change that public perception and make his kingdom less parochial. "Belgium doesn't exploit the world," Leopold lamented. "It's a taste we have got to make her learn." His appetite grew as other European powers started to carve up Africa among them. "I do not want to miss a good chance of getting us a slice of this magnificent African cake."

He took control of what he called the Congo Free State. The new territory was seventy-six times larger than Belgium, an enormous slice of Africa. But it wasn't a slice for Belgium. Instead, it belonged to Leopold. He effectively owned it. The Congo became his personal fiefdom. Leopold had no clue how to manage a colony, though. He quickly found himself in over his head. Debt was mounting. His how-to guide hadn't prepared him for the financial ruin that was approaching. But before that ruin arrived, Leopold was saved, perhaps a bit unexpectedly, by a scientific accident and a lot of bicycles.

Several decades earlier, a rubber craze had swept across the United States. A sticky sap from Brazilian trees promised to make all sorts of exciting new products possible. Investors poured millions into rubber production. But that excitement faded when people realized that rubber melted into a smelly glue when it got hot and broke apart when it got cold. A rubber raincoat would literally drip off the person wearing it during the summer months. Then, in 1839, Charles Goodyear accidentally spilled sulfur into melted rubber. Unlike normal rubber, his inadvertent concoction, which he called "vulcanized rubber," had miraculous properties. It was weatherproof. But even with this breakthrough, there just wasn't much demand for rubber. (Goodyear died at least $200,000 in debt.)

The demand came later. In the late 1880s, decades after Goodyear's death, a Scottish veterinarian named John Dunlop invented a new rubber tire to help his tricycle-riding son coast over bumps in the road. The innovation gave birth to the "bicycle boom." In 1890, forty thousand bicycles were produced in the United States. Six years later, the figure was 1.2 million. Suddenly, everyone wanted rubber. Europeans dreamed of wealth sprouting from the ground as they planted rubber trees throughout their colonies. But those trees would take time to mature. Leopold realized that he was, by a fluke, sitting on a green gold mine. Rubber vines that grew naturally throughout his Congo colony could be tapped immediately to meet global demand. All he needed were workers to collect that gooey gold and send it back to Europe.

When the rubber was brought to Belgium and beyond, E. D. Morel, an eighteen-year-old shipping clerk in England, noticed something odd about the shipments. No money was being sent back to buy the rubber.

Instead, the cargo holds of ships steaming for Africa were full of guns and manacles, the chains of bondage that had largely disappeared from the modern world. Morel had discovered Leopold's secret. The atrocities carried out in Leopold's personal colony are hauntingly documented in an award-winning book, *King Leopold's Ghost*, by Adam Hochschild.

In the Congo Free State, King Leopold's barbarism was largely carried out by an armed group called the Force Publique, a hodgepodge of Belgian soldiers and greedy mercenaries. They forced villagers to extract rubber, an excruciatingly painful process in which the liquid latex from the vine was slathered across a large area of skin, gradually hardened, then was peeled off.

Anyone who resisted would be punished harshly. Leopold's armed troops would grab any women they could capture and take them as hostages. The men of the village were told that the women would only be released when the village chief had supplied the Belgians with the required amount of rubber. If the men didn't comply, the women would be murdered. As the men went off into the jungle to save their loved ones, the soldiers from the Force Publique would rape the women that they deemed most attractive. Once the quota was finally hit, the women would be sold back to the villagers for "a couple of goats apiece." If villagers continued to resist, everyone in the village—men, women, and children—was massacred to send a message to surrounding villages. To ensure that the soldiers had carried out the orders, the Belgian officers demanded proof. The standard method was to bring back the right hand from each corpse. At times, bored soldiers even used Congolese people as target practice. One member of the Force Publique reportedly decorated the flower bed in his garden with twenty human heads.

Back in Belgium, there was considerable interest in the "exotic" Congo. As Adam Hochschild explains, Leopold "imported" an exhibition of Congolese people for the 1897 world's fair in Brussels. The king put 267 men, women, and children on display for the amusement of his fellow citizens. The Congolese people were forced to show off their lives in newly constructed fake villages that were supposed to represent various levels of being "civilized." Attendees found it amusing to give the captive "villagers" Belgian sweets that they'd never before tasted. Some started getting sick from the sugar overload. To put a stop to it, the exhibitors put up a sign: THE BLACKS ARE FED BY THE ORGANIZING COMMITTEE. The "Builder King" had constructed a human zoo.

By the time Leopold died, between 2 million and 12 million Congolese had been killed. (In describing the slaughter of so many people, George Washington Williams, an African American investigative journalist, coined the term *crimes against humanity*.) The death toll was devastating. But the profits were staggering. According to a conservative estimate detailed in *King Leopold's Ghost*, Leopold personally pocketed the equivalent of $1.1 billion in today's value. Some of that money was used to build grand monuments in Belgium that tourists still flock to today, unknowingly standing in the shadows of buildings funded by one of history's worst horrors. Lest we mistakenly believe his atrocities are ancient history, a few people still alive today were babies at the time of Leopold's funeral.

One man, two systems. In Belgium, Leopold faced accountability and oversight. Lives had value. In the Congo Free State, the king was a tyranny of one and his atrocities were hidden. Rubber had value. As political scientist Bruce Bueno de Mesquita has argued, it's the world's worst natural experiment, showing how a racist monster can be constrained by one system and unleashed by another.

Sometimes, though, history is written with the opposite script. What happens when a decent person is thrust into a position of power and has to take control of an awful system?

The Viceroy of Vermont

"What's the difference between a park bench and a ski instructor?" Paul asks.

I smile and shake my head.

"Only one of them can support a family."

Light flurries are falling, fresh snow coating the green pine branches of the trees sprawling across the Vermont mountain. I'm on the Green Ridge Triple, a chairlift whisking us to the peak. With a clunk, the chairlift grinds to a stop. It's breezy, but the chair barely sways. We're directly below a tower, the cable tightly locked into the wheels above that propel the lift toward the Summit Lodge.

"I always tell the kids I teach that when the chairlift stops directly under the wheels like this, it's good luck," Paul tells me. "You have to close your eyes and make a wish—but don't tell me your wish or it won't come true."

I nod and smile awkwardly. It's our first chairlift ride together, and it's not exactly what I had expected. After all, the man next to me, in his uniform of blue snow pants and matching ski jacket, inherited a dictatorship. For months, his 4:30 a.m. alarm clock was the sound of mortar fire trying to kill him as he lived in Uday Hussein's residence and commuted to Saddam Hussein's former palace. Not exactly the standard line on a CV of someone applying to work at a ski resort. Flipping burgers at White Castle? Sure. But Saddam's Palace? And while I haven't actually checked to be sure, I'm reasonably confident that no other ski instructors in Vermont have had a bounty of ten thousand grams of gold placed on their head by Osama bin Laden.

L. Paul Bremer III, known to friends as Jerry, is now eighty years old. He was born nine weeks before Pearl Harbor. He has a robust coif of gray hair, but his face looks two decades younger than he is—something he credits to a lifetime of triathlons and marathons. When his knees could no longer take the impact of all those miles on pavement, his running days were over, so he became a serious cyclist. In the winter, he skis as much as his knees will allow.

Bremer is a lifelong diplomat. He served in posts in Afghanistan, Malawi, Norway, and Washington. President Reagan named him ambassador to the Netherlands, then made him his counterterrorism czar. Bremer was later appointed the chairman of a specially created body, the National Commission on Terrorism. On June 7, 2000, Bremer submitted the commission's report, warning that the "threat of attacks creating massive casualties is growing." In testimony before Congress that summer, Bremer spoke of the risks of another Pearl Harbor, carried out not by Japan, but by a shadowy network of terrorists. Fifteen months later, at 8:46 a.m. on September 11, that unheeded warning became tragically prescient. Bremer's own private offices at the time were in the North

Tower of the World Trade Center, above where the first plane hit. He was lucky to have been in Washington, DC, that morning. Some of his colleagues weren't so lucky.

In the spring of 2003, Bremer got a phone call that would forever change his life. It was from Donald Rumsfeld, George W. Bush's secretary of defense. Rumsfeld told Bremer that he was being considered for "a big job" related to the recent invasion of Iraq. The risks were obvious, but Bremer's wife, Francie, didn't hesitate in supporting him: "If you're asked, you have to do it." When the president asks you to do something, she said, diplomats have a duty to serve. On May 6, 2003, President Bush named Bremer the head of the Coalition Provisional Authority, the body that was charged with creating a smooth transition from dictatorship to democracy in Iraq.

It wouldn't go smoothly.

Bremer arrived in Baghdad in mid-May 2003 on a C-130 troop transport. Despite the scorching heat, he emerged onto the tarmac in the uniform that would become emblematic of his tenure as viceroy of Iraq: a crisp dark suit, a tie, and tan Timberland combat-style boots. A civilian, yes, but one in a war zone.

On his first day, Bremer attended an unnerving meeting. The security situation was disastrous in Baghdad. Armed looters were everywhere, pillaging shops, government ministries, heritage sites, and private homes. It was violent chaos. At the meeting, Bremer raised the possibility of the US military shooting the looters to send a message that order was being restored. Someone leaked his idea to the press. The *New York Times* ran a story about it. The blowback was immediate. If Bremer had tried to issue a similar order in the United States, he'd have been prosecuted for the attempted mass murder of civilians. After all, you can't shoot someone for stealing a TV. Many Americans were outraged.

Many Iraqis, however, weren't. Baghdad wasn't Burlington, Vermont. For decades, Saddam Hussein had imposed order by force. Due process hadn't ever been part of the system. Bremer believed in establishing democracy and rule of law. But he also knew that dictatorships don't morph into democracies overnight. He was trapped between inheriting a brutal system where people expected order to be produced at the barrel of a gun and public opinion back home in a democracy where order was supposed to come from rule of law. Dia Jabar, a man in Baghdad selling soft drinks and cigarettes, told journalists at the time that he hoped Bremer's suggestion to shoot the looters would be carried out. Without a firm hand, he warned, there would be "civil war, a sectarian war—Sunnis and Shi'as" against one another. Soon, the soft drink salesman's fears would be confirmed. Hundreds of thousands would die in the sectarian violence that ensued.

"This is Bella," Bremer tells me, petting his tiny Maltese rescue dog. He's invited me back to his house for coffee after the ski lesson. Bremer lives alone since his wife passed away in 2019, but the house has eight bedrooms. "We wanted enough space to suit all the grandkids," he explains. No longer in his blue ski uniform, Bremer sports a white turtleneck. His belt has American flags on it. He leads me into his study, a room decorated with accolades from a lifetime of public service. Hanging on the wall over his computer screen is an Iraqi flag given to him when he left Iraq with a dedication stitched in it: "For your remarkable heroism, vision, energy, leadership, and unmatched dedication. History will remember you for rebuilding a nation." I can't help thinking that those words about his legacy feel just a touch optimistic.

Sipping espresso as Bella settles at my feet, I ask him about his infamous looting order. A hint of a grimace crosses Bremer's face. "The primary role of any government is public safety," he says. "We had plenty of soldiers, but they didn't have rules of engagement that told them to stop the looting. . . . I believe that shooting the looters would have saved lives." I press him on it, insisting that he wouldn't have dreamed of anything remotely similar if he'd been the viceroy of Vermont instead. "Sure," he says, "but in *everything* we were doing, it was so different from what you do in the United States."

Bremer talks wistfully about the hopes he had when he initially set off for Iraq. Whatever your views on the war, the tragic lack of postwar planning, and its catastrophic consequences for so many Iraqis, Bremer is no cartoon villain. He supported the war, which makes some see him that way. His critics say he was incompetent and dangerously naive. Others accuse him of being an imperialist war criminal. But unlike other warmongers, he was at least willing to put his money where his mouth was and take on one of the world's worst jobs in one of the world's most dangerous places. He did so out of a genuine belief—a misguided one, perhaps in hindsight—that he could make other people's lives better. Many people lie to me during interviews. I have no doubt that Bremer was being sincere about his intentions. He believes deeply in democracy and freedom and thought that he was fighting for both.

But in Iraq, his values were tested. When the radical cleric Muqtada al-Sadr began printing incitements to violence against Americans, Bremer ordered his newspaper closed. Soldiers shut it down, locking the building with chains. Critics said it reeked of hypocrisy. "We don't want another Saddam!" protesters chanted, referencing Bremer. One protester told PBS News, "What is happening now is what used to happen during the days of Saddam. No freedom of opinion." But Bremer had reason to worry. Al-Sadr's Mahdi Army would go on to massacre countless Americans, as he called for a jihad against coalition forces. (Those threats weren't abstractions. Bremer narrowly missed being killed as his convoy was targeted by an improvised explosive device, or IED.) Al-Sadr's role in encouraging violence would significantly contribute to the worst years of Iraq's bloody civil war. Should he have been given the freedom to publish a newspaper that incited violence?

A decent person inheriting a bad system has to make choices that the person wouldn't make in a good system, where newspaper publishers aren't facilitating a bloody insurgency and looters aren't precursors of a sectarian war. Even though Bremer had no direct authority over the military, every decision he made was obviously life and death.

That became clear early on during his reign in Iraq, when Bremer visited a hospital. The lights were off. No machines were beeping. There was no electricity. The national grid was only producing 10 percent of the power compared to prewar levels.

"They showed me to the neonatal unit," Bremer recalls. "There was a little baby there. She weighed six pounds, something like that, and she was nearly six months old. And suddenly it occurred to me that I was responsible to get electricity into that hospital. There was nobody else around who could do it or could make it happen." From then on, Bremer began each daily morning meeting by reviewing a diagram of electrical supply throughout Iraq, trying to find ways to restore supply faster.

As he told me that story, sitting in his study with his dog, I recalled a moment a few hours earlier as we were making small talk on the slopes. Bremer—who had been responsible for restoring electricity, ensuring security, paying millions of Iraqis on the public payroll, and a transition to democracy all at once—was telling me about the resort's plans to relocate a chairlift.

"It's pretty ambitious," he told me, like someone whistling in awed appreciation of an impossibly grand vision. "They're saying they're going to relocate the whole thing this summer. We'll see if they can get it done."

Unlike Leopold, Bremer wanted to do the right thing. He was constrained. His actions were subject to aggressive oversight. Yet, in a broken, brutal system, he figured an idealist wouldn't get far. Due to a lack of planning before the invasion, Bremer was forced to improvise. He'll be the first to admit that some of those improvisations had disastrous consequences. But that doesn't mean they were malicious. Instead, Iraq's system defined his choices. Another system would've caused him to make different choices. He certainly didn't advocate for shooting looters when he was ambassador to Norway.

After several hours of chatting with Bremer, I got up to leave. I walked past his bookshelf, which had a signed picture from President Bush saying, "To Jerry, great job!" Next to it were two other prized possessions: Bremer's Level 1 ski instructor certificate and a hat given to him after his first ski season that says BEST ROOKIE on the brim.

People are complicated.

Few of us inherit dictatorships. But many of us operate in broken systems. With constraints imposed by that context, we don't have absolute free will. Our behavior—good and bad—is shaped by those systems.

Now, consider the previous chapter and this one in tandem. In examining a character such as the megalomaniac janitor Steve Raucci, it's clear that certain people are better at manipulating the system to get power. But it's also clear that bad systems encourage abuse, while good systems prevent it. The solution, as we'll see in future chapters, is to reform systems so they attract fewer corruptible individuals and, then, stop those who become powerful from committing any abuses. It's easier said than done.

But before we figure out how to fix things, we need to answer a key question that has been lurking in the background so far: Does power *actually* corrupt? Or is something else going on?

VII

WHY IT APPEARS THAT
POWER CORRUPTS

Lord Acton and the Inquisition

A man is stripped naked. His hands are tied behind his back. The rope bites into his wrists. His body is raised up, high into the air, with a system of rudimentary pulleys. The knots tear at his skin. The man, helpless, cries out, begging to be released. "Really I know no one. I don't know anything. I haven't lent anyone a book—to no one, to no one! I didn't even read these books myself." He screams. His body falls. At the last second before impact, the rope becomes taut. The pulley squeaks. His feet remain suspended inches from the ground. His shoulders are ripped from their sockets. He screams again, then goes limp as he loses consciousness.

These were standard scenes, meticulously recorded, during the Spanish Inquisition. The torture device, known as a strappado, was used to elicit confessions. It would break the bodies of the accused just enough to still give them a chance to admit their sins and their heresy before death. Many of the accused were executed anyway. Some were strapped to the dreaded rack and stretched to death. Others were placed in the aptly named head crusher, in which a helmet, a chin plate, and tightening screws compressed your skull, little by little, until it buckled. It makes grim reading.

Centuries later, in the late 1800s, a British bishop named Mandell Creighton chronicled this period in a series of historical works. But rather than condemn the Church's brutality, he documented it dispassionately. It wasn't the historian's place, Creighton believed, to moralize. He viewed the role of religious historians as being akin to that of professional apologists: they should give powerful ecclesiastical figures the benefit of the doubt rather than criticizing their abuses.

One reader wasn't impressed with Creighton's chronicle. John Emerich Edward Dalberg-Acton, 1st Baron Acton, 13th Marquess of Groppoli, often known just as Lord Acton (I can't imagine why it's so often abbreviated), started taking Bishop Creighton to task for his indifference to the torture and execution of innocents. In Acton's view, Creighton "prefers the larger public that take history in the shape of literature. . . . He is not striving to prove a case, or burrowing towards a conclusion, but wishes to pass through scenes of raging controversy and passion with a serene curiosity, a divided judgment, and a pair of white gloves." It was as though the historian wanted to keep his hands clean while describing those in the Church who had gotten their hands very dirty indeed. Acton saw Creighton's moral indifference as abdicating the responsibility of history, to hold accountable powerful men for their abuses in a world overrun by impunity for those in authority.

In an 1887 letter to Bishop Creighton, Acton wrote, "I cannot accept your canon that we are to judge Pope and King unlike other men, with a favourable presumption that they did no wrong. If there is any presumption it is the other way against holders of power, increasing as the power increases. Historic responsibility has to make up for the want of legal responsibility. *Power tends to corrupt and absolute power corrupts absolutely.* Great men are almost always bad men." And thus was born one of the most famous quotations in history.

Acton's quote was new, but his idea wasn't. Similar quotes are peppered throughout history. In 1770, for example, William Pitt the Elder spoke to the House of Lords about a similar phenomenon, arguing that "unlimited power is apt to corrupt the minds of those who possess it." Lord Acton just came up with the version that stuck. (Today, the "tends to" is usually omitted. Most know the quote as "power corrupts, absolute power corrupts absolutely.") This widely known, widely accepted aphorism is trotted out in cocktail conversation by those who wish to seem witty to refer to the scandal of the day. But is it true?

We often view power through warped eyes, mistaking inescapable features of power with corruption *caused* by it. Power does corrupt, as we'll see in the following chapter. But our overly cynical view of *how much* power corrupts is wrong. Some of that has to do with four phenomena that are too often overlooked when we praise or condemn authority figures. I call those four phenomena dirty hands; learning to be good at being bad; opportunity knocks; and under the microscope. Each gives us a skewed perspective that causes us to believe that power corrupts people more than it actually does. This isn't to say that people in power behave virtuously, but rather to show that the widely held view that power *makes people worse* is often overblown due to cognitive mistakes we make when assessing those in charge.

Dirty Hands in Bangkok

I check the time on my phone. It's 8:07 a.m., seven minutes after I was slated to meet former Thai prime minister Abhisit Vejjajiva. I'm in the café of the posh Hotel Sukhothai in Bangkok's business district. The high-rise building is set in a carefully manicured tropical garden, a long line of palm trees acting like a shield to deflect the incessant whine of motorcycle taxis and the chaos of street vendors hawking sweet, milky Thai iced teas.

As I sip on my overpriced Americano inside, I scan the café once more. There's only one other patron, a Thai man in a yellow T-shirt, a jarring contrast with the men in dark suits and ties hurrying in and out of the hotel. I unlock my phone and type out a quick message. "I'm here—anything I can get for you before you arrive?" A moment later, my phone buzzes. It's a message from Abhisit. "I'm here too." I look up, the man in the yellow T-shirt smiles, and I join him at his table.

"Sorry, I didn't expect you to be wearing a T-shirt," I say sheepishly.

"No problem. I thought you'd be older."

It's the power delusion at work. Our assumptions about power and status got the better of us. We shake hands. As we do, I can't help fixating on a disturbing thought: I'm shaking hands with a man who has been accused of committing mass murder.

Abhisit speaks with a posh English accent, a by-product of his student days gallivanting with Boris Johnson at the super-elite prep school Eton College and later at Oxford University. He explains that he's wearing the T-shirt because today is his normally scheduled day to donate blood. In the back of my mind, I wonder whether that's a ploy, a sanguine sympathy card that he often plays before he's interviewed. It could go either way. Perhaps he's genuinely selfless and compassionate. Or maybe he's a manipulative Machiavellian. The line between those extremes in politics is often thin.

I start by asking a softball question: When did he realize that he wanted to become a politician? Was there a formative moment that set him on his trajectory?

"I was nine years old when the student protests happened in 1973," he replies. "And they were basically calling for democracy, a written constitution. I was obviously too young to understand what was going on at a sophisticated or deep level. But what inspired me was the fact that we had young people in the streets trying to bring changes to the country."

Thirty-seven years later, Abhisit would be characterized by his opponents as the man who slaughtered people in the streets as they sought to bring changes to the country that he ruled.

Most Westerners think of pristine beaches and raucous red-light nightlife when they picture Thailand or Bangkok. But the country is also home to more coups d'état than anywhere else on the planet. After a 2006 coup, a new prime minister was selected. But he, too, was removed from power after— I'm not making this up—he hosted four televised cooking shows called *Tasting, Grumbling* for which he was paid $350. Those funds were deemed a violation of a rule that prohibited government officials from pursuing business interests while in office. As a result of a bit of allegedly corrupt pad thai, Abhisit was put in charge. He was thrust into the role of an unelected prime minister, picked by generals and a king rather than by the people.

"I was very determined to prove that you can go into politics and come out of it without being corrupted by it," Abhisit tells me. "So I was always very conscious of that. And I wanted to set an example as far as being honest, being straightforward, and sticking to your principles. I hope I've succeeded."

But in early 2010, Abhisit's opponents started to mobilize against him. Some 120,000 opposition supporters descended on the streets of

Bangkok. They demanded Abhisit's resignation. At first, they were peaceful. But in April, the protesters stormed the parliament, forcing the government to flee the building. One evening, the government tried to clear the protest zones. The soldiers were met with a flurry of bullets and grenades. The commanding officer was hit by a grenade explosion and died. Four other soldiers died, too. Troops fired back at the militias. Twenty-six people were killed. Nearly a thousand others were injured.

In response, the heavily armed protesters began speaking of civil war, threatening a mass violent uprising if the government tried to remove them from the streets. Some of the protesters had defected from the Thai military, so a bloody conflict was a realistic possibility. The protesters even started smuggling heavy weapons into the protest zones in trash bags in the dead of night. By mid-May, the city was a tinderbox. Abhisit knew that if the fires were lit in Bangkok, the conflagration could spread across the country in hours.

"It was probably two months where I would only get about at best three or four hours of sleep," Abhisit recalls, sipping his coffee.

As sporadic gunfire became part of the city's soundtrack, Abhisit ordered helicopters to drop leaflets to the protesters and militias below. The leaflets contained a warning: the government was establishing "live-fire" zones as a buffer between protesters and government troops. Abhisit was making clear that he'd given the green light for soldiers to use real bullets on anyone—even unarmed civilians—who entered those no-go areas.

Despite those warnings, militias began conducting systematic arson attacks across the city. Some protesters tempted fate and entered the live-fire zones. Many were killed by government snipers. On May 19, 2010, the Thai military broke through the protest barricades. The protest leaders surrendered. Gradually, order returned. The brutal crackdown accomplished its goal. The bloodshed ended, but at what cost?

In total, eighty-seven people were killed, including two foreign journalists covering the protests. Another few dozen civilians are still unaccounted for, so the death toll is likely higher. More than two thousand people were injured. Many were peaceful protesters.

An election was held the following year. Abhisit lost, winning just 35 percent of the vote. Once out of power, Abhisit was charged with mass murder. But when the Thai military took control yet again in a 2014 coup d'état, the murder charges were dropped.

Back in the posh café, Abhisit fidgets with his coffee cup, looking downward as he speaks. "When you're in power, you are under intense pressure to keep order and to try to put an end to the protests," he says quietly. "But at the same time, you're trying to do your best to make sure that there are no losses. Obviously, we regret the fact that eventually there were losses, but that was the most difficult part of my time in office." Some Thai generals I spoke to echoed that sentiment: "You've seen what has happened in Libya or in Syria. We couldn't let that happen in Thailand. That was the choice Abhisit faced: restore order by killing a small number of 'terrorists' or let hundreds of thousands of innocent Thais die in a bloody civil war." At least that was how they saw it. Or the spin they wanted to put on it.

We've already seen how those with dark triad traits tend to have fewer qualms making a morally repugnant decision. Such moral conundrums—such as smothering a baby to save a village—are often used as thought experiments in college philosophy classes, but those are the kinds of real-world decisions that politicians routinely face in broken systems. When you rule a poor, volatile country of 70 million people, as Abhisit did, most decisions—even budget allocations—are genuinely life-and-death calls. Cut mental health support to increase pay for teachers and people will die. Shut down an economy one week too late during a pandemic and people will die. Allow protesters with rocket-propelled grenades to burn down a city or shoot at soldiers and people will die. And, if an urban uprising metastasizes into a civil war, many, many people will die.

As I sat in the café with Abhisit, I couldn't stop thinking about how his choices caused at least eighty-seven people to die. That appalled me. But nobody knows how many people would've lost their lives had he charted a different course. It could've been far fewer, or it could've been exponentially higher. It's impossible to know.

Now, put yourself in his shoes. Let's imagine that we *could* know what would've happened had he acted differently. This is what social scientists call the counterfactual. Let's imagine that the counterfactual is clear: if Abhisit had allowed the protests to grow, they would've successfully mobilized for a civil war, causing a conflict that led to twenty-five thousand deaths. It's easy to say Abhisit is a brutal murderer. It's harder to say how you would've acted if you were in the seat of power and the lives of thousands of people were placed on your shoulders.

These disturbing, morally nauseating political calculations are being made all the time across the globe by people like Abhisit. Some who make those decisions relish violence and are guided by a compass that only tilts toward self-interest. Others only do horrible things because they believe it's the least bad choice. After meeting Abhisit six or seven times, I hope that he's the latter kind of leader. But I can never be certain.

In Jean-Paul Sartre's play *Dirty Hands*, the fictional Communist leader Hoederer speaks of such impossible dilemmas: "I have dirty hands right up to the elbows. I've plunged them in filth and blood. Do you think you can govern innocently?" For normal people, serious moral transgressions are avoidable. There's *always* another option, another path to avoid doing something repugnant. The overwhelming majority of people don't knowingly make decisions that ruin lives or snuff them out. Instead, we deflect such decisions to others. We elect or appoint or hire people to make unbearable choices that we couldn't face. In turn, the people we delegate authority to are sometimes thrust into situations in which *all* options are immoral. No matter what they do, it could have disastrous consequences. This is not to absolve, condone, or normalize grotesque acts of abuse and violence by those in power—quite the contrary. Political leaders must be held accountable for any human rights abuses they authorize or enable. But it's worth remembering that, sometimes, people in power weigh up two awful options and try to take the lesser evil.

"It is easy to get one's hands dirty in politics and it is often right to do so," argues Michael Walzer, professor emeritus at the Institute for Advanced Study in Princeton, New Jersey. He coined the phrase "the dirty hands problem" to refer to the unique set of moral dilemmas that politicians—and others in positions of authority—routinely face.

Abhisit got his hands dirty. He ordered bullets to be fired at protesters, including some who were unarmed. If that doesn't make your skin crawl, you might want to take the psychopath test. But nobody should be under any illusions: some people were going to die no matter what Abhisit did. That's often true for people who wield enormous power, but it's rarely true for the rest of us.

In 2019, when Abhisit was leading his party into elections, he took a principled stand that cost him dearly. He crossed many senior members of his party to stand up to the ruling military junta, calling for a return to civilian-led democracy. That decision effectively ended his political career. He threw away a chance at regaining Thailand's top job in order to fight for democracy—hardly what you'd expect from someone irredeemably corrupted by power.

However, the dirty-hands problem isn't just for unelected Thai politicians, nor is it just in the realm of dictators and despots in broken countries. It affects everyone who has control over large numbers of people. It's even tarnished some of the most revered figures in British and American history. As Richard Bellamy, professor of political science at University College London, argues, "We desire principled politicians but expect— even oblige—them to commit unprincipled acts."

In late 1941, Winston Churchill had a secret. His government, with the help of the Bletchley Park code breakers, had found a way to decipher the seemingly unbreakable codes of the Nazi Enigma machines. While Hitler was transmitting clandestine coded messages to his military commanders across the world, the British government was reading them. The cracking of the Nazi codes was the biggest secret of the war and the most valuable weapon in Britain's arsenal. If the Germans found out their codes had been broken, they'd replace the Enigma machines. The British would again be flying blind in a deadly war.

Much of the time, Churchill could have his cake and eat it, too: he'd find plausible ways of attributing intelligence gathered from the broken codes to agents and informants. That way, he could act on the stolen information without raising suspicions. But some intelligence was too specific. And it was too risky to share how the information was gathered with many people. As the wartime posters warned, "Loose lips sink ships."

But tight lips sank ships, too. One such ship was the HMAS *Sydney*, a cruiser in the Royal Australian Navy. Historians have suggested that Churchill received intelligence from the broken codes that Australian ships, including the *Sydney*, would soon be attacked. He decided not to share that information with the Australians, knowing full well that keeping silent would put their vessels at risk. Yet, if he warned the *Sydney*, odds were higher that the Germans would wise up that their Enigma codes had been cracked.

On November 19, 1941, the *Sydney* came under attack from a German cruiser and was sunk. All 645 people on board died. Churchill could probably have prevented their deaths. He deliberately chose not to. In doing so, he got his hands dirty to help defeat the Nazis.

Similarly, in early 1865, during the final phases of the American Civil War, Abraham Lincoln—a man known to history as honest Abe—behaved in blatantly dishonest ways. To secure passage of the Thirteenth Amendment, which would outlaw slavery in the United States, Lincoln effectively bribed holdouts in the House of Representatives. He bought their votes with unrelated legislative sweeteners. "The greatest measure of the nineteenth century," Congressman Thaddeus Stevens wrote, "was passed by corruption, aided and abetted by the purest man in America." Pure, that is, except for getting his hands dirty for a much greater good.

Churchill and Lincoln are so revered that these episodes have been whitewashed from their well-known histories. But for most people in power, the dirty-hands problem skews our evaluations of leaders by making them appear worse than they actually are. When we say "power corrupts," we mean that power makes people worse than they previously were. Instead, much of the time, they just have to make worse decisions, which isn't the same. We should all be glad that Honest Abe was willing to play dirty to get rid of slavery and that Churchill had the stomach to do what was necessary to defeat the Nazis. For those in power, immoral acts are, at times, clearly the most moral choice.

But the dirty-hands problem isn't the only reason why we mistakenly believe that power has corrupted someone. Sometimes, people in authority seem worse not because they got corrupted, but because they learned some new tricks.

Learning to Get Good at Being Bad

"I can't remember a time when I didn't steal," Eric says.

"Did it run in the family?" I ask.

"My older two brothers are still alive and kicking. I don't think they've got a speeding conviction between them. And my mother and father were both hardworking but poor."

Eric Allison grew up in a deprived area in the north of England. On his block, only one family owned a car, a fact he noticed early on in life. "About five doors down there was this house, and I thought they were rich because they had a car and they didn't have children," Eric recalls. "So, when I was eleven, I decided to break into their house."

Allison had stopped attending school. "I didn't like school and school didn't like me," he says matter-of-factly. On one of his days at home, he noticed something intriguing. Through a trapdoor, he could access the rafters above. He clambered up, looked around, and noticed that only a low wall divided his family's house from the house next door. The same was true for the next house, and the next house, all down the row. He realized that he could get into any house on the block without even stepping outside.

Enlisting the help of two neighborhood boys as lookouts, Allison waited until the couple with the car went to work. Then, he broke in through the rafters. "I found a very good prize. There was a jar with lots of coins in it. And I'm talking about two-shilling pieces and half crowns, which was quite a lot of money in those days. I think it worked out about twenty quid or something—more than a week's wage."

Allison was cleverer than most eleven-year-olds, so he realized that he'd be caught unless there was an explanation for the break-in that didn't point to an inside job. "I swept the floor, so nobody could see the dust from the rafters. And then, I opened the back door and broke a small window next to it." The police, he figured, would assume it was a random break-in.

He'd have gotten away with it, but Allison learned an important lesson: pick your accomplices wisely. Even though he gave strict instructions to the other eleven-year-olds in on his plan not to immediately spend any of the money, one couldn't resist. "One of the lads, one called John, he bought a pair of flippers, you know, swimming flippers," Allison says. When his father asked him where he got them from, John eventually turned Eric in as mastermind of the caper. He pleaded guilty and got a conditional discharge from the magistrate.

That wasn't the last time that Eric Allison got burned by unreliable coconspirators. He stole a gumball machine from outside a shop. The "prize"—that's what Allison always calls it—was a lot of pennies and quite a few gumballs. He immediately returned home after the theft and was careful to hide his prize, in case the police came looking. His partner wasn't so smart, gallivanting around town with a mouthful of chewing gum. "He grassed me up," Allison says. He was sent to a juvenile detention center.

As soon as the young thief got out, he went right back to stealing. "But I was more careful," Allison recalls. He started thinking about how he could maximize returns and minimize risks. He began vetting potential partners far more carefully. He'd never again repeat a mistake twice.

At the age of twenty-one, he was still stealing, but had also managed to snag a respectable job as a waiter at a fancy restaurant. He could only dream of finding himself in such an environment if he was wearing a uniform. "I realized I'd rather be sat at the table eating the food rather than serving it to somebody. So, I made a really conscious decision to become a full-time criminal. And that's what I did."

Year after year, Allison experimented. Through trial and error, his ambitions grew, his skills expanded, and his mistakes were eliminated. His wallet got fatter, too, as his heists started netting him six figures per year, a substantial sum in those days. "I never cared about the money," Allison says. "I just liked stealing it."

He began doing intensive research before jobs, such as scoping out rich families with "old money," as he calls it, who had entered racehorses in Ascot, the British version of the Kentucky Derby. Then, when he knew they were away at the racecourse with their prized horses, he'd collect his prize from their houses.

Allison also figured out how to commit check fraud, withdrawing money from banks with forged checks. "If a place in those days—from, I suppose you'd say Plymouth to Aberdeen—had more than one bank, I've been there," he explains. It became a competition, a game to test his limits, not for the money, but for the thrill of the theft. He even tried to set personal records for the most banks defrauded in a single day. "My best day was seventy-five," he says proudly.

When Allison wasn't stealing, he was thinking about how to steal better. It occurred to him that his check-fraud schemes would net bigger amounts if he could find some well-padded accounts and figure out which owners didn't verify their statements often, so that a large amount of money going missing wouldn't be noticed. So, Allison and some accomplices—he won't say their names ("I've got to keep some things quiet to protect the guilty," he says)—burglarized the home of a bank employee to steal his swipe card. Then, they got access to some bank records, figured out which accounts were ripe for targeting, and got a massive prize. The problem was extracting the money: "You can't just go into a Lloyds bank in, say, Cheltenham and say, 'Half a million pounds in cash, please,'" he says. But by then, Allison was a sophisticated criminal, so he figured out a way to cash the checks using banks in Gibraltar and Geneva, through an intermediary, who took a cut.

"When we got the phone call saying that the eagle has landed, that the money had actually been taken out in cash and was on its way, I remember going out and I bought a really nice bottle of claret," he recalls. "And I just sat there with that bottle on my own, just sat there thinking, 'Not bad, Eric. Not bad. From a chewing-gum machine to this.'"

Eric Allison got away with countless heists over the years, relying on increasingly sophisticated methods. Over roughly six decades of full-time stealing, he only got caught a handful of times. In his last big job, he stole a million pounds from Barclays, one of the largest banks in Britain. He got caught and spent seven years in prison, giving him plenty of time for self-reflection.

Today, he's left behind his life of crime—his career, as he refers to it—and has a job as the prison correspondent to the *Guardian* newspaper. I ask him whether he misses his old life. "I do miss it," he says, sighing. "I miss the buzz." And, he says, if the *Guardian* hadn't given him a shot, he admits that he'd still be stealing. "I certainly wouldn't be talking to you," he quips, laughing.

Allison was never atop a formal hierarchy, but he nonetheless illustrates a crucial lesson about those who wield power. "I didn't become a worse person," he insists. "That's not accurate at all. I just got better at doing my jobs." He may not be what you expect from the phrase *lifelong learner*, but that's exactly what he is.

Learning is an integral part of getting power and holding on to it. That creates a misperception. If you analyzed the data, it would *appear* as if someone were getting worse over time—that power was corrupting them. In fact, their bad intent may have been static while their effectiveness increased. They were always corrupt. They just got better at it.

Among dictators and despots, this phenomenon has a name: authoritarian learning. Sometimes, dictators hold summits to share ideas. If it were a conference, there would be seminars such as "Crushing Protests: A Case Study" or a panel on "How to Make Dissidents Disappear." In one particularly exotic real-world example from 1958, Mao received the Soviet leader Nikita Khrushchev in a swimming pool. Khrushchev couldn't swim, so he had to wear water wings as they conducted diplomacy and swapped strategies. Their translators walked up and down the length of the pool as they spoke.

Other times, dictators simply innovate. Just as Allison used trial and error to get better at stealing, dictators do the same to get better at stealing elections. In the past, election rigging used to be done primarily with ham-fisted ballot-box stuffing. It was crude. Perpetrators were likely to get caught. People could see it happening, and sometimes henchmen screwed up. When they did, it was hard to explain why a thousand ballots had been counted in a ballot box for a precinct of just five hundred voters. It was a primitive realm ripe for innovation.

In the early 2000s, the government of Ukraine developed an ingenious strategy. In areas that had a high density of opposition voters, election day seemed normal. People cast their ballots as usual. But when officials went to count them, all the ballots were blank. They weren't protest votes. Instead, the regime had replaced the pens in the opposition precincts with ones containing disappearing ink. After a few minutes, the X disappeared. Their rigging had gotten smarter.

In Zimbabwe, the government even developed a plan that took eighteen years to come to fruition. Officials would systematically fail to provide birth certificates to babies born in opposition areas. When those babies became adults and went to register to vote—against the ruling government, most likely—they couldn't because they were unable to prove their identity. "You have to wake up very early in the morning to beat us," one Zimbabwean government official told Professor Nic Cheeseman of the University of Birmingham.

These are all instances of corrupt, malevolent governments getting better at becoming corrupt and malevolent. They got worse because their tactics improved, not because power corroded a previously upstanding moral character.

But whenever someone—often someone obnoxious who has memorized quotes to seem witty at a cocktail party—trots out the well-worn adage from Lord Acton, one phenomenon often gets trotted out, too: megalomania. "Why is it," that person might ask, "that every dictator goes crazy? Did you know that Kim Jong Un claims to have learned to drive when he was a toddler? Why do dictators all invent bizarre myths about themselves that nobody in their right mind could possibly believe?" And then, because the person is obnoxious, he or she will answer the question with a smug smile, "Because power corrupts, and absolute power corrupts absolutely."

This is an instance—and certainly not the first—of the pompous cocktail-party raconteur being wrong. Dictators behave in crazy ways. Their myths (known in political science as cults of personality) are frequently bizarre. But that behavior is actually strategic and rational, adopted as a result of learning how to stay on top.

In North Korea, the Kim dynasty has invented an entire theology around their rule called *juche*. Memorizing its eccentric myths is essential to staying alive, because challenging official state dogma is likely to end with a death sentence or a one-way ticket to a gulag. But the stories about the Kims are objectively absurd. According to official wisdom, the Kims have composed thousands of operas. They don't need to go to the bathroom like mere mortals. They even invented hamburgers (known locally as "double bread with meat," which, to be fair to them, is a far more accurate name).

All of this serves a crucial purpose that dictators learn over time: it's a loyalty test that sorts people you can trust from people you can't. If people are willing to publicly embarrass themselves by spouting obviously absurd lies about the "Dear Leader," then they're more likely to be worthy of the regime's trust. A henchman who parrots absurdities is a henchman worth investing in. The problem, though, is that eventually those myths surrounding the leader become commonplace in society, so nobody is going out on a limb to repeat them. The solution? Just keep inventing crazier and crazier myths, constantly testing people within the regime and within society to see who goes along with it and who doesn't. That strategy creates a ratcheting effect: if the lies don't get more extreme, your loyalty tests become useless. It appears that dictators' thirst for absolute control is warping their minds, when it's often just a sharpening of their strategies. Power didn't corrupt them. They learned to be good at being bad.

Opportunity Knocks

Now, let's imagine an alternate world. In this imaginary world, human morality is governed by a precise statistical probability. Every time a person is presented with an opportunity to do something immoral or abusive, they'll behave badly precisely 10 percent of the time. Every ten times that people come across a wallet full of cash on the sidewalk, they'll pocket the money once. Nine times out of ten, they'll return it to the owner intact.

In such a world, who would be the least moral people?

That question has two plausible answers. The first is that everyone is equally moral. They're all behaving badly an equal proportion of the time. Mystery solved, case closed.

But the second answer—the way we normally seem to answer—is that the least moral are those who behave immorally most often, or who inflict the most harm on others. To see how arbitrary this view is, let's imagine two people in this world, one who lives on a farm on a dirt road in the countryside, and another who lives on the busiest avenue in a bustling metropolis. The person on the country road comes across a lost wallet once a year. The person on the busy avenue comes across a lost wallet five times a year. After ten years, the city dweller has come across fifty wallets and has pocketed the money five times. The country resident has come across ten lost wallets and pocketed the money once. Does that make the city person five times worse? Surely, such logic doesn't make sense. Their goodness or badness would simply be a function of population density. If we follow that line of thinking to its extreme, then the most moral person in the world could be a sadistic psychopathic serial killer stranded alone on a desert island. That person could never behave immorally toward another person. The person would be virtuous by default. That doesn't seem like a sensible way of making moral judgments, does it?

Yet, even though that logic seems badly warped, it's how we tend to assign blame in our world. Our intuition is to determine who the "bad people" are by how often they do bad things. We make those judgments without any reference to how often an individual faced an easy opportunity to behave badly and hurt other people. That's a particularly relevant insight for people in power, because being put in a position of authority necessarily produces more frequent—and more consequential—opportunities for wrongdoing.

Take, for instance, what can happen when humans have to play God. Two hundred years ago, during the Napoleonic Wars, a French surgeon named Dominique-Jean Larrey changed how battlefield injuries were treated. In the past, the emphasis had been on saving soldiers who could quickly return to fighting. Others who might have survived but would never be able to fight again were left to die. Larrey changed that, putting an emphasis on soldiers who most urgently needed care to survive. By World War I, patients were placed into one of three categories: those who would survive no matter what; those who would die no matter what; and those who would be more likely to survive if they received urgent care. Modern triage—from the French word *trier*, "to sort"—was born. When battles rage, or disaster strikes, doctors become immensely powerful. They're gods in white coats, as they must decide who is—and isn't—worthy of urgent medical care as the clock ticks and time runs out.

New Orleans isn't a Napoleonic battlefield, but in a redbrick hospital three miles west of the city's French Quarter, triage played a central role in a horrifying tragedy. In 2005, the hospital was known as Memorial Medical Center, a name that would become infamous after the city's levees broke. When Hurricane Katrina struck, floodwaters rushed into the hospital. It became a dystopian island, with surrounding treetops and the rooftops of ambulances seeming to sprout out of a murky gray-blue sea. Trash and debris floated outside the windows. Two hundred patients and six hundred employees were still trapped inside.

City power had failed, so the hospital was running on a backup generator. Food was running out. Without air-conditioning, inside temperatures quickly soared to well over 110 degrees Fahrenheit (43 degrees Celsius). Then, in the early hours of Wednesday, August 31, the backup generator cut out. The lights went dark. Lifesaving breathing machines switched over to emergency battery power. Thirty minutes later, the machines stopped beeping. The batteries had died, so patients started to die, too. Dr. Anna Pou, a highly respected physician known by colleagues for being dedicated to her patients, tried to manually pump air into the lungs of someone who needed mechanical breathing to survive. In the race against the clock, doctors kept some patients alive long enough to be evacuated by the coast guard. Others, including the one with Dr. Pou, didn't make it.

The next morning, the severity of the crisis had become clear. Dr. Pou and her colleagues decided that they should triage the remaining patients into three categories. As the Pulitzer Prize–winning journalist Sheri Fink reported, "Those who were in fairly good health and could sit up or walk would be categorized '1's' and prioritized first for evacuation." The 2s were worse off and would probably make it but needed help. The 3s were the sickest and would be evacuated last, as they had the lowest chance of survival. Controversially, the 3s also included people who had signed do-not-resuscitate orders, as though a DNR gave permission to be abandoned during a crisis. Pou played a key role in the grim task of sorting patients. When doctors reached a decision, the triage number was either written on a piece of paper and taped to the patient's chest or written directly on the patient's hospital gown in permanent marker.

Meanwhile, the situation was getting desperate. Nobody was coming to rescue them. The hospital was running out of supplies, so staff started rationing them. The doctors and nurses had barely slept since the storm hit. Some patients were in a horrific state, the relentlessly sticky heat compounding their already-serious conditions. One doctor, Ewing Cook, looked around and saw a lot of people who probably wouldn't make it. He considered whether to euthanize patients who were likely on their deathbed anyway. When he later explained why he didn't act on that impulse, his answer was simple: he didn't have the opportunity. "We didn't do it because we had too many witnesses," he told Sheri Fink. "That's the honest-to-God truth."

But Cook still thought euthanizing patients was a good idea. He eventually left the hospital by boat (to try to rescue some of his family members who were also affected by the hurricane). When he left, he spoke to Dr. Pou and told her "how to administer a combination of morphine and a benzodiazepine sedative" so that some of the patients would "go to sleep and die." One nurse later said that Dr. Pou had then told her that "the decision had been made to administer lethal doses" of sedatives for some of the 3s. That list included several who weren't dying but were so obese that rescue didn't seem plausible. (Dr. Pou's lawyer disputed that she'd used the phrase "lethal doses.") Without electricity, the patients would have to be carried up and down stairs to their rescue. Some weighed nearly four hundred pounds (180 kilograms). It was difficult to imagine how they'd get out.

One such highly obese patient was Emmett Everett, aged sixty-one. Everett had been made a paraplegic from an earlier injury and had been awaiting a fairly routine surgery, but was otherwise doing all right. He was healthy enough that he'd fed himself breakfast on Thursday morning and, according to Fink's reporting, asked a staff member, "So are we ready to rock and roll?"

According to statements later made to investigators, Dr. Pou nonetheless went up to the seventh floor, where Everett was, carrying vials of morphine and a drug called midazolam, which is used to sedate patients before surgery. If used in sufficient doses alongside morphine, it can be fatal. As Fink describes, "Pou disappeared into Everett's room and shut the door." Shortly after Dr. Pou went into Everett's room, he died. Eight other patients on that floor died, too.

When the floodwaters began to recede, forty-five bodies were discovered at Memorial hospital. Twenty-three—more than half—had either morphine, midazolam, or both in their bloodstream, even though only a handful had previously been prescribed either of those drugs for pain management. When two forensic experts were brought in to evaluate the cause of death for Everett and the patients on the same floor, they agreed that eight of the nine deaths had been caused by homicide. Another expert believed all nine were homicides. One forensic examiner summed up his view succinctly: "For every patient on a floor to have died in one three-and-a-half-hour period with drug toxicity is beyond coincidence."

Dr. Pou was charged with murder. However, the grand jury refused to indict her. The charges were eventually dropped. Three civil lawsuits against Dr. Pou and others were settled. (Fink later wrote about this disturbing saga in her award-winning book *Five Days at Memorial*).

There's no other evidence—before or since—that Anna Pou has ever tried to harm patients. Yet, experts agreed that it's highly likely that her decisions during those catastrophic few days caused the premature deaths of several people who would likely have survived. Some argue that makes Dr. Pou a murderer. Others say that she did the best she could during a horrific crisis, in which hindsight is twenty-twenty, but decision-making in that unfathomable moment was clouded by uncertainty, panic, and fatigue. You be the judge. But one truth goes unsaid in the debate: Had Anna Pou been a custodian or a security guard or a hospital administrator instead of a physician, she wouldn't have been accused of murdering patients. That she was in a position to decide the fates of others gave her the *opportunity* to do harm. The same phenomenon applies to everyone in positions of authority. They face more situations in which they can hurt others. When they make the wrong call, more people suffer. Does that mean that power made them worse people? Or do they just *appear* to become worse because of that increase in opportunities and the magnification of consequences? Often, it's the latter.

Under the Microscope

Let's again return to our mythical world of predictably corruptible people who behave badly with clocklike regularity, precisely 10 percent of the time. But now, let's imagine that rather than picking up a lost wallet, these people are prone to embezzling from their employer. One woman works for a midsize paper company in, say, small-town Pennsylvania. Another works for a midsize paper company in a grim commuting town outside London. Both have the same number of opportunities to embezzle. But there's one difference: in this fictional world, the anti-embezzlement watchdog group in Britain has ten employees, and the anti-embezzlement watchdog group in America has just one employee, due to budget cuts. What would happen if we examined the embezzlement data? It would appear that the British embezzler was much, much worse than the American one, because she'd be caught far more often—even though they were behaving identically. After all, Eric Allison's long career as a thief looks a lot better on paper than it actually was, because only a tiny sliver of his crimes showed up on his rap sheet. When it comes to evaluating people who behave badly, the level of scrutiny they face is an essential variable in correctly evaluating someone's actions.

This is particularly important for those in positions of immense power, because many operate under the constant gaze of a microscope. Sometimes, the rich and powerful can use their considerable resources to divert that gaze, or to disguise abuses or crimes as legitimate activity. But much of the time, seemingly worse behavior by those in power can be chalked up to an explanation that we consider less often: they're simply more scrutinized than the rest of us.

Take Bernie Madoff, for example. In late 2008, as the global economy collapsed, the largest Ponzi scheme in history was uncovered. Madoff had orchestrated a massive fraud, clocking in at around $64 billion. Families were ruined. Life savings were lost. But when the dust cleared and Madoff ended up in jail, the victims were left with a single, maddening question: How had he gotten away with it for so long?

Madoff had been committing fraud since at least the 1990s, with some investigators suspecting that his operations had been based on fabricated returns since the 1970s. But Madoff had two major advantages that allowed his crimes to go undetected for decades. First, nobody looked too closely because nobody was complaining, so long as their money kept growing. Second, even when whistleblowers tried to sink his operations— and they did on multiple occasions—investigators didn't look too closely because Madoff had established close friendships with many of the people who could destroy him. For an extra layer of protection, Madoff served on the board of the Securities Industry Association.

Some critics alleged that Madoff may have been subject to less scrutiny because he had personal links to the Securities and Exchange Commission, the main financial regulatory body in the United States. Madoff himself boasted at a business event of those close relationships with SEC lawyers, saying "my niece even married one." (The SEC's internal investigation later found no wrongdoing related to that potential conflict of interest.) But the SEC had dropped the ball. They'd been tipped off in a 2006 email that Madoff was potentially running "the biggest Ponzi scheme ever." This came after Harry Markopolos, a securities executive, had provided the SEC with evidence of Madoff's fraud no fewer than three times between 2001 and 2005. Markopolos realized within five minutes of looking at one of Madoff's funds that the returns were made up. Four hours later, he'd mathematically proven that they were fabricated. His repeated complaints—backed up by hard evidence—never led to anything more than a cursory investigation.

Madoff's ability to avoid detection for decades is the exception that proves the rule. Had it not been for his masterful manipulation of the authorities who were supposed to be doing rigorous oversight, he'd probably have been caught quickly because he was managing quite a lot of money. Meanwhile, millions of cases of small-scale fraud are likely left undiscovered because the perpetrators don't need to bother greasing the wheels to avoid detection. They just don't control enough money to warrant a second look.

A perfect illustration of this "tip of the iceberg" problem arose when the US Congress made a seemingly insignificant tweak to its tax forms in 1987. In the past, to get a tax break, families just needed to list their dependents on a form. One employee wondered whether people were claiming fictional dependents, or even listing family pets, to get tax breaks. So, a new and improved form added a line next to each dependent that required also writing each dependent's unique Social Security number.

Seven million people disappeared. There were 77 million American dependents claimed for tax deductions in 1986, but just 70 million in 1987. That abrupt shift suggests that up to 1 in 10 "people" claimed as dependents for tax breaks in the United States did not exist. The IRS even found eleven thousand particularly bold families who had mysteriously lost at least *seven* dependents from one tax year to the next. The government received an additional $2.8 billion in tax revenues the following year. That money would've been distributed to the people who were committing tax fraud year after year without anyone noticing. Clearly, a colossal iceberg of bad behavior was under the surface. We often just see the tip of it when people in power are exposed because someone bothers to look out for it. If that's true, then perhaps we're all worse than we appear, but the powerful get caught more because they're scrutinized more.

The picture is starting to come into focus. Corruptible people are drawn to power. They're often better at getting it. We, as humans, are drawn to following the wrong leaders for irrational reasons linked to our Stone Age brains. Bad systems make everything worse.

Yet, our intuitions about power can be flawed and mistaken. Four phenomena—dirty hands, learning, opportunity, and scrutiny—make it *seem* that power makes people worse than they actually are. We sometimes confuse the effects of power with intrinsic aspects of holding it. However, these four mitigating factors are only part of the story. They don't fully explain away the corrosive effects of power. That's because, as we'll see, Lord Acton was right.

Power does corrupt.

VIII

POWER CORRUPTS

Rancho Rajneesh

In north-central Switzerland, six miles south of the Rhine River, lies a picture-postcard village. With lush green foothills and chalets that look as if they've been ripped out of a glossy tourist magazine and slapped on the hillside, you can practically smell the fondue. But if you blink as you drive onto its blip of a main street, you'll miss it. Halfway up one of the village's idyllic slopes is a midsize care facility. It's home to two dozen disabled people and the woman who looks after them—a petite, frail, Indian-born septuagenarian who also happens to be the worst bioterrorist in American history.

"Do you want some water, maybe?" a nurse asks, as I get out my notebook.

I hesitate. "No thanks, I've already had some." It's not a normal response when offered water, but I panicked and couldn't think of a more natural refusal. Under no circumstances was I going to consume anything offered to me.

In late 1949, just after an independent India was born, so was Sheela Ambalal Patel. She grew up in a loving family—and one that had sufficient resources to ensure that she'd have opportunities that most Indians didn't. In 1967, at the age of eighteen, Sheela set off for the United States to study at Montclair State University in New Jersey. "I wanted to study fine arts and become an artist," she tells me. "Now, I have learned to be an artist of how to live life!"

Sheela's path to Montclair initially set her up for an all-American life. She married a man from Illinois. But in 1972, like many other young people in the wake of America's 1960s cultural awakening, Sheela and her new husband sought something more than the standard-issue suburban existence. They wanted a spiritual awakening. So, together, they set off for India in search of a guru. They joined an ashram, a monastic collective devoted to the teachings of Bhagwan Shree Rajneesh—a tall, thin man with bug eyes and a wizard-like long gray beard who promised enlightenment to his disciples. He was known to them as Bhagwan or Osho. His followers became known as sannyasins or Rajneeshees. Bhagwan's new age religious movement was always a bit ill-defined. But its core tenets seemed to be a blend of free love and sexual liberation combined with enjoying the excesses of capitalism in an ostensibly classless commune. The Rajneeshees engaged in experimental "therapies," which included long group-sex sessions. (These were later alleged to have also involved violence and sexual abuse.)

As a convert to Bhagwan's teachings, Sheela adopted the sannyasin name Ma Anand Sheela. In 1980, her husband died of Hodgkin's disease, leaving Sheela a young widow. But her real love was Bhagwan. The guru had taken a shine to her, too. They grew closer. "I was just a simple young person," Sheela says with a wistful smile. "I didn't know what I was doing." Nonetheless, by 1981, Sheela had become Bhagwan's right-hand woman. Everything related to Bhagwan filtered through her.

Sheela was soon tasked with finding a place to build a new age utopia, where the entire world could revolve around Bhagwan. After jetting across America to various plots of land, she came across the Big Muddy Ranch in central Oregon. It was enormous: sixty-four thousand acres, or around one hundred square miles, of dry, sunbaked hills dotted with sagebrush. Sheela bought it. She renamed it Rancho Rajneesh.

The nearest town was seventeen miles northwest, where you would be greeted by a green sign saying ENTERING ANTELOPE. POPULATION: 40. DRIVE CAREFULLY. The locals were immediately suspicious of their new neighbors. The sannyasins seemed like aliens to the ranch hands in cowboy hats who ate at the no-frills café on Antelope's main street. The newcomers dressed exclusively in red. They wore beaded necklaces called *malas*, complemented by a locket containing a picture of their bug-eyed guru. It was clear they were planning to stay.

By 1982, tensions were running high. The old-timers of Antelope wanted to stop what they saw as the invasion of their town by a foreign sex guru and his thousands of young disciples. A sizable chunk of those disciples were Americans, swapping their new age Californian spiritual awakening for a great experiment in a remote stretch of the Pacific Northwest. Many of the Americans brought their Hollywood money, which poured into Bhagwan's coffers. But they brought something even more valuable: their right to vote. As the townspeople sought to block the Rajneeshees' plans to build a massive commune, it occurred to Sheela that there were more American Rajneeshees than there were Antelope residents. They could just take over the town.

In November 1982, the sannyasins won the local elections and took over the Antelope city council. They changed the name to Rajneeshpuram and tripled taxes on the locals. The sign just outside town was swapped out. It now read CITY OF RAJNEESH: WELCOME TO YOU. The café was rebranded Rajneesh Zorba the Buddha Restaurant. Truckers in blue jeans didn't know what to make of the herbal teas, the alfalfa-sprout sandwiches, and the portraits of an Indian man with a long beard staring down at them as they stopped in search of a pot of black coffee.

Around this time, Sheela began to get a taste for power. As Bhagwan's powerful sidekick, she suddenly had vast resources at her disposal. She built an airport. "I had a crazy idea," Sheela tells me. "Why don't we buy a plane? We can have a very cheap DC-3. And then I would bounce it off on Bhagwan and he would say, 'Okay. Do it.'" The DC-3 became the flagship of Air Rajneesh, complemented by an executive jet, a couple of helicopters, and a few smaller propeller planes. With the help of free labor (the Rajneeshees worked twelve-hour days, seven days a week, to build Bhagwan's utopia) Sheela also oversaw the construction of a shopping mall, a Medical Corporation, a 350-million-gallon reservoir created by a four-hundred-foot dam, a post office, a public bus system for the Rajneeshees, and a farm that supplied 90 percent of their food. Soon, thousands of "red people" were on the ranch. And all learned an important lesson almost immediately: cross Sheela at your peril.

While she was building a physical empire, Sheela built a media empire, too. As press interest in the commune grew, Sheela's star was born. She flew around the world, becoming a lightning rod of controversy. In one menacing interview that foreshadowed what was soon to come, Sheela was asked about those in Oregon who sought to stand in the way of her implementing Bhagwan's utopian dream. "They haven't learned their lesson," she said with a knowing grin. "Yet."

But as Sheela was basking in the glow of her own cultlike stardom, she was also consolidating power behind closed doors in Rajneeshpuram. Bhagwan had taken a vow of silence. That gave Sheela a unique kind of power over the group: she was the voice of their god. She used that power like a cudgel. As Win McCormack, a reporter for the *Oregonian*, put it in a mid-1980s investigative report: "Sheela indisputably turned out to be the most tyrannical, amoral, and ruthless of Bhagwan Shree Rajneesh's executive assistants."

Sheela also developed a heavily armed "peace force." They conducted target practice with semiautomatic assault weapons. They scanned the juniper-laden hills from helicopters, guns at the ready. Any visitors had to go past four surveillance outposts and checkpoints. Some in the Oregon press began to worry that a Jonestown-style incident—with mass violence or a mass suicide—could happen.

The locals, well aware of such ominous possibilities, decided to try to take back control of their community. They were outnumbered and outmaneuvered at the town level, but the numbers were on their side at the county level. All they needed to do was get the county government to hold Bhagwan, Sheela, and the Rajneeshees accountable for violating all sorts of building and land-use regulations. But Sheela, who had now drunk at the trough of her guru's power, wasn't about to let some county officials take her down. "Donkeys can only understand a kick," she told Frances FitzGerald of the *New Yorker*.

On August 29, 1984, three county government officials came to inspect the ranch. Two were known opponents of the Rajneeshees, while the third was sympathetic. At the end of their visit, a representative from the Rajneesh Medical Corporation offered them a glass of water. It was a hot day, so all three happily gulped it down. The next morning, the two known enemies of the Rajneeshees awoke with "unbearable stomach pain." Both were hospitalized, severely ill from potent bacteria that had been stirred into their water. They survived. The more sympathetic county official was unharmed. Around that same time, Sheela told her subordinates, "If there is a choice of saving one thousand unenlightened people or one enlightened master, you should always choose the enlightened master." She'd soon show that she meant it.

To avoid the county-level crackdown, Sheela decided to try to rig the election by reducing turnout. In late September and early October, two of Sheela's trusted lieutenants drove around local restaurants and sprinkled little doses of *Salmonella typhimurium* on the salad bars of local restaurants. It was to be a test run for the November elections. In that "experiment," the Rajneeshees poisoned just under a thousand people. Many were hospitalized, including one infant who nearly died. The poisonings were initially chalked up to food mishandling, but when investigators later raided Rancho Rajneesh, the truth became known. "We had salmonella in their Medical Corporation, and we had samples of sick people that got salmonella poisoning," former prosecutor Barry Sheldahl tells me. "And we sent those to the Center for Disease Control in Atlanta, and they matched them up and they said these are identical strains of *Salmonella typhimurium*. Exactly identical." Law enforcement also found purchase orders for that salmonella in the Rajneesh Medical Corporation. Witnesses said that Sheela had been the mastermind behind the poisonings. (They also testified that there had even been serious talk of pureeing beavers into the county water supply, since the animals were notorious for harboring harmful bacteria in their guts.)

But investigators also uncovered something much worse: alternative plots that hadn't yet been put in motion. According to witness statements, Sheela had considered using *Salmonella typhi*, which is far deadlier. There was evidence that the Rajneeshees were exploring the possibility of weaponizing HIV, a new, mysterious virus at the time. Another plot was uncovered to assassinate a US attorney. Sheela had also allegedly written on a napkin a list of thirteen people who needed to be "bumped off" and had handpicked a group of sannyasins to become what was referred to as an "assassination team." She'd also allegedly been plotting to kill Bhagwan's personal doctor, someone she apparently saw as a potential threat because of his proximity to the guru. And lest anyone mistake the intent, investigators also seized some light reading in the Medical Corporation building, including the following books: *How to Kill*; *Deadly Substances*; *Handbook for Poisoning*; and *The Perfect Crime and How to Commit It*. The impressionable young student who hoped to become an artist and "didn't know what she was doing" had figured out how to do quite a lot.

In 1985, everything fell apart. Sheela fled the ranch, but was later arrested. She was given a long prison sentence but spent just four years behind bars before being deported. Bhagwan turned on Sheela and denounced her. He fled the United States and died in 1990. Rancho Rajneesh is now the Washington Family Ranch Young Life Christian summer camp. There's no trace of the ranch's origins on its website.

Today, in her picture-perfect Swiss village, Sheela is as feisty as ever—though her raven-black hair has turned gray and her 1980s diva sunglasses have been replaced by reading spectacles. She's warm and gentle in person, hardly the monster I'd come to know from court transcripts. In her spartan room in the care home, two portraits watch over her: one of her parents, and one of Bhagwan. Sitting across from her, as schizophrenics walk past her open bedroom door, I can tell that what excites her is talking about her lost past, that powerful existence on Rancho Rajneesh that is now just a distant memory.

I ask her whether she thinks power corrupted her.

She doesn't hesitate. "My power was the power of love for Bhagwan and his people. Power was not corrupted from me. World can say what they want to say, but I'm telling you my feelings."

I wasn't sure what to make of that answer. But I'm sure that Sheela's experience is extreme. Most people who taste power don't end up trying to weaponize HIV, assassinate prosecutors, or contemplate poisoning water with shredded-up beavers. Her journey from innocent aspiring art student to bioterrorist hell-bent on eliminating the enemies of her guru does seem to jive pretty well with Lord Acton's maxim. After all, now that Sheela has lost power, there's no evidence that she's hurt anybody—so much so that the Swiss government has granted her a license to care for vulnerable people. Is Sheela an example of a good person who was turned bad by power?

As social scientists love to point out, the plural of *anecdote* isn't *data*. So, we have to turn to the data. What does power actually *do* to you?

Horsepower Corrupts

Dacher Keltner isn't the guru of a new age cult, but he is *the* scholarly guru when it comes to studying the cognitive effects of power. With long blond hair that could blend in on a pro surfing tour and a broad, welcoming smile, Keltner is the antithesis of many of the abusive people he studies. The first thing Keltner asked when he welcomed me into his home was "Have you had a snack?"

At his lab at the University of California–Berkeley—called the Greater Good Science Center—Keltner cranks out an astonishing amount of research on emotions, feelings, power, awe, and the science behind what makes us tick. His studies, which have been cited by other researchers an impressive 58,851 times, formed much of the basis of the emotional science behind the Pixar film *Inside Out*. He regularly advises Silicon Valley's aspiring leaders. Many of the most prominent people who study power in top psychology departments around the United States were once his PhD students.

Humans have been fascinated by power for thousands of years before Keltner. But power studies became more systematic after World War II as researchers tried to make sense of the evil that had just been unleashed on the world. In the 1960s, there were the Milgram experiments, in which many ordinary participants showed a willingness to shock people to fatal levels on the instructions of an authority figure. The Milgram experiments dovetailed nicely with Hannah Arendt's concept of "the banality of evil," which sought to explain how normal people could be active participants in the atrocities of the Holocaust. In the 1970s, Philip Zimbardo made waves with the Stanford Prison Experiment, which we've already explored.

But for decades, the scientific literature on how power affects us was limited. This was partly due to the imposition of long-overdue ethical limits on what researchers could do to subjects. (Neither the Milgram nor the Zimbardo experiments would be allowed today.) Then, in 2003, Keltner, along with Deborah Gruenfeld and Cameron Anderson, developed a new theory that launched a flurry of research. Called the Power Approach and Inhibition Theory, it is—apologies to Keltner and his coauthors—not exactly a memorable phrase that slips off the tongue. But the ideas behind it are easily digestible. Essentially, power leads to "approach" behaviors: people become more likely to take action, to pursue goals, to take risks, to seek rewards, and to self-promote. The powerful approach life like a gambler: if you don't play, you can't win. Power makes more people play and more confident that they'll win. By contrast, the powerless are inhibited. They're reactive rather than proactive. They're cautious, trying to protect what they already have rather than risking it. They're more attuned to threats and danger from others. If the powerful are life's gamblers, the powerless are more likely to cling to the few chips they already have.

Keltner's approach is informed by both experiments and observational data, in which he tests hypotheses in the real world. Sometimes, his theories are generated by observing himself. ("When I've felt more powerful, I swear more," he tells me. "I can't help it." And sure enough, he's found that gaining power tends to make others swear more, too.) Other times, his theories come from lived experience.

One day, when Keltner was cycling to work, he almost got hit by a guy driving a jet-black Mercedes, the kind of car that exists to be a status symbol. It got him thinking: Why does it always seem as if those close calls happen with expensive cars rather than beaters, particularly given that drivers of rich cars have much more to lose in a collision? Such experiences, which are annoyances to most of us, are hypotheses to Keltner. And when he has a hypothesis, he tests it.

Keltner came up with an experiment. He had one researcher hide in the bushes on a busy Berkeley road to note down the make and model of cars that approached. Meanwhile, another researcher would wait for a car to approach and then enter the crosswalk. It was timed so that the car could just about get by, but it would require somewhat aggressive driving. What happened?

"Zero percent of the drivers of poor cars—the Yugos and Plymouth Satellites of the world—drove through the pedestrian zone," he explained to National Public Radio in 2016, while "46.2 percent of our drivers of wealthy cars—you know, the Mercedes and the like—drive through the pedestrian zone." When Keltner publicized his research, one particularly offended driver of a pricey Toyota Prius hybrid wrote to him and patiently explained that it didn't matter whether the cars were expensive, but rather what *kind* of expensive car was involved. This was a rival hypothesis: rich Prius drivers were more considerate than rich Mercedes and BMW drivers. So Keltner tested it. "Prius drivers were actually the worst," he says with a laugh.

Keltner's work on power highlights a clear effect, in which powerful people tend to lose their inhibitions. Being "drunk with power" is an apt description. Increase people's sense of feeling powerful and they won't care as much what others think of them. They'll become less effective at reading people because they'll feel less of a need to empathize with others. They'll start to feel as if the rules don't apply to them. As Keltner explains, "People who enjoy elevated power are more likely to eat impulsively and have sexual affairs, to violate the rules of the road, to lie and cheat, to shoplift, to take candy from children, and to communicate in rude, profane, and disrespectful ways." Lord Acton was right.

Keltner wrote *The Power Paradox* in 2016. The book's thesis is straightforward. He argues that being a good person—someone who is affable, altruistic, competent, and kind—helps you get power. Those traits make others admire you. They put their trust in you. They speak highly of you to their bosses. All of that allows you to rise through the ranks. But then (and this is the paradox) those same traits that helped you get to the top are swiftly eroded by the corrosive effects of power, such that you're more likely to abuse your authority once you're on top.

The systems and the people that Keltner studies are mostly in America, whether it's in dormitories, the streets of college towns, or boardrooms. That's quite a different environment for wielding power than what I explore in my research studying dictators who rig elections in Belarus and rebels who recruit child soldiers in West Africa. So, when I spoke with Keltner, I had one big question. Isn't it possible that the rosy part of the "power paradox"—the idea that being "good" helps you climb the ladder—applies best to, say, highly regulated Fortune 500 companies in rich industrialized democracies with rigorous HR departments and boards providing oversight? Would the same be true if you were trying to rise through the ranks in a small business led by a petty tyrant or if you wanted to be a drug kingpin, a cult leader, or a manager at Gazprom, the Russian energy giant? After all, the rosy side of the power paradox doesn't seem to ring true for the Ma Anand Sheelas of the world.

Most academics with sweeping theories like Keltner would get defensive at that kind of pointed question. But Keltner is a true scientist, more interested in accurately explaining the world than protecting his ego. He immediately conceded the point with a warm smile: "Sure, that could be true, and that's one of the big limitations. We have a problem that many of our findings are biased by our samples."

Modern psychology research is plagued by two chronic issues: the replication crisis and the WEIRD problem. The replication crisis, which we already discussed in reference to the dubious "power pose" studies, refers to research findings that aren't replicated when another, independent team of scientists conducts the same study. If you add vinegar to baking soda, it fizzes—no matter who does the adding, where you are on the planet, or what brand of baking soda you use. Similarly, if you conduct the same psychology study twice in different contexts with different participants and you get the same results, there's good reason to believe it's a "real" finding and not just a fluke driven by statistical noise. "If it's a single finding in one place, you should be voicing caution," Keltner tells me.

Then, there's the WEIRD issue, an acronym that stands for Western, Educated, Industrialized Rich Democracies. When you start reading psychology research, one of the most common sentences in the methodology section is something like this: "Participants were 31 undergraduate students at a private college on the east coast of the United States (17 female, 14 male; mean age = 19.7 years) who took part for course credit." Translation: I made my elite undergrads participate in the experiment if they wanted to pass my class. Such practices are known as convenience sampling, in which the subjects of a research project are selected not because they're representative of the general population, but rather because they're available or cheap or easy to sample. That wouldn't be a problem if your research was strictly trying to figure out what makes disproportionately rich, highly educated American college kids tick. But psychology is trying to figure out what makes *humans* tick. In that pursuit, the WEIRD college-kid issue is a seriously problematic bias.

A 2010 study in *Brain Sciences* found that two out of every three psychology studies from the United States exclusively used undergraduate students as subjects. In other countries, that figure was four out of every five. The overwhelming majority of those students are Western. Given what we learned in chapter 6 with the rice theory and the ways in which people in collectivist societies reason differently from those in more individualist cultures, this is no trivial matter. As the study puts it bluntly, "A randomly selected American undergraduate is more than 4,000 times more likely to be a research participant than is a randomly selected person from outside of the West." If that sounds like a lot, it's because it is.

As Keltner argues, this crucial issue needs to be fixed, because many of the power studies in academic literature are tapping into insights that might apply to WEIRD frat boys but not to an aging Chinese executive. Trying to use a nineteen-year-old psychology undergrad to infer lessons about bloodthirsty dictators or even cutthroat CEOs is a pretty big leap. Keltner often avoids convenience sampling, and he regularly checks his work (his car study replicated in other contexts), but other researchers aren't as diligent. This is an important caveat before we move on, because some of the research below is affected by the WEIRD phenomenon. Still, these studies are worth exploring, partly because their findings are comparatively robust and partly because, even with skews, they're instructive in understanding how power changes us.

There are four main ways that researchers study how power changes our behavior. The first is with "structural manipulations," which is academic jargon for experiments in which people make decisions that directly affect other people. This is often more reliable because the feeling of power over another person is real, not imagined. Next, there's the priming approach, in which an experiment subject is randomly assigned to one of two groups. The first group is, for example, instructed to write a short essay about a time when they felt particularly powerful. The second (control) group is instructed to write a short essay about what they did, say, last Tuesday. The idea is to have one group activating the part of the brain associated with feeling powerful and then compare that with people who haven't been put in that mindset.

The remaining methods are, in my view, the least reliable. In the third approach, people are primed with subconscious cues about power (for example, by having them complete a word-search puzzle in which words associated with power or control, such as *authority* or *boss*, frequently appear). And the fourth has people assume certain physical poses, such as the power pose. (I haven't included any findings from research that uses these latter two approaches.) With those words of caution out of the way, what does the science seem to suggest about the effects of power?

Most studies find that power makes us worse. One common experimental design uses the "dictator game." A pot of money is to be distributed among the people in the experiment. At random, one person is assigned to be the dictator and is granted the power to decide who gets what—all using real money. The idea is to vary conditions and see whether people behave in selfish or selfless ways.

In one 2015 study, researchers played the dictator game in three different arrangements. In the first, "low power" scenario, the dictator had control over only one other person. The dictator could divide the pot of money in a 60/40, 50/50, or 90/10 split. The "middle power" condition gave the dictator control over three people, with the same split choices. The "high power" condition gave the dictator control over three people, but added in the option of an even more uneven split, 96/4. Dishearteningly, the researchers found that as power increased, so, too, did selfish behavior. In the low-power condition, there was a 39 percent chance that the dictator would screw the others. In the middle-power iteration, that number rose to 61 percent. And in the high-power condition, in which the dictators could really stick it to three other people, they took the money and ran 78 percent of the time.

Then, with a separate group of people, the researchers conducted the same experiment with a slight tweak. Before the dictator game was played, they asked participants how a leader *should* behave in a situation in which they're tasked with sharing resources. As you'd expect, most said that a leader should be magnanimous and share fairly with others. Yet, when they soon found themselves in a leadership position faced with that exact choice, only half of the people in the low-power group actually behaved as they said a leader should. In the high-power group, only one in five stuck to their stated principles and shared fairly. Power doesn't just corrupt, it also makes you more of a hypocrite.

For an added (and especially dignified) twist, the researchers also had participants drool into a straw. This allowed the researchers to measure testosterone levels in those who signed up for the experiment. When the researchers analyzed the data, they found something conspicuous: those who were in the high-power group *and* had high levels of testosterone were exceptionally likely to take the money for themselves. (Other studies have shown an interaction effect between power, testosterone, and narcissistic abuse. In one experiment, researchers injected testosterone into talapoin monkeys and found that the dominant males became much more aggressive toward their subordinates after the injection.)

Another finding, which is robust and replicable, is that power increases risk-taking. In one study, volunteers were randomly assigned to take on the role of either a boss or an underling in a task. Then, they played blackjack. Those who had been in the boss role in the previous task were more likely to "hit"—to take an additional card—even when it was risky to do so. This finding makes intuitive sense. People who find themselves in positions of power are, by definition, life's winners. When they've rolled the dice in the past, they've won. Plus, because they're comparatively powerful, they can afford to lose more and still stay on top. Powerless people in precarious positions avoid unnecessary risks because they can't afford to lose. (Eventually, once people are so down-and-out that they feel they have nothing left to lose, they might be more prone to risky behavior.)

Bizarrely, feeling powerful doesn't just make you want to take risks, it also gives you a false sense that you can control those risks even when you quite clearly can't. This notion is referred to by scientists as illusory control. In one study, participants were randomly assigned to three groups. One group wrote a short essay about a time they felt powerful. Another wrote about something neutral. And a third wrote about a time that someone else had power over them. Then, they were told that they'd get paid if they accurately predicted the outcome of a dice roll—something that's completely random. Next, they were given the choice to either roll the dice themselves or have the researcher roll it for them. Even though it would make no difference to the outcome, all of the people in the powerful group chose to roll the dice themselves, compared to around half in the power-less group. (This study was a bit flimsy as it was based on only thirty-eight undergraduates, but the concept of illusory control is well-documented in other research.) It's not hard to imagine how damaging it can be in the real world when powerful people wrongly believe they have the ability to manage risks—and roll the dice themselves, gambling with other people's lives based on that false belief.

Other findings are similarly bleak. In a 2008 experiment, researchers used a standard measure to determine how powerful a given person felt. Then, they had participants speak to each other one-on-one about events or moments in their life that had caused them pain or suffering. Some of the stories were devastating. The researchers measured the responses of those who were listening to those traumatic experiences. The participants who felt more powerful were less affected by what they heard. They empa-thized less, a finding that Keltner has also seen in his own research.

The idea that powerful people care less about the people below them in the hierarchy isn't particularly new. It was explored by the German phi-losopher Georg Wilhelm Friedrich Hegel in 1807, when he wrote about an abstract relationship between a master and a slave. As Hegel explains, the master need not know much about the slave. Whether the slave is outgoing or has a favorite color isn't important to the master's prospects. But for the slave, knowing the master—understanding him—is crucial to avoiding beatings and staying alive. As a result, the asymmetric power relationship causes subordinates to be more attuned to those who have control over them than vice versa. In modern times, this dynamic explains why you might know your boss's birthday even if the boss doesn't know yours.

Beyond these findings, a laundry list of studies show that gaining power tends to make people behave in worse ways. The powerful inter-rupt others more, stereotype more, use less moral reasoning when making decisions, and are more judgmental of behaviors in others that they them-selves exhibit. The scientific evidence is occasionally blurry on precisely *why* having control over others affects us so negatively, but few studies suggest that power makes people more virtuous.

There's still a big problem with these research findings: they mostly took place under controlled conditions. Even if the sample isn't too WEIRD, and even if you find a representative group of the population rather than college students, you still have the issue that the people involved know that they're not *actually* powerful. Everyone playing the dictator game knows it's just a game. You can't confer real, lasting power on someone inside a lab no matter how hard you try. And manipulating real lives to make some people powerless and others powerful for the sake of an experiment isn't possible (thankfully) because of ethics rules.

We're therefore stuck between two flawed methods of testing whether power corrupts. The first, which observes power in the real world (as with Ma Anand Sheela) is usually biased by a self-selection effect. Sheela wanted power, she got it, and then it seems to have corrupted her. But it's impossible to tell if the underlying cause for her destructive behavior was Sheela's personality flaws, or the cultlike system she found herself in, or the power itself. The same problem exists when measuring the real world as with Keltner's car-crosswalk experiment. Were people aggressive drivers because they drove BMWs? Or are aggressive people more likely to get rich and buy BMWs *because* they're less considerate? We can't say for sure.

The second approach, using experiments in a controlled setting, is a bit of a flimsy cardboard cutout for the actual experience of real power. Divvying up even $100 in a lab isn't remotely like the experience of becoming a CEO or a dictator or even a sports coach. Those studies are certainly better than nothing, but it's still just not the same.

Nonetheless, despite these reasons for caution, all the available evidence points in one direction. Becoming powerful makes you more selfish, reduces empathy, increases hypocrisy, and makes you more likely to commit abuse. Lord Acton was right: power does tend to corrupt. The problem, then, isn't that the conventional wisdom is wrong, but that the conventional wisdom only focuses on a tiny part of the picture. We fixate on the tip of the iceberg—the powerful people we can see. But as we've already seen, focusing on that pinnacle means that we're missing the much-larger dangers that lurk beneath the surface: why corruptible people are drawn to power, why they're better at getting it, and how they exploit cognitive biases in our Stone Age brains to convince us that they deserve it.

Much of our focus so far has been on our minds. We've explored what personality traits make people more likely to seek power and seen how holding power affects decision-making. But we're still missing a key piece of the puzzle, because becoming powerful doesn't just change the way you think. It also physically changes your body.

IX

HOW POWER CHANGES YOUR BODY

This Is Your Monkey Brain on Drugs

When the US Drug Enforcement Administration makes a major bust, they corral reporters into a room with a podium, a microphone, and a table that's overflowing with drugs. A politician or a DEA official then proudly tells the crowd of reporters the street value of the haul. It's the human equivalent of a primate thumping its chest. But once the cameras are switched off and the podium is empty, where do the drugs go? Is some government warehouse full of green forests of decaying weed next to the white slopes of cocaine mountains?

Most of the drugs seized in major busts are burned (with careful attention to ensure that nobody accidentally gets high in the process). But some end up at a facility in Maryland called the National Institute on Drug Abuse. There, a select bit of cocaine is refined, purified, and sent to the Nader Lab at Wake Forest University.

"The investigator has to get a DEA license," Dr. Michael Nader tells me. "I have a schedule II license." The cocaine he receives is completely pure, so it would have enormous street value. It's kept in a secure hallway in a safe with two locks on it. Two people have to be present to take it out and put it away.

But even though the precautions exist to prevent people from getting their hands on the cocaine, Nader doesn't do research on humans. Instead, he gives cocaine to monkeys.

"When you look at the phylogeny of old-world primates and where we broke off on that line millions of years ago," Nader says, "the closest species that can be used in biomedical research are baboons and macaques." (It's not considered ethical to do drug research on chimps or gorillas. They're too humanlike.) But when you narrow it down to a choice between experiments on baboons or macaques, there's a clear winner. "Baboons are three or four times bigger than a macaque," Nader explains. "They've got huge canines. They're carnivores, so not the kind of animal you'd want to socially house for research and work with closely." Instead, Nader and his lab work with rhesus macaques, a cute monkey species with red faces and gray-brown fur.

Several years ago, Nader and his team of researchers came up with a novel idea. They decided to test how hierarchy, rank, and status affected the experience of using drugs. It was a question worth exploring because drug addiction does seem to affect humans differently depending on their social strata. Who is more likely to get hooked? The alphas on top or those who have fallen to the bottom of the social hierarchy?

Here's how Nader's experiment works. They take twenty-four macaques and put each in individual pens. No other monkeys, no social hierarchy. Then, once the macaques have gotten used to being solitary, they pull the partitions up. Suddenly, there are six groups of four monkeys. The pecking order is established almost immediately, with a clear ranking from one at the top to four at the bottom. "They figure out the hierarchy pretty quickly and it stays that way," Nader says.

Once the social order is set, the researchers scan the macaques' brains. They do that to measure the number of dopamine receptors. Dopamine is the main neurotransmitter that's associated with reward pathways in the brain. The receptors, as you might surmise from the name, receive the dopamine. Our brains have two kinds of dopamine receptors: D1 and D2. When dopamine locks into a D1 receptor, it gives us pleasure, thereby reinforcing the allure of whatever behavior has elicited the release of dopamine. When dopamine locks into a D2 receptor, by contrast, it doesn't reinforce that behavior. Hypothetically, if you exclusively had D1 receptors, any release of dopamine would get you hooked on the preceding behavior (such as taking drugs) quickly and powerfully. If you exclusively had D2 receptors, the effect would be blunted. You could stop cold turkey.

What Nader and his fellow researchers found when they scanned the macaques was dumbfounding: you can change the proportion and number of dopamine receptors simply by creating hierarchies. "What we have shown," Nader explains, "is that if the animal goes from an individual housing situation to a social group and he becomes dominant . . . when he gets access to cocaine, it's not that reinforcing." Becoming a dominant monkey should, hypothetically, make you less likely to get addicted to coke.

But that hypothesis needed to be tested. In the subsequent experiment, each monkey was fitted with an intravenous drip. Then each macaque was placed into a specially designed "primate chair" and wheeled into the lab. There, they sat in front of an "intelligence panel," which gave them a set of controls to operate. Pull one lever and a light gets illuminated, followed by a series of banana pellets being dumped into a feeding cup. Pull another lever and there's a light, the noise of an infusion pump, and a steady drip of cocaine piped straight into the bloodstream. Over time, the macaques learn to associate the levers, the light patterns, and the noises with each kind of reward. They understand that right means sugary food and left means cocaine.

At high enough doses, all the macaques would choose cocaine. (This is true of humans, too.) But at low to moderate doses, subordinate monkeys were much more likely to pick cocaine over food. The less powerful macaques would get hooked. The dominant monkeys chose food.

In a later experiment, Nader and his colleagues took monkeys from one group of four and placed them into another colony of four others that had already established their social hierarchy. Switching groups is stressful, sort of like the macaque equivalent of being the new kid at school trying to sit down among an existing clique in a high school cafeteria. Shortly after that disorienting social experience, the researchers ran the cocaine-versus-banana-pellet test. Subordinates were even more susceptible to self-medicating with cocaine, whereas the dominant monkeys were resilient and kept picking the food over the cocaine.

After the experiments, they scanned the macaques' brains again. Sure enough, the number of D2 receptors in the dominant monkeys had increased. The chemical composition of their brains had been altered by power.

Some people object to these experiments. But Dr. Nader insists that he and his colleagues work hard to give the macaques a good life. The doses of cocaine aren't sufficient to cause suffering. "When veterinarians come to the lab, they're under the impression the macaques are going to be strung out and they're going to look awful," Nader says. "Every single veterinarian has been surprised at how healthy they look. You probably had this vision of, you know, a monkey that's just skin and bones and just a little bit of fur. And that's not it at all. They're well taken care of."

Most important, Nader says, these macaques are unwitting heroes in trying to save human lives from the clutches of destructive addiction. The goal of the research is to better understand addiction so that its magnetism can be broken in humans. "I'm trying to get it so that when the animals get a stimulus that says cocaine is available, they say, 'I'm going to stay over here and I'm going to take the banana pellet,'" Nader tells me. "That's what I want." Our version of a banana pellet is perhaps more likely to be a healthy green salad, but the idea is the same.

Nader's studies raise an intriguing possibility. If the chemical cocktail within the brains of monkeys changes when they gain power and dominance, it would be surprising if we—their primate cousins—*don't* develop biological changes when we gain control over others. The monkey cocaine studies seem to point to a simple conclusion: that power is good for our bodies. It makes us more resilient. Is that true?

The answer isn't so simple.

Biological Stress Is Bad, Control Is Good

How do rank, power, status, and physical health fit together? How can we be sure that those factors are the *cause* of biological changes in our physical well-being rather than coincidence?

Those are two of the questions that Professor Sir Michael Marmot of University College London has dedicated much of his life to answering. In most observational studies (studies that look at data from the real world rather than through a carefully controlled experiment in a lab), it's difficult to disentangle cause and effect. If you just compared, say, CEOs to custodians, you'd certainly find big differences in health outcomes. But the two groups have so many other differences that any relationships you found between status and health could've been caused by hundreds of different variables: education, childhood experience, nutrition, you name it. It would be impossible to show that status, or climbing the hierarchy, had altered anyone's biology.

Whenever Marmot suggested power and health were related, most people chalked it up to one of two things: stress or money. Either people who were powerful would have worse health outcomes because they were stressed, or they'd have better health outcomes because they were rich.

In 1985, Marmot decided to test those hypotheses. He launched the Whitehall II Study to examine health inequalities, with a special emphasis on hierarchy and status. Whitehall is the name of a road in the Westminster area of London, where many of the British government's offices are located. The study set out to track 10,308 British civil servants over their careers in government. Because the comparisons were being made between people in the same profession and often among people who started at the same rank, Marmot could neutralize a lot of the other confounding variables that might get in the way of figuring out which effects were caused by rank and hierarchy and which weren't. It compared apples to apples much more than previous studies.

Moreover, because the same people were being measured over time, Marmot was able to see how relative status changes affected health in the same individuals. "At the entry to the study," Marmot tells me, "you take people of a certain seniority level and look at the trajectory of that cohort. Where would the average be for that group ten years later? And then you look at whether those people were above or below that average—in other words, had they done better than the average or worse?" With that method, Marmot's team could track a group of people who entered the civil service at the same time, even at the same rank, and then see how their health outcomes diverged over time in relation to their promotions. Plus, because the band of civil service salaries is narrower than what you get in the private sector, money wouldn't be as much of a factor. Participants were surveyed initially in 1985, and every two to five years ever since.

In the data, Marmot discovered a crude but clear relationship: the higher up the hierarchy you climbed, the lower your mortality. Marmot calls this the Status Syndrome. Those in the lowest strata who stayed there had triple the mortality of those who ascended to the higher echelons of power. This was, at first glance, perplexing, because it went against the assumed relationship between higher-stress jobs and health. "People said, 'Well, stress can't be important,'" Marmot tells me. "Surely high grades are under more stress than low grades—you know, if you've got deadlines and ministers calling on you all the time. And I thought, 'Yeah, higher-ranked people *are* under more stress.'" But Marmot got a stroke of insight when he began looking at questions that focused less on rank and more on control—the ability to shape events in the workplace. "I realized it's not just the pressure," Marmot says. "It's the combination of high demand and low control. And I realized: that explains everything in our data."

The more Marmot and his team of researchers sliced and diced the data, the clearer this relationship was. People who faced immense pressure at work (what Marmot calls demand) were fine so long as they also felt a high degree of control. But for people who felt under a lot of pressure and *didn't* feel that they were in the driver's seat (or able to at least move the steering wheel from time to time), their health outcomes were much worse. We don't need to be dictators, but we do need to feel that we have a say over decisions within our professional lives.

Marmot had found that the conventional wisdom—that more power would cause bad health outcomes because of added stress—is wrong. The reason it's wrong, however, is surprising. It turns out that there's quite a big gap between what we often call stress and what actually stresses our bodies in harmful ways.

Stanford biologist Robert Sapolsky has found—in studying both baboons and humans—that stress is a crucial tool in survival. When our bodies are functioning properly, stress causes a series of biological changes that help us. Again, let's think back to our Stone Age ancestors. Say you're out for your morning walk, hoping to do a bit of hunting and a dash of gathering before breakfast, when, suddenly, a saber-toothed tiger comes over a ridge and bares its fangs in your general direction. Both you and the tiger have a stress-induced reaction. The body pauses its normal digestion, redirecting energy from producing long-term fat stores and injecting it into the bloodstream right away. This makes sense. You and the tiger are both going to need extra energy for what's about to happen. Because digestion is paused, saliva production slows (which, as Sapolsky notes, explains why we get dry mouth when we're nervous). Long-term processes that are necessary for good health, such as growth and tissue repair, are put on hold, too. This is a welcome bit of bodily triage, since you might not have any tissues left to repair if the saber-toothed tiger catches you. The hypothalamus simultaneously tells the pituitary glands to spring to action. The sympathetic nervous system kicks into high gear, releasing hormones that raise your heart rate and blood pressure. Adrenaline floods into your bloodstream. If everything works the right way, it gives you a better chance at survival. We know this in colloquial terms as the fight-or-flight response.* Stress is designed to help save us.

But just as so much else in our modern lives has diverged from our Stone Age evolutionary design, so, too, has the stress response. Anyone who fears public speaking and has gotten in front of a crowd to deliver an address has felt something similar to what our ancestors felt in the presence of a predator—a classic stress response. It's perfectly normal and isn't usually a big deal. But the problem, as both Marmot and Sapolsky argue, is that our fight-or-flight stress response has, in some workplaces or lifestyles, become a chronic condition rather than a short-term emergency one. The grind of certain jobs, rather than an exceptional break-the-glass moment in the face of a deadly predator, puts us into stress mode. What should only be acute stress is now, for too many of us, routine.

One reason why this relationship is so difficult to understand is because modern society uses the word *stress* to refer to things that are intense, but not biologically stressful. Plenty of high-powered jobs are intense (or have "high demand" as Marmot would say) but aren't stressful because we enjoy them immensely and are able to shape their outcomes (by having "high control"). The CEO who is watching his or her start-up take

---

* Recent research has suggested that the fight-or-flight response differs in men and women, with women more likely to have a "tend-and-befriend" response. The *tend* refers to protecting the vulnerable (such as children), and the *befriend* refers to finding others to help with mutual defense.

off might say that their meteoric rise is "stressful" when it's not remotely stressful in physiological terms. It's exhilarating and wonderful. Intense, hard work doesn't inhibit normal health processes the same ways that biological stress does. Because we conflate the two in our daily speech, we often misattribute to stress what is actually passion or intensity.

According to Marmot's research, however, you *do* get a harmful biological stress response if you hold a low-status position. But the same effect also exists for high-status positions that combine high demand with low control. A mistreated custodian is always likely to face adverse health consequences from lack of control, but a CEO can, too, in certain circumstances. So how does this manifest in the real world? Unfortunately (even though it would make good reality TV) we can't answer that question with experiments that permanently swap CEOs and custodians to see what happens. Instead, we have to turn back to our primate cousins for answers.

Alpha Males from Baboons to the Boardroom

Most PhD students pore over dusty books in libraries, stare at spreadsheets, or toil as grunts in a lab. Not so for Professor Jenny Tung's student Jordan Anderson, who spent part of his early doctoral research at Duke University practicing his skills at hiding out of sight while shooting blow darts through a tube. "You get the hang of it after a while," he tells me.

The blow darts are used to tranquilize baboons from a distance so that they can be studied. But crucially, to avoid messing up the research, it's essential that the source of the tranquilizer is neither seen nor heard by the baboons, lest they start to associate their human handlers with the strange experience of feeling a sharp prick followed by a sudden feeling of intense drowsiness as they keel over and sleep.

Anderson, Tung, and a postdoctoral researcher, Rachel Johnston, conduct studies on baboons in Kenya's Amboseli National Park, near the slopes of Mount Kilimanjaro. They explore the lives and biology of baboons to gain insights into human evolution, aging, and health. If we could understand what a baboon was thinking or communicating about hierarchy and status, perhaps we could better understand ourselves. For, as Charles Darwin once put it, "He who understands baboon would do more toward human metaphysics than Locke."*

Tung's research team wanted to know whether power and status affect the rate of aging. To figure that out, they relied on an innovative method that examines rates of change within our genes. The biological script of our lives (or the lives of baboons) is composed of a DNA sequence that never gets edited no matter how long we live. It's fixed. Yet, our bodies change significantly over time. The secret to understanding how a static script can produce massive change lies with gene regulation—the "switching" of genes on or off. Some of that regulation is irregular, meaning those genes switch on and off at various times depending on a whole host of external factors. But certain sections of the genome switch on and off at regular intervals, like a ticking clock.

One such clock is a process called DNA methylation. Of the A's, G's, C's, and T's that make up our DNA, the C's (or cytosine) are most likely to get affected by that process. As Tung tells me, it produces "a little chemical mark, just an extra carbon and some hydrogens that gets sort of welded on to bases in our DNA, particularly in things like baboons and things like us." If you measure the rate of methylation over time, you can get a good proxy measure of our "genetic" aging, which is completely separate from how many birthdays we've celebrated.

"It's really clear to us that some individuals who are sixty are physiologically much less healthy than the average sixty-year-old," Tung explains. "And some individuals who are sixty are much more healthy than the average sixty-year-old, in a way that sort of percolates down to the level of the cell." If you look around you, this isn't surprising. We notice all the time when someone's age diverges from how the person appears. The method used by Tung's team is a much more precise way of measuring that divergence, exploring whether an individual baboon is aging faster or slower in biological age than its calendar age would predict.

With students such as Jordan Anderson blow darting the baboons (245 of them, to be precise), the team tested the genetic aging of the ba-

* This refers to the British political philosopher John Locke.

boon colony and saw how it matched up with social rank within that colony. The most obvious theory would be that low social rank would lead to faster aging and that higher social rank would lead to slower aging, precisely because higher-ranked baboons get more food along with their pick of mates. But the findings were more surprising. High-ranking males aged much faster. One ambitious male baboon who was rapidly ascending in social rank was tested once at a reasonably low social rank and then tested ten months later after his position had substantially improved. Even though only ten months had passed, his predicted aging (based on biological markers) had increased by nearly three years, as though time had been sped up. In the baboon data, the two individuals who saw the biggest slowdown in their predicted biological aging were the two individuals who *descended* the social hierarchy fastest. As Tung, Anderson, and Johnston put it in their study, rising to the top does confer significant advantages in finding a mate, but it comes with a significant cost—a "live fast, die young" strategy for baboons.

However, there's also considerable evidence that it's quite bad to be a low-ranking baboon. Over thirty years of studying hundreds of baboons in the Kenyan savanna, Stanford's Robert Sapolsky has demonstrated that low-ranking baboons have worse rates of high blood pressure, lower levels of good cholesterol, worse immune systems, and a slower return to normal bodily functioning when they face a stressful situation. However, Sapolsky—more in line with the findings from Tung's group—also demonstrated that life at the top can be stressful for alpha males, particularly during power struggles. Sapolsky's theory was straightforward: it's good to be the baboon king, but when there's the risk of an uprising, it's just as stressful—maybe even more so—than being a baboon peasant.

Sapolsky's theory was bolstered by a 2011 study led by Laurence Gesquiere of Princeton, in which his team measured glucocorticoid, a stress-related hormone. They found that the higher up the primate hierarchy an individual climbed, the less stress it had. But there was an exception: the alpha males at the pinnacle were extraordinarily stressed. It led the researchers to a conclusion at odds with our conventional thinking. The best position to occupy was the *beta* male slot, where you could get access to all the spoils of power without the risk that comes with being the baboon sovereign.

But is this all just baboon trivia or do the same dynamics exist in modern humans? Is it good to be a manager but bad to be a CEO? And how do these baboon studies intersect with Marmot's Whitehall II research and his concepts of high demand and low control?

Four economists may have found answers in a 2020 study—one that helps us determine whether Darwin was right that baboons offer a compelling, albeit slightly furrier, glimpse of humanity. Led by Mark Borgschulte of the University of Illinois, the economists decided to answer two questions. First, do CEOs age faster when they're under more stress? Second, do CEOs die faster when they're under stress? To explore those questions, they started by exploiting a brilliant natural experiment from American corporate history.

In the mid-1980s, American states began passing "anti-takeover" laws, which made it harder for a corporate raider to take over a company. These laws made it less stressful to be a CEO because they ensured greater job security while reducing the risk of an abrupt hostile conquest. Using clever research techniques, the researchers compared nearly two thousand (mostly male) CEOs who had been in charge during the higher-stress condition—the Wild West of corporate raids before the laws—and the lower-stress condition, after the laws protected them. CEOs who spent more time being in charge after the laws were put in place lived longer than CEOs who were in charge during the more stressful period. As the authors put it, "For a typical CEO in our sample, the effect of experiencing the [reduced stress from the] anti-takeover laws is roughly equivalent to that of making the CEO two years younger."

Of course, CEO jobs aren't all equally stressful. To put it more precisely, while all CEOs might describe their jobs as "stressful," some CEOs are likely to face more biological stress than others. Being in charge of, say, Delta Airlines or British Airways during a devastating pandemic probably puts more damaging stress on you than being the CEO of a company that sells webcams or home gym equipment. Working under that assumption, the economists compared CEOs who reigned over companies that were experiencing substantial industrywide crises to those who weren't. Sure enough, CEOs who oversaw a company during a disastrous period for their industry died sooner than those who didn't. (Similarly, a study, published in the *British Medical Journal*, that spanned several centuries and included seventeen countries found that politicians who won elections and subsequently served in office died sooner than runners-up who lost elections and never served. The burden of stress that comes with serving in the political fray appears to shorten the lives of politicians.

So, some evidence suggests that becoming the top dog makes us die sooner. But what about during life? Do CEOs who faced particularly stressful periods appear to age faster than those who don't? That aging is separate from the aging that Tung and her team measured using the DNA clock with baboons, because it focuses on how we look outwardly, not on chemical markers inside our genome. Still, the concept of stress-based aging shouldn't be unfamiliar. We've all seen the before-and-after photos of American presidents who enter the White House youthful but emerge after four or eight years with many more wrinkles and a large outcropping of gray hairs. But the researchers—led by Mark Borgschulte—wanted to systematically test whether that effect that we seem to notice holds up under scientific scrutiny.

To check, they used machine learning. The computer code involved is complex, but the idea is simple. They fed 250,000 individuals' faces into a computer so that it could "learn" to identify physical markers of human aging. A wrinkle or a bit of gray here, a bit more ear hair sprouting there. Over time, the model is refined, getting better and better at spotting subtle differences that change over time—differences that the human eye might not even be able to pick out. Then, they had the model analyze pictures of CEOs at various times throughout their tenure as the alpha of their company. When the model spit out the results, the verdict was clear: genuinely stressful periods make us appear to age faster. The CEOs who oversaw a company hit hard by the Great Recession of 2008–9 looked as though they'd aged a full year faster over the following decade than those CEOs who didn't oversee a company during such a stressful shock. Forget the expensive wrinkle cream. Instead, be sure to ditch the stress that comes with high status and low control.

So, how can we reconcile Marmot's theories generated from the

Whitehall II Study, the findings from baboons in Kenya's savannas, and subordinate monkeys getting hooked on cocaine in the lab? What they all have in common is an agreement that being low on the social pecking order is terrible for your health. That research is clear: being low status kills you faster.

The picture becomes murkier as individuals rise toward dominance. Studies do seem to point to a much more complex interplay between power, control, rank, and health at the higher echelons. Results are mixed. It seems safe to say, however, that being higher status does insulate you from bad health outcomes—but only to a point. Being high status without high levels of control over your destiny can damage your body. Being high status in a moment of crisis can make you age faster and die younger. And being an alpha—all alone at the top—can be disastrous for your health, particularly when the risk of being toppled from that position is real. In baboons, that risk of losing power is always lurking in the savanna, so elevated rank always seems to accelerate biological aging. CEOs are different, with some constantly worrying about getting fired while others have job security. That variation in stressors creates discrepancies in the health-related effects of power for humans. Regardless, the evidence suggests that having too little or too much power can damage your health, whereas ascending to somewhere in the upper-middle part of the social ladder is often just right.

However, before you start reevaluating whether you *really* want that promotion after all, there's some good news. Whether you're a low-status worker stressed by precariousness, a high-status CEO weathering the aftermath of a pandemic, or a drug kingpin just trying to stay alive, there are some ways that you can protect yourself from the corrosive health effects of having too little or too much power. That protection is within everyone's grasp.

We Get By with a Little Help from Our Friends

Between 1997 and 2001, 159 men and 175 women willingly walked into a lab, had a bit of the common cold virus squirted into their nose, quarantined for six days in separate rooms, then walked out $800 richer. This was for a study about the biology of disease—but with a twist. Prior to the quarantine period and the deliberate addition of the virus into the volunteers, researchers had participants fill out a series of questionnaires. One related to social relationships. The researchers asked participants how many people they had spoken to that day, how many conversations that lasted more than ten minutes they had had in the previous twenty-four hours, as well as the social roles they generally occupy (mother, husband, colleague, mentor, coach, etc.). Using these metrics, the researchers developed a "sociability" score to rank participants from extroverted social butterflies to Unabomber-style hermits. Then the researchers collected other data to ensure that any correlation they sought and found wasn't due to something else (such as preexisting health issues, body mass index, race, education level, and the like). Once they had all the data they needed, the participants got the virus injected into their nostrils and began their quarantine.

The researchers sat back and waited for the sniffles to appear. On each day of the six-day quarantine, the participants were assessed for symptoms of the common cold. The scientists measured mucus production, gave people some dye through the nostrils and jotted down how long it took to reach their throat (compared to pre-infection levels), and used a series of similar objective metrics that allowed patients to be compared with scientific rigor. When the numbers were crunched, those who had low sociability scores were three times more likely to develop common cold symptoms than those who had high sociability scores, even though all had received the same dose of virus. That striking finding suggests that having a robust social network can improve our health by reducing stress and improving our overall well-being. In contrast, being low status, powerless, and lonely is a deadly mix. (This finding may partially reflect that more social people get exposed to more viruses and are therefore more resilient once exposed in a lab experiment. But that doesn't explain all of the variation.)

It's not fully clear how social networks boost immune function on a biological level, but some preliminary insights are offered by other species. Professor Tung at Duke (with the blow darts and the baboons) has also examined how status affects the disease-fighting prowess of macaques, the same species used in Nader's cocaine studies. Tung's group artificially varied status among the macaques, taking dominant individuals and putting them into groups where they'd become subordinate and vice versa. By manipulating status experimentally, they could isolate cause and effect. They would first take a sample from a monkey in a dominant role, then take a sample from the same monkey once it entered a subordinate role. Because it's the same individual and the only thing that has changed is the status, the researchers can figure out what effect status is having on the monkey biologically. (Experimentally varying the status of humans would violate ethics rules, which is why such experiments have only been done in some nonhuman primates.)

Monkeys who moved from dominant to subordinate status had worse immune system functioning. Similarly, monkeys who moved from subordinate to dominant status had a boosted immune response. But because the real world is often surprising, the data had two interesting wrinkles. First, dominant monkeys had immune responses that were fine-tuned to fight off viruses, whereas subordinate monkeys were better equipped to fight off bacteria—a perplexing finding that shows the baffling complexity of social rank and biology. Second, much like with the study of colds and social relationships, subordinate monkeys who were frequently groomed—a social practice that involves cleaning but is also used to reinforce bonds between two individuals—had more resilient immune systems than those who weren't.

Our primate cousins can therefore teach us some important lessons. People who are facing significant biological stressors due to powerlessness and low status, or high status with a lack of control, can likely ward off the negative effects of stress by building better social relationships. Our biology *will* be affected by our place in the social hierarchy, but we can blunt the negative effects with a little help from our friends. Crucially, unlike with non-human primates, our social status isn't monolithic. People who are low on the pecking order within their company might nonetheless be high on the pecking order at their church or synagogue or mosque. They might be a revered captain within their community softball team. Or, they could just be well respected by a loving, supportive family in which they feel powerful and in control. The densely woven tapestry of our modern social life gives us opportunities to cheat the risks of death and aging that are uniformly tied to a more one-dimensional social rank in less socially complex species.

If you want to be healthy, increase how much control you have over your life whenever possible—particularly if you're low on the social ladder, or you're near the top of it. But since most people can't just wave a magic wand and find themselves more in control, the easier path is, if you're going to go for that promotion, make sure it doesn't come at the expense of those you care about and love.

On that cheerful note, we now turn to the most daunting puzzles of the book. If corruptible people want power more, are better at getting power, and some good people are corrupted by wielding it, how can we invert those dynamics? What can be done to fix it? It's time to figure out how to make sure that more good people seek power, get it, and stay good once they're in charge.

X

ATTRACTING THE INCORRUPTIBLE

Lesson 1:
Actively Recruit Incorruptible People
and Screen Out Corruptible Ones

In the early hours of October 16, 2010, Didacus Snowball and his girl-friend, C.T., were getting ready to turn in for the night. It was well below freezing outside, with a brisk coastal wind howling around their house. That wasn't particularly unusual for late autumn in Stebbins, a little Alaskan village of around five hundred residents right on the Bering Sea, just two hundred miles south of the arctic circle. But it was warm inside as the couple climbed into bed. Then, they heard a loud knock. Didacus moved across the room and opened the door to see who it was.

As the door swung open, the man outside rushed in. He attacked Didacus, punching him in the face, pinning him to the ground, and strangling him with his bare hands. C.T. screamed, shouting at the man to get out of the house and telling Didacus to run and get help from the nearby police station. He wrestled free of the man's stranglehold and bolted out the door, hoping to find an officer on duty. But with Didacus out of the house, the intruder set upon C.T., knocked her to the ground, wrapped both hands around her neck, and started choking her. As she tried to cry out, her breath faded under the tight grip of his fingers. Everything went black. She lost consciousness.

When she came to a few minutes later, the intruder—she recognized him as a local resident named Nimeron Mike—was on top of her. She looked down and, with horror, saw he was trying to remove her jeans.

Eventually, C.T. managed to wriggle out from under the weight of his body. She grabbed an unloaded rifle just within reach. C.T. hit Mike in the head with it. It bought her time to move away.

Just in time, the police arrived. Mike was arrested. He was convicted and placed on Alaska's sex offender registry for attempted sexual assault. It wasn't Mike's first brush with the law. In total, he'd served six years behind bars for a variety of crimes: domestic violence, assault, reckless driving, groping another woman, drunk driving, and stealing a car.

A decade later, if Didacus Snowball and C.T. had been attacked in their home by an intruder, Nimeron Mike might have been involved again. But this time, he'd have shown up in uniform and carrying a badge. That's because Nimeron Mike, a man with a rap sheet as long as the Stebbins airstrip, had become one of the village's sworn police officers.

"I'd have this fact—that someone was a current police officer," Kyle Hopkins, an investigative reporter for the *Anchorage Daily News*, tells me. "And I would look up their background and it wouldn't make sense because they would have these convictions that would seemingly preclude them from being a police officer." For years, Hopkins kept seeing this pattern: criminals becoming cops. The pattern stood out most in Alaska's remote, isolated villages.

Hopkins decided to do a deep dive. Partnering with ProPublica, he broke a major story. His reporting won a Pulitzer Prize for uncovering a startling fact: convicted repeat offenders were being hired as police officers with astonishing frequency in Alaska. It shouldn't have been happening. But it was. And in Stebbins, Hopkins discovered another shocking fact. Every officer—every single one—had been convicted of domestic violence. If your boyfriend or husband was beating you, calling the cops just ensured that another abuser would come to your house. The rot went right up to the top, too. The police chief had been convicted of seventeen crimes, including felony assault and sexual abuse of a minor. The crooks had taken over the station.

How could that have happened?

The answer is simple. There weren't any qualified applicants. The Stebbins residents who were qualified didn't apply. And the criminals who couldn't find work elsewhere were only too happy to trade an orange jumpsuit for a blue uniform. The city administrator, Joan Nashoanak, stresses that the job postings always specify that applicants can't be felons and can't have been convicted of a misdemeanor within the last five years. But whenever a new officer was needed, the city had to waive that requirement. The choice the city faced was between an officer who was a felon, or no officer at all. "We can't find anybody else without a criminal background," Nashoanak told Hopkins. When Hopkins tracked down Nimeron Mike as part of Hopkins's investigative reporting in Stebbins, Mike said that mere hours after he applied for the job, he was sworn in as an officer. "Am I a cop now? It's like that easy?" he remembered wondering at the time.

Stebbins is an extreme cautionary tale for what happens when you don't have a deep enough applicant pool and you don't think carefully about recruitment. You'll scrape the bottom of the barrel and end up with lots of awful people in positions of authority.

So here's the trillion-dollar question: How can we make sure that better people try to gain power?

When it comes to recruitment, there are three main answers. First, get plenty of applicants. Second, proactively seek out the kind of people that you want in power. And third, devote sufficient resources to screen out the corrupt and corruptible people who self-select into positions of authority. Stebbins failed on all three fronts. It's an extreme case, but it's far from unique in that trifecta of failure.

When trying to expand the pool of applicants, you need to pursue both *deepening* and *broadening.* A deeper applicant pool is one in which you get a larger number of similar applicants to what you already have, which allows you to be pickier. A broader applicant pool is one in which you recruit applicants who are significantly different from what you already have, which allows you to innovate and improve. Both are useful for improving outcomes, particularly when they occur in tandem.

Think of assembling a packet of M&M's that contains thirty candies. If you manufacture precisely thirty green ones and no others, there's no room for error. You have to include all the chipped, broken, and discolored ones. All will be green. If you make sixty green ones instead, you'll still have a green-only pack, but you can at least pick the thirty best ones. The broken ones will get discarded. That's deepening.

If your candy scientists have a eureka moment and start to crank out brown, yellow, red, orange, tan, and blue M&M's, that's broadening. Better yet if they discover peanut M&M's. The best pack of M&M's is likely to be drawn from a deeper pool of candies within each color (so you can pick the best of a uniform bunch), but also from an expanded pool to include colors and kinds that didn't previously exist—the human equivalent of fresh ideas, fresh skills, and fresh perspectives.

Broadening can also create a virtuous circle. Matthew Syed, author of *Rebel Ideas*, has convincingly shown how diverse thinking sparks innovation within organizations. But it also causes people who wouldn't normally put themselves forward for leadership positions to start seeing themselves as future power holders. In an experiment in India, for example, some villages were randomly assigned a female leader. Others were randomly assigned a male leader. What happened? There was a clear-cut "role model effect." Parents in the villages led by women started to expect more of their daughters, raising them to be more ambitious. And girls in those villages started to see themselves as potential future leaders, shifting their life choices in empowering ways. Broadening produces positive effects immediately, but it yields future dividends, too.

Think of someone in your life who would be a powerful moral force as a representative in Congress or Parliament, or who would be an inspiring, responsible CEO. Everyone knows plenty of people who would be phenomenal leaders if given the chance. But many, if not most, of those people wouldn't want to touch politics or the corner office of a major corporation with a ten-foot pole. The challenge facing us is figuring out how to get more of those shy incorruptibles to start competing with the overconfident narcissistic corruptibles who were born believing that they *deserve* power because they're God's gift to man.

However, many organizations never think about this problem when designing recruitment protocols. When it's time to find someone to put in charge, too many follow a predictable pattern: do what was done last time. I call this a QWERTY mistake, because they're making the same kind of error as the one that explains why you're used to typing out emails and text messages on an illogically designed keyboard.

In the late 1860s, the American inventor Christopher Latham Sholes produced the prototype for what would become the typewriter. The early versions of typewriters were set up with an intuitive keyboard design: a lower row that ran alphabetically from *A* to *M* and an upper row that continued from *N* to *Z*. If you knew the alphabet, you knew where to find each letter. But there was a problem. The mechanical machines were prone to jamming if people clicked the keys too quickly, especially if two letters in rapid succession were next to each other. So, Sholes gave his son-in-law, a school superintendent in Pennsylvania, a crucial task: figure out which letters occur together most often in the English language. The results of his amateur analysis were used to design a new keyboard layout that aimed to separate sequential letters in the alphabet that were likely to be needed back-to-back, such as *S* and *T*, or *N* and *O*. They came up with a design that's almost identical to today's QWERTY layout. Their arrangement of the keys had an added bonus. Because the layout was utterly confusing, nobody could type fast enough to jam the machines.[*]

Fast-forward 120 years. Computer keyboards had eliminated the problem of mechanical jamming. But everyone who was typing on a computer had already learned the QWERTY layout. The early tech companies faced a choice: optimize computer typing forever with something better, or stick with the existing way of doing things even though the problem it was designed to solve had disappeared. As you're well aware, they chose to stick with the old way. (Social scientists refer to this phenomenon as path dependency—in which a new decision is based largely on previous decisions. This often results in a worse outcome, but is viewed as the path of least resistance at the time.) When recruitment efforts replicate the old model by fishing out the same language for the job advertisement, or recruiting out of the same pool of people as before, that's the QWERTY approach to deciding who's in charge. It's time to get rid of it.

Recruitment on autopilot isn't just problematic because it fails to deepen or broaden the applicant pool. It also too often reproduces biases,

---

[*] One team of Japanese researchers has recently disputed this account. They argue that the origins of the QWERTY keyboard was more a response to the needs of quickly transcribing Morse code, but the parable is just as relevant regardless of which version is correct.

because organizations that have changed their culture to be more inclusive haven't always updated their recruitment process in the same way. Multiple randomized experiments have demonstrated that the language used in recruitment advertisements for leadership positions makes an enormous difference in who applies. For example, language is often subtly gendered. Researchers have found consistent evidence that a recruitment ad that refers to something like establishing "dominance over the competition" is perceived by prospective applicants as indicating a more male-heavy organization. Such aggressive language has been shown to reduce the number of women who apply to those positions of authority. Because the bias is subtle, you need to consciously counteract it.

Getting it right isn't rocket science. At Carnegie Mellon University, the faculty noticed that just 7 percent of computer science majors were women. They tossed out their old way of doing things—got rid of the QWERTY typewriter so to speak—and completely revamped the way they spoke about computer science. They reformed inflexible prerequisites that could scare off potential majors. They proactively sought out a deeper and broader pool of potential majors. The result? Within a few years, the department went from 7 percent women to 42 percent women. They didn't need quotas. They just thought more carefully about what factors might broaden out the pool of students that would come to them. It worked.

Here's the takeaway: if you're trying to find the right person for a powerful position, you should think carefully about what kind of person you want to apply, join the police academy, or run for office. It shouldn't just be about lines on a résumé or specific skills, but should also consider other measures such as personality traits and the person's past track record with teamwork. To get better political candidates, political parties and civil society organizations need to do a much better job of drafting in morally principled people who would grudgingly go into politics as a public service, not eagerly as a way to enrich themselves, get famous, or grandstand for their ego. Plenty of innovative leaders are within the ranks of apolitical professions—leaders in education, health care, and science to name a few—who would likely make excellent public servants, but have never seriously considered it. With a bit more effort put into breaking the QWERTY recruitment mold, that can change.

Better screening is also essential. In a single job interview, a charming narcissist can present a very different impression from what might be gleaned from a more thorough review. More rigorous vetting might seem as if it'd be costly. But for those seeking significant power, a more thorough review at the early stages is likely to save a ton of time, money, and avoidable damage later. And for positions of enormous consequence, such as heads of state or CEOs of major companies, psychological evaluations for dark triad traits are probably wise, even if they're currently considered unusual or insulting. At that level of power, the stakes are simply too high to worry about a brief bit of intrusive questioning. Whatever specific interventions are adopted, a big part of the battle is acknowledging a core problem: those who shouldn't be in power are more likely to seek it. We need to design *every* system to try to screen out the corruptible, power-hungry candidates.

We shouldn't pretend, however, that better recruitment will be a panacea. Getting sensible, moral people to put themselves forward for the responsibilities and risks of leadership will always be a challenge. As we've seen throughout earlier chapters, corruptible people are drawn to power like moths to a flame. So how else can we ensure that more incorruptible people get thrown into the mix? The answer may lie with an English ox and a bizarre little machine invented in ancient Greece.

Lesson 2:
Use Sortition and Shadow
Governance for Oversight

Francis Galton, an English polymath eugenicist with pork-chop sideburns, was obsessed with data. His personal motto was "Whenever you can, count." This affinity for quantification, combined with his vile prejudices, caused him to behave in bizarre ways as he sought to translate the world into numbers. As Galton traveled across Victorian Britain in the late nineteenth century, he observed young women with particular interest. Using a contraption he called a "pricker," which "consisted of a needle mounted on a thimble and a cross-shaped piece of paper," he poked holes in his custom-designed record of female attractiveness. Then, he compiled his rankings from the pricker and created a "beauty map." The results were admittedly of limited use. (In his subjective judgment, London came out on the top of the table. Aberdeen, in Scotland, was at the bottom.)

But many of Galton's less loathsome attempts at quantification yielded more useful results. In 1906, he attended a rural-country fair. One of the amusements was a competition in which fairgoers were invited to guess the weight of an ox. Galton didn't expect anyone to get the weight right, but he decided to do a statistical analysis of the responses nonetheless. When the competition closed, Galton analyzed the 787 guesses. What he found was remarkable. The median guess—the one smack-dab in the middle of all 787—was 1,208 pounds.* The mean guess—the statistical average—was 1,197 pounds.

The actual weight of the ox? Also 1,197 pounds.

Galton's parable of the ox-weight-guessing competition (which was repopularized in the 2004 book *The Wisdom of Crowds* by James Surowiecki) doesn't always work. Humans are sometimes badly wrong, even when our thoughts or opinions or guesses are aggregated. But when a reasonably random distribution of people puts their collective mind to solving a problem, they can sometimes perform exceptionally well. Some people will always be badly off, guessing three hundred or thirty thousand pounds. But if there are no systematic skews in the group of people guessing, then the low guesses usually just cancel out the high ones. What you're left with is a large number of reasonable guesses.

The problem is that the group of people making decisions is just about *always* systematically biased in some way. It's often as far from random as you could get. For example, since 1721, there have been fifty-five British prime ministers. Forty-one studied at either Oxford or Cambridge. And as we've already seen, people who seek power aren't randomly distributed. They're often quite abnormal relative to the rest of the population. The county-fair attendees were likely to be a much more representative slice of the local population, perhaps with the possible exception of the eugenicist hanging around with his pricker.

---

* Galton initially reported this figure incorrectly as 1,207 pounds, and it was only corrected by a review of the evidence in 2014.

Real randomness can be particularly useful because it neutralizes the influence of people with an ax to grind or a hidden agenda. When guessing the weight of an ox, you're likely motivated only by trying to get the right answer. The fairgoers weren't influenced by political expediency or morally compromised by an urgent need to be reelected. Galton's parable of the ox is therefore at odds with the way that decisions are usually made.

But the parable of the ox also offers another insight. If someone was trying to rig the contest, it would've been a lot easier to bribe the one person tallying the votes than to bribe 787 individuals to change their guesses. If power corrupts, it's much harder to corrupt random groups of people than it is to corrupt the small, self-selecting group of corruptible people who thirst for power.

Several thousand years ago, the ancient Athenians believed in the incorruptible strength of random numbers. As a result, they designed a democratic anticorruption machine, a gargantuan slab of stone with rows of holes carefully carved into it. It was called the *kleroterion*. To make key decisions, citizens would place their *pinakion*, a personalized piece of wood or bronze, into the slots of the machine. Then, an official would turn a crank that would randomly release either a black or a white ball from the machine. If the ball was black, the top row of citizens were dismissed from consideration. If it was white, the randomly allocated row was tapped for duty. It was effectively like an ancient version of the lottery machines that have balls bouncing around, except in this case it was used to select decision makers rather than winning digits for a sweepstakes jackpot.

Using randomness to put citizens in positions of authority is called sortition. Some advocates of sortition argue that we should replace elections altogether and instead introduce governance by drawing lots. That proposal has many problems. It would undermine democratic choice. And some political tasks—such as negotiating a nuclear-test-ban treaty—require specific expertise cultivated over a career. But that doesn't mean that sortition should be discarded altogether. Instead, it should be used to advise elected officials rather than to replace them.

Here's how it could work. In politics, you could have a large annual Citizen Assembly chosen by a computerized version of the *kleroterion*. Think of it like paid jury duty on steroids. The assembly would serve for one year.

It would select something like ten big issues to tackle for the year, perhaps with the input of elected officials. One year it might be issues related to climate change and tax reform, the next year health policy and transportation. Additionally, elected officials could request quick advisory opinions from the Citizen Assembly—answers to yes-or-no questions that are urgently being debated in the legislature. Is it a good idea to legally mandate wearing masks in crowded public spaces during a pandemic? Should we bomb Syria? Is it finally time to buy Greenland? The assembly would have the same access to expert opinions and advice as elected officials. Once the assembly members had discussed and debated, they would issue publicly available advisory opinions. Elected officials would be under no obligation to follow this advice, but the wisdom of the randomly selected crowd would be visible to everyone. If politicians had a different view, they'd at least have to explain why they were deviating from the assembly's proposed solution.

The same model could be adapted for any large organization, from transnational corporations to police departments. Big companies could use sortition to create a shadow Board of Directors from the rank and file within the organization. Every time a major decision needed to be made, the shadow board would release its own views. That would force any aloof, out-of-touch boards to at least grapple with the view from below. Divorced from the myopia of the quarterly profit rat race, shadow boards could help prevent catastrophic failures by forcing their higher-ups to see big-picture concerns that are too often ignored. For public bodies, such as police departments, civilian review boards that evaluate misconduct could be supplemented by a shadow board of citizens that weighs in on major decisions that affect the operation of the department. The crowd will sometimes be wrong. But it's healthy for those in power to have to sometimes listen to the carefully considered views of a random slice of people who are affected by their decisions.

Oversight by sortition has several virtues. First, because it's random, it wouldn't suffer from the problem of corruptible people seeking a position on a shadow board or a Citizen Assembly. Instead, many of the people in Citizen Assemblies and shadow boards would most likely be there grudgingly—and that would be a welcome change.

Second, when leaders are acting out of immorality or self-interest, it would often become obvious because it would be such a glaring contrast with the advice of the assembly or shadow board. The public would have confidence that those drafted into service by sortition aren't making decisions to avoid upsetting lobbyists or because they're worried about alienating a narrow interest group. Cronyism and nepotism would become much harder. Within business, a shadow board would have every reason to think longer term than the quarterly press release and be an antidote to those who are too myopic.

Third, while political systems are often geared toward deadlock, normal people tend to be geared toward compromise. When you and your friends can't decide whether to go to Olive Garden or TGI Fridays, it's rare to have someone walk away and launch attack ads at their rivals about the quality of the breadsticks. But politicians behave like that all the time. Including more normal people in decision-making would put pressure on those who are actually in power to gravitate toward sensible solutions rather than performative posturing.

One recent study provided concrete support for this approach. An experiment involving 864 participants in Zurich, Switzerland, compared power gained randomly to power gained via a competition. The researchers found that those who ended up in power by chance behaved with less hubris. Random selection is humbling in a way that winning a competition (such as an election) isn't. While it's just one study, it provides encouraging results. People who *don't* want power might be most honorable at wielding it.

Better recruitment, combined with oversight by sortition, can make it less likely that bad people will make bad decisions. But because sortition can't and shouldn't be used for every position of authority, there's still an important question: What about those bad apples that inevitably sneak through? What can we do to minimize the harm they can inflict on us?

Lesson 3:
Rotate to Reduce Abuse

When Helen King was a police officer, one team in her department consistently seemed to punch above their weight: the undercover plainclothes officers who specialized in drug busts. "Everyone thought they were great," King tells me. "Anytime a bit of intelligence came in, even late on a Friday night, they volunteered, they'd research it, they'd get a warrant, and they'd execute it. It was all really productive and really helpful." On paper, they were standouts.

King later found out the real reason behind their eagerness and enthusiasm. Each time that team carried out a raid and found drug plants growing under heat lamps, they harvested them and sold them back to drug dealers. This profitable racket escaped detection for quite some time. How were the officers able to act like criminals and not get caught?

The team, by design, had become a sealed-off unit. Everyone in that unit was in on the racket. That meant no outsiders poking around or asking unwelcome questions. As long as they kept working hard to show off seemingly productive drug busts, the results spoke for themselves. (This sort of thing happens more often than you'd think. In 2014, one policeman in England was discovered with eleven kilos of cocaine in his washing machine, which is impressive mostly because British washing machines are tiny. Fitting eleven kilos of anything inside one is an astonishing feat.)

When King rose through the ranks and ended up as the assistant commissioner for the London Metropolitan Police with a focus on recruitment and training, she realized that the crooked drug cops had given her a valuable insight. "If you allow teams, whether it's just two uniformed officers or an entire drugs team, to work in isolation from others and to work very closely over a long period of time, that's where quite a lot of corruption cases will come out," King warns. The solution is simple: rotate people around so nobody gets too comfortable. Fresh blood doesn't just bring fresh perspectives. It also provides antibodies against corruption.

Rotation is important for two reasons. The first is obvious: anytime a group of people are colluding, an outsider presents a risk. The more outsiders pass through, the harder it is to successfully collude without getting caught. Plus, when insiders who know about crooked dealings move elsewhere, they might spill the beans. Some organizations, countries, or teams have such an ingrained culture of corruption that no amount of rotation will make a difference. Rotten in, rotten out. But much of the time, the added risk of exposure from rotation is a deterrent. It stops abuse before it happens. (The logic is similar to that of banks that require employees in sensitive positions to take two weeks of consecutive vacation time each year. It's akin to a two-week rotation. Without someone to cook the books for a few weeks, ongoing fraud is often uncovered when someone fills in for the fraudster.)

Rotation is also important for an unexpected reason, related to something called the Peter Principle. The concept, which was coined by its namesake, Laurence J. Peter, asserts that people tend to rise to the "level of their incompetence." If a system is broadly meritocratic, people who perform well will rise up in the pecking order. But eventually, we all hit Peter's Plateau—the level at which our skills simply aren't up to the job. We find ourselves in over our head. We're no longer beating expectations. So, what happens? No more promotions. No more stellar performance. And that's where lots of people stagnate.

Unfortunately, stagnant people are corruptible people. And the prospect of advancement is a powerful carrot to make people behave properly. When people hit Peter's Plateau, they lose that carrot *and* they're more likely to get bored with their job, which is a dangerous combination. Suddenly, someone who was following the rules while hoping to climb to the top might start to skirt the rules out of increasing frustration.

Rotation helps solve both problems. If variety is the spice of life, then rotation is just the kind of anticorruption paprika we need. If someone still doesn't find life spicy enough even after rotating around, at least the movement of people across teams and units will ensure that any bad behavior is detected sooner.

This isn't just an abstract concept dreamed up by social scientists during naps in our ivory-tower armchairs. It's been tested—both in the real world and in experiments. For example, the German federal government has designated certain areas of the civil service as particularly prone to embezzlement, bribery, or corruption. For those positions, nobody can occupy a given role for more than five years. If an exception to that rule is ever made, the reasons for that exception have to be formally justified in writing. At first glance, it has seemed to work. There's not much corruption around those positions. But Germany is already a low-corruption country. As a result, it's hard to isolate cause and effect. Is corruption low because the staff are rule-following Germans working in Germany, or is it because they're being moved around?

To find out, Christoph Bühren of the University of Kassel decided to conduct an experiment. Participants were put into pairs, with one designated as the public official in a game that provided real payouts. Multiple strategies could be used to get the highest payouts, but bribing other people was one option. To make things more interesting, researchers tweaked the setup. One group in the study had repeated interactions with the same person. Another group had their partners constantly shifted. The results were extraordinary. When the study was run in Germany, bribery happened 32 percent of the time when people were left with the same partner. But when they were working with a different stranger each time, that rate fell to just 13 percent. Repeated interactions made people trust more, which made them more comfortable to launch a secret scheme. Lest we think this effect only works in comparatively clean countries, the study was replicated in China. There, the rates of bribery fell from 41 percent with consistent companions to just 19 percent with rotating strangers.

Rotation isn't a miracle. But it helps. And it works best when a higher proportion of the people in the organization or political party or police department are already honest and decent. If you're recruiting better people and aren't stuck in QWERTY-style autopilot, rotation is more likely to become a virtuous circle. The better people you get into the rotation, the more it becomes an effective tactic at deterring and suppressing malfeasance by those in power. And if everyone is overseen by a random hodgepodge shadow board or a Citizen Assembly selected by sortition, all the better.

Sadly, even these interventions are *still* not enough. There's another problem: as we saw when we encountered clever psychopaths who rose up the ranks, the human versions of rotten apples are good at disguising themselves as pristine ones because we rarely look much below the surface. The way we evaluate leaders too often rewards cunning manipulators who *appear* to be honest and successful. We're going to need to change that, too.

Lesson 4:
Audit Decision-Making Processes, Not Just Results

When I was an undergraduate at Carleton College, in rural Minnesota, an enterprising group of student volunteers decided to start a free bike-sharing program called Yellow Bikes. The idea was heartwarming. People would donate their old junk bikes. Students would repair them and paint them bright yellow. Then, they'd be left around campus, unlocked, so anyone who wanted to ride rather than walk to class would just need to pick up a discarded bike and start pedaling. Despite some close calls with students drunkenly discovering an unfortunate lack of functioning brakes while careening downhill on campus (or so I've heard), the program was a raging success. One student even completed the cycling leg of the Carleton Triathlon competition on a rickety yellow bike.

Four years earlier, my brother had told me that his fellow students at Dartmouth College tried something virtually identical. The only difference was that the bikes were painted green. Shortly after the project produced the initial fleet of brightly painted green bikes, a group of students decided it would be fun to build a ramp and launch the bikes, rider and all, into the Connecticut River with a splash. Much merriment was had by all as the fleet of bikes sank to the riverbed.

Two identical initiatives. One success, one failure. If you only evaluated the Green Bikes program, you certainly wouldn't waste your time replicating it on your campus. The idea was doomed to fail. If you only evaluated the Yellow Bikes program, you'd start spray-painting. The idea was destined to succeed.

Humans are wedded to the false notion that there's a straight and predictable line between cause and effect when decisions are made. The green bikes ended up in the river *because* it was a stupid idea. The yellow bikes worked *because* it was a smart idea. That's not how it works. The real world is mind-bogglingly complex. Minor variations and flukes can drastically shift outcomes. That causes us to wrongly attribute failure to some excellent ideas while heaping praise on terrible ideas that produced improbable success. The lesson is simple: Don't always focus on results and outcomes. Instead, scrutinize the decision-making *process* much more carefully.

This is particularly important for three reasons when it comes to evaluating people in power. First, if you reward someone for a job well done—when their success was due to luck—then you're more likely to end up with a costly failure from a bad but lucky leader. Second, people who are good at getting into power are also good at creating narratives that cast them in a better light than reality. They're skilled at making us think they did a good job even when they screwed up. Better scrutiny of decision-making processes can counteract that. And third, good leaders sometimes look bad during selected snapshots in time, even though they're doing everything right. That can cause us to wrongly jettison good leaders or hang on to bad ones.

An instructive example comes from baseball. In 1989, the Minnesota Twins were a mediocre team, winning just under half of their games. Fans were furious at the team's leadership, including manager Tom Kelly. The club had just traded Frank Viola, the American League Cy Young Award winner, for three other pitchers. A year later, the Twins' win-loss record had gotten worse. They ended the 1990 season as the worst team in their division, winning just 74 of their 162 games. The manager, Kelly, found himself on the ropes. Fans and sportswriters started grumbling that it was time for fresh blood. The team's owner decided to brush off the criticism. He gave Kelly one more chance. But by mid-April of the 1991 season, the Twins looked worse than ever. They started off with two wins and nine losses, including a dire stretch of seven losses in a row. It seemed Kelly would soon be looking for a job in minor league baseball.

Then, in June, something remarkable happened. The Twins won fifteen games in a row, one of the longest winning streaks in baseball history. The pitchers that they'd acquired in that apparent blunder of a trade in 1989 started to pay off. The wins kept coming. By the end of the season, the Twins were in first place. Over the history of professional baseball at that point, 245 teams had ended a season in last place in their division. Zero had ever finished the following season in first place. That is, until the 1991 Minnesota Twins. In October, the Twins completed their turnaround, winning a nail-biting World Series in the seventh and final game against the Atlanta Braves.

What would've happened if the team's owners had caved to the pressure and fired Kelly as a result of two losing seasons? We can't say for sure, but Kelly's management was surely a key factor in the Twins march to the 1991 championship. If the team's owner had just looked at the team's win-loss record in a snapshot, he might have done something we often do: get rid of good leaders for bad reasons.

To understand why firing Kelly would've been a mistake, it's worth looking at the Twins' record in context. Baseball teams have vastly different payrolls. In 2019, for example, the Boston Red Sox paid their players a total of $222 million, compared to just $60 million for the Tampa Bay Rays. In other words, Boston had $3.70 to spend for every $1 Tampa Bay spent. Because more money can buy better players, any comparison between two managers has to take payrolls into account. Plus, because even the absolute-worst teams in history usually win at least a third of their games, there's a floor to poor performance. The worst Major League Baseball team in history, with the world's worst manager, will still probably win about 54 of the 162 games on the schedule. As a result, statisticians have come up with a much better metric to evaluate performance: How much money did you have to spend per win beyond the 54 wins that even the worst team will have? For example, if a team won 104 games and spent $100 million, it would be $100 million for fifty "extra" wins (104 − 54 = 50). In this example, the team paid $2 million per extra win.

In both 1989 and 1990, when Tom Kelly's job was in jeopardy, the Minnesota Twins were spending far less per extra win than many other teams. The New York Yankees, for example, were spending twice as much money per win. Kelly was doing a reasonably good job with a meager payroll, but that didn't show up in the league standings. Kelly's rebuild of the team in 1989 and 1990 also needed time to work, as it hinged on developing younger players into top-notch talent.[*] Because the owners were patient, it paid off in a big way with a world championship in 1991. But many owners would've fired Kelly after 1990.

Baseball therefore teaches an unexpected lesson for leadership: we often look at the wins and losses rather than evaluating the decisions that produced them. That tunnel vision causes us to wrongly conflate good results with good leadership and bad results with bad leadership. Reality is more nuanced.

---

[*] Furthering the point, baseball managers only have limited say over which players are on the team. Those decisions are often left up to an off-the-field official: the team's general manager. As a result, we often blame on-field managers for poor performance when they're working with decisions made by a far less visible leader in the team's front office.

This seemingly subtle point matters because many slippery, slimy leaders who rule realms more consequential than baseball diamonds are *really* skilled at making their results seem impressive. Remember Steve Raucci, the psychopathic janitor from Schenectady? To get a promotion he went to extraordinary lengths to make his predecessor's energy-saving record seem worse than it was. Raucci even used violent intimidation to obscure his own poor performance. Baseball managers can't massage their win-loss record, but politicians, CEOs, police officers, and others in positions of authority do frequently juke the stats or manipulate data to create a rosy, but misleading, impression. Some bad leaders are exceptionally good at timing. The worst leaders are all too willing to saddle their successors with impossible challenges that they delayed dealing with, creating the illusion of smooth sailing *until* the new leader took control. Such manipulations make it even more likely that we'll reward those who did the wrong thing but managed to get away with it by spin, deception, or gaming the system. To avoid that trap, we must assess the decision-making itself and carefully scrutinize results in proper context.

History is littered with leaders who received undeserved praise because of a good PR campaign. Take, for example, Benito Mussolini. While Il Duce is rightly regarded as a fascist monster, one bit of acclaim has stayed affixed to his legacy, like a lonely beauty mark stubbornly poking out of an authoritarian carbuncle. I'm referring to the adage "He made the trains run on time." There's one problem with that statement: he actually didn't.

Italy's railroads were in a sorry state after World War I. But most of the investments made for their repair and reform occurred before Mussolini took power. Once he became a dictator, Mussolini focused on vanity infrastructure, creating ornate train stations on rail lines for the country's elite, while ignoring commuter trains that served the masses. Hundreds of people died in construction projects under Mussolini—and most of the trains still didn't run on time. For the trains that did run on time, the decisions made by Mussolini's predecessor played a much-bigger role in making that possible. Nonetheless, the Italian fascist did what so many in power do masterfully: he took credit for decisions made by others. If you only focus on surface-level results without examining the underlying context or the decision-making itself, you'll end up reinforcing bad behavior rather than deterring it.

The problem is that nobody investigates how a decision was reached when everything turns out well. We have commissions for disasters, not successes. That needs to change. Because chance plays such an enormous role in success or failure, we should also routinely investigate successful outcomes that may have been produced by procedural failures.

For example, the Space Shuttle *Challenger* explosion in 1986 could've been avoided if more attention had been paid to damaged O-rings during cold-weather launches. Instead, these were ignored by too many with the power to fix it precisely because the problem hadn't resulted in an explosion—yet. All the warning signs were there. The postlaunch reviews were a procedural disaster, in which red flags were ignored and whistle-blowers ignored or silenced. But because the shuttle had safely returned to Earth, nobody paid much attention. If the *Challenger* somehow hadn't exploded in 1986, it would probably have exploded later. Learning from accidental success is just as important as learning from catastrophic failures. But we, as a species, just don't usually see it that way.

We've already seen how corruptible people seek power and are often better at getting it. These four lessons provide a road map to put better people into positions of authority: recruit smarter; randomly select people to perform oversight; rotate people around more; and audit decision-making processes, not just results. Implement all four strategies, and you're well on your way to having better people in power. But we're still only part of the way there. That's because no matter what we do, some corruptible people will become powerful. So, what can we do to ensure that once people are in charge, they aren't swayed by the corrosive, corrupting effects of their authority?

XI

THE WEIGHT OF RESPONSIBILITY

Lesson 5:
Create Frequent, Potent Reminders of Responsibility

If you think you've ever had a stressful first day on the job, think again.

When British prime ministers take office, they're often tired, but euphoric. Having spent the previous night celebrating victory, they all arrive at 10 Downing Street smiling and optimistic. Robin Butler's job was to wipe that smile off their face.

"The prime minister will arrive and have to take up the job after only about two or three hours' sleep," Butler tells me. But once at the office, the new leader is hit with a massive pile of papers—appointments to make, official statements to sign, decisions that can't wait. Among those papers, Butler would place one seemingly innocuous set of documents. Yet, it was a moral land mine, the hardest decision a human can possibly face. Butler had the unenviable task of explaining it.

His explanation would go something like this: The United Kingdom has four nuclear submarines, known colloquially as Trident—named after the nuclear missiles they carry on board. As you read this, one of the four is patrolling the world's oceans, a hidden behemoth with unimaginable destructive power lurking in the deep. Its onboard payload comprises 6.4 megatons of explosive power, the equivalent of around 430 Hiroshima bombs. If the weapons engineer pulls the trigger—a trigger that's the modified handle of a red Colt .45 revolver—entire countries can be wiped out in minutes. Once a missile is launched, there's no recalling it.

For months, the patrolling Trident submarine doesn't transmit or broadcast any messages. It runs silent, only dangling a long antenna behind it to receive incoming orders. Secrecy is paramount because nobody can be allowed to know the submarine's location. The reason for that is simple: that submarine is Britain's nuclear deterrent. If its location is known, a surprise attack on the submarine could knock out that deterrent in an instant, leaving the country vulnerable. As long as its location is unknown, an enemy will fear that any nuclear attack on Britain will prompt orders for a swift retaliation, a fear that's known as mutually assured destruction. Nuke the UK, and you'll have good reason to worry that you'll get nuked right back.

But what would happen if a surprise nuclear attack struck London, quickly eliminating the British government in a single horrible plume of smoke and radiation? Who would give the order to retaliate? That ominous question has been answered with an ingenious—but disturbing—protocol known as the Letters of Last Resort. For several prime ministers, that protocol began with Robin Butler handing them four pieces of paper and four envelopes, one for each of the Trident nuclear submarines.

"I would then explain this ghastly moral problem," Butler tells me as we sip tea in his Westminster flat. Butler, who is now both a knight and a lord, is tall and imposing, a holdover from his days spent playing competitive rugby in his youth. Despite being in his early eighties, he's far more active than his snow-white hair might suggest. But when he provided the briefing about the letters, it was the new prime minister's face that turned white.

Butler's guidance was straightforward, even though the choice facing the incoming leader wasn't. The leader was to handwrite instructions for what to do if Britain was attacked with a nuclear weapon and the government ceased to exist. There are no formal rules for what the prime minister must write, but four main options are suggested: retaliate, don't retaliate, put the submarine under the control of the US Navy, or leave it up to the commander of the submarine to decide what to do. The rub is that the nuclear deterrent only works if Britain's adversaries *believe* that the letters contain retaliation orders. If it was known that the letters said *not* to retaliate, then an enemy could strike without fear of being hit by British nuclear weapons in return.

Butler would explain to the prime ministers that their beyond-the-grave orders must be written in advance, with no knowledge of who attacked Britain, or why. Retaliation could set off a chain reaction that would end life on the planet, a tit for tat with weapons powerful enough to produce nuclear winter, making humans go extinct. Without knowing the context, the prime minister must decide, Should I give orders that, if followed, could eliminate our species? Put yourself in the prime minister's shoes. What would you do?

"It comes as a shock to the prime minister," Butler recalls. "But it must be, above everything else, the thing that brings home to them what the weight of their responsibility is."

It seems that the British government has, quite by accident, designed the ultimate system for reminding those in high office about the burdens of power. From day one, the new prime minister must realize how much his or her decisions can destroy lives—and even end human life altogether. So, how did it actually affect the prime ministers? To find out, I needed to call former prime minister Tony Blair on Zoom.

He popped up on my screen holding a mug—presumably of tea—while wearing a cozy sweater.

"Sorry I'm dressed so casually—it's lockdown and everything," he explains.

I ask him what it was like to have the experience of winning the election, moving into 10 Downing Street, and then getting hit by Butler's bombshell briefing.

"Whereas everyone else was euphoric, I really wasn't," Blair says. "I was oppressed by the weight of the responsibility that was descending upon me and very conscious of it—very conscious of the fact that campaigning for office and governing in office are two very different things."

But, he says, the Letters of Last Resort weren't nearly as much of a burden as I might have expected. "To be very honest about it, I thought that the likelihood of nuclear conflagration was so remote that . . . yes, of course, I paid a lot of attention deciding how I drafted the letters," Blair says, pausing to reflect. "But it didn't seem to be anything other than an extraordinarily remote possibility, so I can't say it occupied my thoughts greatly." However, Blair does say that he got the same "responsibility effect" from other briefings, which hammered home the scale of his duty. He insists he was always aware that when you were making decisions for millions, you needed to always think about those affected as individual people, not statistics.

"I was always very conscious of that distinction," Blair says. "The French author Georges Duhamel has a character in one of his books that loved humanity in general, it's just that he hated them in particular." Blair says he was determined not to behave like that character.

"A lot of my changes and reforms came from frontline visits," Blair recalls. "I would do one public event and then I would spend several hours, for example, with frontline health-care workers or police officers. That tends to keep you grounded. . . . The most important thing for a politician is, don't go into politics unless people interest you. Actual people. Individuals."

In British politics, Blair is now a lightning rod of controversy, largely because of his decisions related to the Iraq War. But whatever your political views, his insights about what it *feels like* to be in power are worth considering. For Cold War–era prime ministers, the Letters of Last Resort were probably more sobering because nuclear conflict felt like a real possibility. For Blair, it was frontline visits with ordinary people that gave him pause. That's a crucial lesson: for most people, constant reminders of how their decisions could affect others can create more self-reflection and therefore improve behavior. It's not a magic elixir. But it helps.

Wherever power can be abused, it's crucial to remind those who wield it of their corresponding responsibility. Sometimes, such reminders are created by design, as with the Letters of Last Resort. Other times, you don't need to design anything. The harrowing reminders are built in. Surgeons, for example, are haunted by patients who died on their operating table. As awful as those experiences are, many surgeons will tell you that they focus the mind in a productive way. There's no escaping that every scalpel movement matters.

Others are thrust into roles in which the stakes are both obvious and unrelenting. Cornell William Brooks, for example, felt that responsibility when he was president of the National Association for the Advancement of Colored People (NAACP). It was clear to him that his actions wouldn't be judged as any other executive's, but rather as a standard-bearer for an entire group of people—black people—in the United States. "You realize that you're speaking not just on behalf of yourself," he told me when I met him in his office at the Harvard Kennedy School. "You are speaking on behalf of people who don't get a chance to speak. It's humbling."

Kim Campbell, the first female prime minister of Canada, told me something similar: "Nobody who looked or sounded like me had ever done that job before. How do you manage the challenge of being seen as appropriately feminine? But at the same time, being appropriately strong and commanding and trustworthy in terms of dealing with crises or difficult situations?" It was constantly on her mind that she was being viewed as a test case—not of her party or of herself—but of having a woman in charge of the country. "I don't ever see anybody saying that Kim Campbell is an object lesson for why you don't want a woman as prime minister," she says. "That would have worried me."

For pioneers who are the first to occupy a position of authority, or for those who carry an official banner on behalf of a group that has historically faced discrimination, the weight of responsibility doesn't come as an occasional reminder. It's a constant. While it's difficult to get precise data, it's likely that such heavy burdens do cause people such as Kim Campbell and Cornell William Brooks to insist even more on clean, virtuous leadership. They know it's not just about themselves.

However, having an intellectual understanding of responsibility will not guarantee a magical translation into good behavior. Take, for example, one of the most amusingly depressing studies ever conducted. In 1973, students who were studying to become priests at Princeton University were asked to meet with researchers to talk about their motivations for taking the cloth. Then, the seminary students were told to prepare a brief talk about the biblical parable of the Good Samaritan, in which two callous people pass by a robbery victim in distress without helping before a Samaritan stops to care for him. After the students had prepared their speeches about the Good Samaritan, they were instructed to go to an adjacent building and give their talk.

Here's where it gets interesting. A third of the students were told that they had plenty of time to get to the other building. A third were told that they'd make it on time if they went right away. And a third were told that they were running late and needed to rush to the building.

The researchers were being mischievous. On the way to give their Good Samaritan talk, each of the students encountered a stranger in agony in the alleyway between the buildings. The alleyway was so narrow that the students would have to physically step over the suffering man to get past. The stranger in distress was part of the experiment, but the future priests didn't know that. Sixty percent of the students running early stopped to help. Half of those who were on time stopped. But only 10 percent of the seminary students running late helped the stranger. This was particularly ironic because they were future priests rushing to give a talk about the biblical parable telling them to stop if they encountered a stranger in agony. Reminders of responsibility can work, but other factors can override them.

So, to create better behavior, you have to twin reminders of responsibility with another psychological tweak: show people in positions of authority the costs and consequences of their actions. If those in authority aren't made deeply uncomfortable by human faces right in front of them from time to time, they're probably not doing their job right.

Lesson 6:
Don't Let Those in Power See People as Abstractions

Ken Feinberg is the spitting image of a high-powered, high-paid lawyer: immaculately pressed white shirts, shiny silver cuff links, tortoiseshell spectacles. At seventy-six, he looks young for his age, but his bald head shows wrinkles across his brow, as though the agonizing decisions that he's grappled with for decades have been etched onto his face. He speaks in a booming voice, every word laced with an almost-over-the-top caricature of a Boston accent. When he gets ready to emphasize a point, his voice rises until he is shouting, like the human embodiment of capital letters. Yet, the shouting is no substitute for exactness. Feinberg deploys words like a twenty-first-century weapons-targeting system. This skill proved crucial in a career built around speaking to families who have faced horrific suffering.

For the last thirty-five years, Feinberg has overseen every single major compensation fund in the United States. The Sandy Hook school massacre. The BP oil spill. The Boston Marathon bombing. If a horrific event with a long list of victims takes place in the United States, Ken Feinberg's phone rings. But the most difficult task he's been given was, without question, the September 11th Victim Compensation Fund. After 2,977 people were murdered in New York, Pennsylvania, and Washington, DC, Feinberg had to answer one impossible question: What were each of their lives worth?

The fund was enormous, so Feinberg had leeway. In a way, that made the job harder—because not everyone would be equal. He came up with a pragmatic solution: try to figure out how much money the person would've earned over the remaining years of life had he or she not been the victim of the September 11 terrorist attacks. That was an uncomfortable method, boiling down people's worth to their financial earnings and embedding huge disparities into the compensation decisions. But it could solve a key problem: higher-earning victims often had more financial obligations than lower-earning victims, so this would try to minimize the disruptions to families who had already gone through so much. Nobody wanted a widow or widower to default on a mortgage signed under the expectation of a steady paycheck for years to come. Feinberg's model would make sure that the expected paycheck—or a rough approximation of it—would keep coming indefinitely.

In case the initial financial offer to a family was contested, Feinberg established a system to allow a personal appeal. He'd meet the family in person, hear about their loved one, then decide whether their circumstances warranted an adjustment. "Eight hundred and fifty separate victims and their families came to see me personally," Feinberg tells me. "The trauma and the horror of 9/11—and the loss of loved ones turned to dust without even a body—I found to be debilitating." Meeting these people face-to-face was heart-wrenching.

Feinberg couldn't bring anyone back from the dead. But he could resuscitate a grieving family's finances. So day after day, month after month, Feinberg listened. I asked him whether he grew numb to the horror stories once it became part of his routine. He immediately objected, "No matter how many times you do it, you're not any more able to divorce yourself from the emotional overhang of the tragedy. That, you never get over."

The financial calculations weren't straightforward either. Young people working low-paid jobs as World Trade Center baristas who were disabled from the attacks could reasonably have expected to earn more later in life. "'Mr. Feinberg,'" he recalls many saying to him, "'I had this low-paying job, but I had a contract where I was going to get five times more next year.' Show me the contract. Show me the documentary evidence. 'Mr. Feinberg, I'm only earning X, but I just was admitted to Harvard Law School.' Show me that you were admitted." If he deemed the assumptions were reasonable, Feinberg would adjust the compensation upward. If they weren't, he'd turn people down.

Imagine having to tell a grieving mother that her son's life simply wasn't worth as much as she said it was, at least in financial terms. Imagine having to look families in the eye and tell them that their lost loved ones' career dreams and aspirations, their plans for future career advancement and the salary it would entail, just weren't credible. That was Feinberg's standard day at the office.

Feinberg was even forced to make decisions that could tear apart families, compounding the horrors of victimhood. One woman came to see him, not to ask for more money, but just to talk to someone about her husband. He was a firefighter who died trying to rescue people from the Twin Towers. She told Feinberg that her husband was the center of her universe, a model husband and a perfect father. She called him "Mr. Mom." When he wasn't at the fire station, he was teaching their six-year-old to play baseball, teaching their four-year-old to read, or reading a bedtime story to their two-year-old.

"The only reason I haven't gone up to the roof of our building and jumped to join him is our three children," she told Feinberg, through tears. "But without Mr. Mom, my life is over. I don't care how much money you give me." Then, she left. The next day, Feinberg's phone rang. It was a lawyer.

"Mr. Feinberg, did you meet yesterday with the woman with the three kids, six, four, and two? With the dad they called Mr. Mom?"

"Yeah. Terrible."

"Mr. Feinberg, I want to tell you something. I don't envy what you have to do. You've got a tough job. But she doesn't know that Mr. Mom had two *other* kids, five and three by his girlfriend and mistress in Queens, New York. I represent the mistress and the two kids. And I just want you to know, because when you cut your 9/11 check, there's not three surviving children, there's *five* surviving children. But I'm sure you'll do the right thing."

Click. The lawyer hung up.

Do you tell the widow? Or do you keep your mouth shut?

"What I ultimately did," Feinberg recalls, "was I never told them. I made two calculations. I cut one check to his wife as the guardian of the three children, and without her knowledge, I cut a separate check to the girlfriend as the guardian of the two kids. That was it."

After decades of dealing with those kinds of dilemmas, Feinberg says he's learned two lessons. The first is that life can unexpectedly change in an instant, so you had better cherish it. But the second lesson—the one we'll focus on—is something that we don't normally associate with the cold detachment of lawyers.

"You better be a benevolent despot," Feinberg insists. "You better be empathetic. You better add to your political and substantive power a healthy dose of empathy and sensitivity. Because without those characteristics, without the perception that you are empathetic and understand the plight of the victim, you're doomed."

This insight had a strategic side. Without empathy for the victims, the people getting compensated were less likely to accept the agreed amount, and the victims could be embroiled in court battles for years. But Feinberg also recognized a crucial human side about himself. He sat face-to-face with 850 victims and their families. He saw each family's pain firsthand. For survivors, he had to look at the disfigurements and scars that they were stuck with forever.

"Unless you have a heart of stone, you're going to be impacted by the emotional vulnerability and expressions of these people in one-on-

one confidential meetings," Feinberg tells me. "There is a certain degree of human nature that prevents me from thinking I'm Julius Caesar or Alexander the Great. And that's a check on self-serving aggrandizement."

In total, over $7 billion has been awarded to roughly thirty thousand victims and their families, mostly based on decisions that Feinberg made. He recognized that he controlled their financial fate. As a result, he went to great lengths to ensure that the people he was affecting weren't amorphous abstractions. He wanted to picture them, to hear their voices break, to agonize with them, *before* he reached a decision. If he was going to say no to someone, he was going to do so after looking the person in the eye.

Unfortunately, Feinberg's insistence on eliminating the abstract nature of decision-making is rare in today's world. It's easier than ever before to be a desk monster—someone who damages, destroys, or even ends lives without leaving the comfort of an office chair or seeing the suffering inflicted firsthand. Entire industries exist to divorce uncomfortable decisions from the visual fields of those who make them. These jobs often have euphemistic names such as *corporate downsizing specialists* or *termination consultants*. They can save your boss the trouble of feeling a bit of emotional discomfort from firing a longtime employee, outsourcing it to someone else. But why does that matter? What happens when serious harm gets sanitized down to a euphemism and the people who are deciding to inflict pain on others never see it firsthand?

On a crisp, sunny January day in Berkeley, California, I walk past students clutching Nalgene water bottles. One has a backpack emblazoned with slogans opposing war and championing justice for victims of human rights abuses. I pass by the crush of students, make my way through the hallways of the law school building, and knock on the door of the most controversial member of Berkeley's faculty: John Yoo. He's wearing a dark suit and tie, in marked contrast with other faculty members, who are typing in their offices in jeans and polo shirts. Yoo welcomes me warmly with a smile. I shake his hand, well aware that many people see the man standing before me not as a law professor, but as a war criminal.

Twenty years earlier, shortly after the September 11 attacks, Yoo, as the deputy assistant attorney general of the United States, was tasked with helping President George W. Bush determine what conduct was and wasn't lawful. Yoo was young and ambitious, a lawyer in his early thirties who was already advising the president. He'd come to the Bush administration's attention after writing a series of legal briefs arguing for expansive authority for presidents during periods of crisis. He was, as one law professor later put it, "a true believer."

On January 9, 2002, Yoo wrote a now-infamous memo, arguing that the Geneva Convention protections—protections that prohibited torture of detainees during conflict—didn't apply to combatants who were apprehended in Afghanistan. The purpose of the memo was, in part, to ensure that American officials and soldiers wouldn't be charged with war crimes even if they abused prisoners during interrogations. Yoo, along with a small group of other lawyers and administration officials who called themselves the War Council, were determined to find a legal justification for what they would later euphemistically call "enhanced interrogation." As a result, they cut out other government lawyers from the decision-making, most likely because those lawyers held the understandable view that international law did, indeed, apply to the United States. Many legal scholars and government attorneys have subsequently argued that Yoo's legal opinions are far outside the mainstream consensus about executive authority and international law. Whether right or wrong, Yoo's views were certainly convenient for the White House.

In August 2002, Yoo authored another memo. It green-lighted interrogation techniques that most people would consider torture. Specifically, Yoo's memo provided legal justification for waterboarding (in which the detainee is given a prolonged sensation of drowning and suffocation), confining prisoners in a tiny box and then pouring live insects in with them to make them panic, and keeping prisoners awake for up to eleven days straight. Some, such as Yoo, argue that those techniques were necessary to stave off future attacks. But subsequent reviews have also shown that some detainees who were tortured by the US government after 9/11 were innocent.

When you meet someone who has grappled with a deeply moral

problem with profound consequences for human suffering, you inevitably put yourself in the person's shoes. What would it be like to have that gnaw at your conscience? So I asked him the obvious question: How had it affected him personally? Had he lost sleep over it?

His response was nonchalant: "No, I don't think I had any sleeplessness—because as a scholar, I think about these things all the time already. I don't personally feel a lot of stress about making decisions."

I pressed him on that answer. I told Yoo that I had made plenty of scholarly arguments, but that I would feel a big difference between stating my opinion in an intellectual debate and issuing a legal opinion that could lead to people being deliberately made to feel as if they're drowning. Yoo nodded. "It is different, sure. And there are people who I worked with in the government who I think kind of had a breakdown over working on these issues." But despite the internal struggles raging within his coworkers, Yoo says he didn't share them.

"I had this view," Yoo tells me. "With interrogation methods, there was like one through twelve or whatever. So we could stop it at four. Maybe that's too little. People might criticize us later for being too reluctant to try to protect national security. You go to twelve and people will say we allowed too much. Everything is a trade-off. You can choose whatever line you want in terms of interrogation methods. There's going to be a benefit and there's going to be costs to each place you stop."

Some of you will side with Yoo and applaud a hard decision that aimed to save lives. Others will think he's a war criminal. But what struck me most wasn't whether he was right or wrong. It was how he made his arguments. No matter how I pressed Yoo, I got the same detached, analytical answers. He was affable, polite, and thoughtful in his replies—even when I tried to push him. With methodical calm, he outlined the logic of each decision. He has clearly thought deeply about these questions. But at no point did I detect any hint of emotion, or a pause of hesitation.

As I said goodbye and walked back out into the Berkeley sunshine, it dawned on me that torture likely remained an abstraction to Yoo. The answers he sought were in books and briefs, not faraway jail cells. He'd presumably never looked into the eyes of a man who was made to believe that he was drowning. Perhaps Yoo's staunch legal views wouldn't have been changed by such experiences. The law, after all, is supposed to be dispassionate, cold, unswayed by emotion. And Yoo's views are strikingly consistent. A disturbing trip to a black site that used torture might have had no effect on his thinking.

But perhaps a healthy dose of discomfort is precisely what's needed for people who are making morally uncomfortable decisions. Both Feinberg and Yoo were grappling with the limits of the law in the aftermath of September 11. Feinberg made sure that he looked into the eyes of those who were hurt by his decisions. Yoo never saw them.

These aren't just anecdotes. It turns out there's good reason to believe that we'd have a society with fewer callous abuses if we made sure that more CEOs and police officers and politicians followed the Feinberg route rather than the Yoo route.

Bambi, Dehumanization, and Artificial Intelligence

Human relationships are mediated by a concept called psychological distance. Our social lives are a bit like an onion. In the center are your immediate family members—your spouse, your children, your parents and siblings. One layer beyond that is your extended family, then perhaps your friends, then your coworkers, and so on. All of those layers, like an onion, can make you cry if something happens to them (depending on your coworkers). But eventually, once you've added enough layers, you start to get to the skin—the bits that are disposable. You won't give their loss a second thought. One layer beyond that and it's not even part of the onion any longer. Those people don't even enter into your thoughts.

Naturally, our onions aren't all alike. Sentimental types might have a larger onion. Others get to the skin much faster, only being moved by concern for their closest personal relationships.

But whether a given layer matters to us isn't fixed. It can change over time. As the moral philosopher Peter Singer has written, the story of humans and humanity is one of an "expanding circle." As babies, our moral universe is small, limited to our parents and perhaps a jealous sibling. But as we develop, we care about more and more people. Singer also argues that the history of our species has been defined by an expanding moral circle. People used to care only about people immediately around them. Now, we can be deeply moved by stories of a tsunami or a terrorist attack halfway around the world with people we'll never meet or know. So, can you deliberately expand your moral circle or grow your moral onion?

The way that someone is portrayed or framed in our minds can radically change our view of that person or group of people. Americans, for example, often think of Iranians as enemies. But American Christians might feel solidarity with persecuted Iranian Christians. Hollywood directors have long understood the power of such framing by manipulating our sense of psychological distance. When a character dies on-screen, we're not supposed to react much if we've barely learned anything about the person. Anonymity doesn't move us. The unnamed characters who are mown down in a war scene have limited effect on most of us, even though we implicitly understand that they surely had families and aspirations. Out of sight, out of mind. But when a protagonist dies—a character that we feel we understand, that we're rooting for and identify with—well, those are the tearjerker moments of cinema. That effect can be so powerful that the death of a deer, such as Bambi's mom, for example, traumatizes us more than the on-screen deaths of just about every unnamed human victim in an action flick.

Specificity matters. You might have different views about "computer nerds" in general than you do about Vanessa, the violinist from IT who brings sourdough into the office every Monday. Or, you may have different views about "migrants" than you do about José, who plays on your company football team and is a first-generation immigrant. (Indeed, there's consistent evidence that the places most opposed to immigration tend to have the fewest immigrants.) The more we encounter a person, the less the person becomes a category. As we peel back the layers of people's personality and their inner life, they move closer to the center of our social and psychological onion. The opposite is true, too. If someone remains an abstraction, it's much easier to not care about the person.

That insight provides a blueprint that can be used for good or for evil.

According to Yaacov Trope, a psychologist at NYU, psychological distance has four dimensions that determine whether a decision lies within the onion we care about. First, there's social distance (no, not the dreaded pandemic variety). Social distance refers to how much you identify with the person who will be affected by your behavior. Firing a neighbor who is the dad of your daughter's best friend is harder than firing someone you've never met. Second, there's temporal, or time, distance. How long of a delay is there between the moment you make a decision and the effects it's likely to have? The CEO of a chemical company will find it easier to let toxic substances slowly leach into groundwater than to poison someone's glass of water at a restaurant. Third, there's spatial distance. It's easier to harm people who are physically far away than those who are in the same room as us. And fourth and finally, there's experiential distance. It's easier to inflict harm on or abuse others if you just have to imagine it, as Yoo did, rather than viscerally feel it, experience it, or watch it.

Warfare provides a particularly instructive example of how psychological distance determines human behavior. Throughout most of human history, warfare has been fixed with regard to three of the four dimensions. Whether it was the Spartans or William the Conqueror at the Battle of Hastings, killing on the battlefield was up close, immediate, and visceral. Jab a spear into someone else's stomach and there's no escaping the utter lack of temporal, spatial, or experiential distance. This lack of psychological distance is problematic for generals trying to win battles for one simple reason: plenty of humans have an instinctive aversion to killing.

In the nineteenth century, the French military officer Ardant du Picq found evidence that a significant percentage of French soldiers in the 1860s were deliberately firing their weapons high into the air rather than shooting into the living, breathing human beings across the battlefield. Dave Grossman's book *On Killing* provides an overview of this phenomenon throughout history, showing striking evidence that a surprising number of soldiers don't actually use their weapons during combat. After the Battle of Gettysburg, 90 percent of the 27,574 muskets collected after the battle were either still loaded or had been loaded twice without firing. And when soldiers use their weapons, some are averse to actually shooting someone. In the Vietnam War, it's estimated that up to fifty thousand bullets were fired for every person killed. Grossman's work points to police and soldier training that now uses more humanlike targets rather than paper bull's-eyes to try to better prepare shooters for the real-world shooting of a person. Such small adjustments have been shown to increase firing rates during armed conflict.

However, it's a lot easier to overcome any trigger-finger hesitations you might have with a disturbing trick: don't think of the person you're killing as a human being. Instead, mentally transform the person into a disposable subhuman abstraction. History's worst atrocities are usually preceded by language that equates human beings with insects, vermin, even objects. Slaves were referred to as stock. Native Americans were called savages. Rwanda's perpetrators of genocide depicted Tutsi as cockroaches.[*] Nazis referred to Jews as rats and depicted them on posters as lice.

But even under murderous regimes, visible reminders that targeted groups are, in fact, humans can have a potent effect. One of the only successful acts of resistance to the deportation of Jews under Hitler was the Rosenstrasse protest, in which non-Jewish German women protested the detention of their Jewish husbands. Because the detainees were officially linked to non-Jewish Germans, who were viewed as fully human, the protest worked. The Jewish detainees were eventually released and spared. But in most of the worst acts of human cruelty and abuse, the perpetrators tried to create social distance between themselves and their victims. Unable to change the temporal, spatial, or experiential aspects of killing, the focus remained on devaluing the lives of the "enemy." It helped overcome the perpetrators' human instinct, our aversion to killing.

These days, overcoming that aversion is even easier. Innovations in modern warfare have expanded psychological distance. Drone strikes, for example, create more spatial and experiential distance, in which a pilot with a joystick can kill large numbers of people on a video screen thousands of miles away. The sounds, smells, and sights of warfare have been removed. For example, drone pilots who commute to Creech Air Force Base in the Nevada desert have a radically different experience from pi-

---

* The Rwanda case is the exception that proves the rule. The genocide was extremely vicious, with ordinary people hacking their neighbors to death with machetes. This extreme physical and psychological closeness is a further testament to just how potent dehumanization can be to overcome that proximity.

lots who land fighter jets on aircraft carriers in the Persian Gulf. After launching a deadly missile at enemy combatants, some Nevada drone pilots would hop in their cars, pick up some milk, and sit down for a family dinner with their kids. Killing, for them, could feel too much like a video game. Even when dehumanization isn't deliberate, it's harder to think of people as part of your beloved moral onion if they just look like tiny, far-away specks on a video screen.

Thankfully, few of us will ever kill someone. But understanding the concepts behind these extreme examples of psychological distance can help ensure that powerful people behave better. Whether it's monstrous managers, embezzling executives, or petty-tyrant immigration officials, tweaking how those in charge experience psychological distance is key to creating a better society.

To see how, let's focus on spatial distance for a moment. In the past, companies such as the Dutch East India Company—enormous behemoths that sprawled across the globe—were the outliers. Now, small, locally owned and operated companies are the outliers. It's become routine for executives in Western capitals to make decisions that drop toxic sludge half a world away or drive up the price of lifesaving drugs in the world's poorest countries without ever setting foot in them. It's increasingly common to get fired by people who work in a corporate headquarters that you've never visited. That should give us cause for concern because our moral inhibitions are lessened as the space between us increases. In a 2017 experiment, participants were asked to operate a machine that killed ladybugs. One cohort was physically in the same room as the machine and could see it, though they controlled it remotely. Another cohort was given the same instructions, but they couldn't see the machine as it was in another location. Those who were spatially distanced from the machine were willing to kill more ladybugs than those who were in the same room. (Those of you with oversize moral onions will be relieved to know that no ladybugs were actually killed in the experiments. The machine was a convincing fake.)

The ability to feel social distance from the people you harm has also radically expanded in the modern era. In the Stone Age, if you stole some berries from your neighbor, you'd almost always see the victim, and the victim would see you. If you got caught, you'd have to face the consequences or live with the stigma in your community. But nowadays, stealing can be done by taking money from faceless accounts in Excel spreadsheets. Eugene Soltes, in his book on white-collar crime, *Why They Do It*, points to a series of embezzlers who had no issue lying on paper or on spreadsheets, but fessed up almost immediately when confronted by another human being.

So, it seems obvious that the best way to set up systems of accountability is by minimizing the psychological distance between ruler and ruled. Not so fast. We probably don't want CEOs of Fortune 500 companies spending every waking moment getting to know each employee, nor is it the best use of time for them to be firing people. Plus, do we want police officers to be playing poker on the weekends with gang members they're supposed to arrest if they commit a crime? Surely not. That's a recipe for corruption and favoritism.

Similarly, it's probably not a great idea for surgeons to be so moved by the humanity of their patients that they're unable to carve into their bodies with cold, methodical precision. Researchers have found that the brains of physicians are far more adept at being unmoved by the pain of others. There's also evidence that nurses who humanize their patients too much end up with higher rates of job stress and burnout. Mild dehumanization in health care can act as a necessary coping mechanism. On my brother's first day of medical school, he had to dissect a cadaver in a class aptly titled Gross Anatomy. Like many aspiring doctors, he found the experience deeply uncomfortable. He asked the professor whether he was supposed to try to think of the person on the dissection table as a piece of flesh or as someone's grandpa. "Both," the professor replied.

Psychological distance is therefore a dilemma that can be solved by what social scientists call a Goldilocks solution. Anyone making tough and potentially damaging or deadly decisions needs to have *just the right amount* of emotional proximity. Get too psychologically close and your judgment will be clouded by inescapable sentimentality. Get too far away and your healthy dose of concern and caution will fly out the window. In many spheres of the modern world, the pendulum has swung too far toward an unhealthy amount of distance. We need more CEOs who take an interest in their employees, more government lawyers who see the human face of their briefs, and more community policing.

In reality, the world is moving in the opposite direction. Computers that use opaque algorithms driven by machine learning are replacing psychologically distant humans, who themselves replaced psychologically close humans. While machine learning and AI have huge potential to improve living standards and create a more just society, they can also create control without accountability.

We've now covered how to get better people into power and how to ensure that powerful people behave better. We can go a long way toward making the world a more just place by reminding powerful people of their responsibilities while ensuring that they see others as individuals rather than abstractions. The problem, as any social scientist will tell you, is that the people are only part of the equation. You can give a sobering lesson to a prime minister with the Letters of Last Resort, just as you can show mid-level managers the human costs of their reckless or callous behavior. That's always worth doing, because human compassion and empathy can be powerful forces for good. But if the underlying systems they work in are broken, even well-intentioned people are still prone to behaving badly. Good people in badly designed systems may still give in to darker impulses.

And there's yet another uncomfortable truth: plenty of people in positions of authority simply won't be moved by reminders of responsibility or efforts to ensure that people never become abstractions. Psychopaths, for example, wouldn't be much affected by the Letters of Last Resort, nor would they particularly care about seeing the faces of their victims. Some would even relish the opportunity to inflict suffering. But it's not just psychopaths we have to worry about. As we've seen, a lot of run-of-the-mill corrupt and corruptible people end up in power—nefarious people who aren't even *trying* to do good in the first place but are instead motivated by self-interest, greed, or narcissism.

So, if bad systems are still a problem and corruptible people in power are still a menace, how can we improve systems to stop corruptible people from behaving badly?

XII

WATCHED

If God did not exist, it would be necessary to invent him.

—Voltaire

Lesson 7:
Watched People Are Nice People

If you were a time traveler deciding when and where to commit a crime spree, one place you wouldn't want to pick was ninth-century England. The punishments and methods of execution weren't exactly pleasant (to put it mildly). But the trial itself could be deadly, too. In cases in which there wasn't enough evidence to determine whether the accused was innocent or guilty, the judgment would be determined by a process known as an ordeal. These rituals relied on a belief in *judicium Dei*, or judgment of God. The accused would be forced to endure something that would normally produce horrific suffering. For example, in "hot water" ordeals, the alleged criminal would be required to retrieve a ring or a stone from a cauldron filled with boiling water. If that burned the person's flesh, it was divine proof that the accused was guilty. If a miracle intervened and the flesh was unharmed, God had clearly spoken: the person was innocent. The "hot iron" ordeal, as its name helpfully implies, wasn't pleasant either. An alleged criminal was forced to carry a red-hot piece of iron precisely nine paces, then the burns (or lack thereof) determined the guilt of the accused.

Such ordeals weren't exclusive to medieval England. In some bedouin communities, the Bisha'a is used to determine whether a person is lying. The alleged liar is asked to lick a hot metal object, often a spoon. If their tongue is burned, they're deemed a liar. In medieval Germany, Poland, and Scotland, cruentation was used, in which the corpse of a murder victim was believed to spontaneously bleed if the murderer was brought nearby. In Madagascar, suspected criminals were asked to eat three pieces of chicken skin that were laced with a deadly poison produced by the nuts of the indigenous *tangena* tree. If they died, they'd be declared a sorcerer and buried in disgrace. During the reign of Queen Ranavalona I in the nineteenth century, one estimate suggests that one out of every fifty people in the population died *every year* as a result of these ordeals.

If you think these systems are a bit insane, you're not alone. Toxic nuts, boiled hands, and scalding spoons don't seem—at least at first glance—to be the ideal foundation for a criminal justice system. But Peter Leeson, an economist at George Mason University, disagrees. To him, ordeals were a bizarre, but perfectly rational, way of figuring out the guilt of the accused whenever you couldn't gather all the facts and you didn't have the Anglo-Saxon equivalent of Hercule Poirot or Sherlock Holmes hanging around your village. The logic of these ordeals can help us understand how to stop people in authority from abusing their power.

Leeson doesn't suggest that God intervened to save the limbs of innocents from boiling water. Rather, he says that the ordeals worked because the accused *believed* that they would work. More precisely, they provided a mechanism to effectively sort the guilty from the innocent for a simple reason: everyone believed that God was *always* watching.

Leeson asks us to imagine Frithogar, an Anglo-Saxon farmer accused of stealing an animal from his neighbor. If there isn't sufficient evidence one way or another, Frithogar may be asked whether he'd be willing to undergo a hot-water ordeal to prove his innocence. If Frithogar is guilty, he'll believe that God will know of his guilt and punish him accordingly. He'll therefore expect to get scalded by the boiling water. As a result, Frithogar will insist on paying a fine or avoiding the ordeal at all costs. By resisting the ordeal, he's snitching on himself. But if Frithogar is innocent, he'll willingly accept the ordeal, believing that God will also know of his innocence and spare him with a miracle. In a way, it's a bit like Solomon and the baby, in which the woman willing to give up the baby rather than have it cut in half shows herself to be the true mother. In the face of dire consequences, the truth often comes out.

Remarkably, the innocent Frithogars of medieval England would often get a miracle. Because belief in divine intervention was so widespread, once someone eagerly accepted trial by ordeal, the priest would (probably correctly) believe that person to be innocent. As Leeson explains, "Knowing this, the priest can fix the ordeal to find the correct result. For example, if Frithogar chooses to undergo his ordeal, the ordeal-administering priest can lower the water's temperature so it does not boil him. Frithogar plunges his arm into the cauldron expecting to be unharmed. His expectation is fulfilled—not by God but by the newly informed priest." There's evidence that precisely this rigging of the ordeal trial happened, in which a suspect's willingness to subject themselves to divine scrutiny caused a priest to spare them. It sorted the guilty from the innocent better than holy boiling water ever could.

Ordeals provide a crucial insight: we behave better when we believe we're being watched by a force that could punish us. We're more honest, too, because there's a greater risk that our lies will be exposed. Crucially, just the threat of punishment is often enough to induce better behavior. But it seems pretty dystopian to imagine that mass surveillance is the solution to society's woes. So, is there a better way? And what do ordeals or religiosity have to do with stopping police officers from using excessive violence or deterring politicians from lining their pockets while they fleece the country? To find out, we need to think a bit more deeply about the role of religion in human societies.

For thousands of years, our devil within has partly been subdued when humans have feared the watchful gaze of a deity looking down from above. Today, billions believe in a God who will punish us for our sins. That belief is so common that it seems as if it must be a natural human impulse. But it's not. Back in the Stone Age, people didn't likely see gods as moral enforcers. As Ara Norenzayan, professor of psychology at the University of British Columbia, explains in his book, *Big Gods*, the gods of hunter-gatherers "are typically unconcerned about moral transgressions such as theft and exploitation. . . . Many gods and spirits are not even fully omniscient to be good monitors of moral behavior—they perceive things within villages but not beyond; they may be tricked or manipulated by other rival gods. Religion's early roots did not have a wide moral scope." Go back far enough and our ancestors probably weren't as afraid of divine wrath. That all changed with the arrival of what Norenzayan calls the Big Gods—the gods of major modern faiths that are said to be aware of everything we do and are willing to punish us for our sins.

The world's major religions are overflowing with reminders that God is watching. Abrahamic religions (Judaism, Christianity, and Islam) make it clear that nothing can be hidden from Him. Even if no human ever finds out that you stole from the church collection plate or that you had impure thoughts about your neighbor, God knows. Other religions send similar messages to believers. In Tibet and Nepal, Buddha Eyes are dotted around villages. This isn't a recent innovation. Incans had to worry about the gaze of Viracocha, a god who oversaw the empire. As Norenzayan points out, such divine monitoring dates back even further, as "one of the oldest and most significant deities in ancient Egypt was Horus, the sky god, also known as 'Horus of Two Eyes.'"

Norenzayan argues that the specter of divine surveillance served a useful purpose for society. Because people believed they were being watched, they behaved more virtuously than they would've otherwise. Big Gods made people fear being caught well before detectives or investigative journalists existed. Furthermore, because society held a shared belief in the same God or gods, Norenzayan says that religiosity built up social trust. If everyone believes in divine punishment, then a shopkeeper can have more faith that you'll pay back a debt. Both of you know that you'll inevitably pay for it—either in this life or the next. Just as nuclear weapons act as a deterrent because of "mutually assured destruction," religion produces another form of MAD: mutually assured damnation. Shared belief creates social cohesion.

In Norenzayan's estimation, the Big Gods filled a power vacuum that existed because premodern governments were notoriously weak. Policing didn't exist. Especially in rural areas, the presence of any government was effectively invisible. The farther out of sight from the palace you were, the less likely you were to feel watched by mortals. This is beautifully captured by a scene in *Monty Python and the Holy Grail*, featuring an exchange between King Arthur, an unnamed peasant woman, and a dissident peasant named Dennis:

KING ARTHUR: I am Arthur, king of the Britons. Whose castle is that?

PEASANT: King of the who?

KING ARTHUR: The Britons.

PEASANT: Who're the "Britons"?

KING ARTHUR: Well, we all are. We're all Britons, and I am your king.

PEASANT: Well, how'd you become king, then?

KING ARTHUR: The Lady of the Lake, her arm clad in the purest shimmering samite, held aloft Excalibur from the bosom of the water, signifying by divine providence that I, Arthur, was to carry Excalibur. That is why I am your king.

DENNIS: Listen. Strange women lying in ponds distributing swords is no basis for a system of government. Supreme executive power derives from a mandate from the masses, not from some farcical aquatic ceremony.

Dennis had a point. Neither he nor the peasant woman would've had much to fear from Arthur's government in their daily lives. The Knights of the Roundtable weren't gallivanting around in search of common criminals or disloyal peasants. Without government enforcement, something else had to fill the void. Norenzayan argues that Big Gods filled that role—and says that without them, many such societies would've descended into far worse chaos and disorder. Who needs Big Brother if you've got Horus and Viracocha?

But Norenzayan's Big Gods argument takes this idea one step further. Not only was a belief in constant divine surveillance helpful for creating a more peaceful society, it also created winners and losers *between* societies. Religious belief could determine whether any given society died, survived, or thrived.

Specifically, he argues that societies that stuck with the amoral hunter-gatherer-style deities—the ones that couldn't keep an eye on the people who worshipped them—tended to do worse than societies that felt watched. Without any heavenly deterrent, people cooperated less. Without a shared omniscient deity, they trusted each other less. Endless internal conflict destroyed progress. Those societies fizzled—or got conquered and subsumed by more cooperative ones. (There's even a scholarly theory, called the supernatural punishment hypothesis, that belief in divine retribution provided an evolutionary edge at the individual level. The theory suggests that those who believed in punishment from above were less likely to behave aggressively in ways that would get them killed or imprisoned, thereby giving them a better chance to have kids. In Darwinian terms, we could call that the "survival of the holiest" hypothesis.)

Norenzayan isn't the first to argue that supernatural beliefs can create social success. Similar arguments have been advanced by the father of sociology, Max Weber, who suggested that the Protestant devotion to the godliness of hard work created self-perpetuating prosperity.

But if the Big Gods argument is right, then it's no accident that the overwhelming majority of the world's population believe in moralizing omniscient gods. Instead, belief in those gods helped create successful societies, leading to a spread of those kinds of religions while others died out. The alternative explanation advanced by believers is that religions thrive or fail based on whether they're true. Christians believe that Christianity has thrived because it's the true faith, as do Muslims with Islam, and Jews with Judaism. That's at odds with Norenzayan's more functional, pragmatic view of religion, which was perhaps best captured by Voltaire. As he put it, "If God did not exist, it would be necessary to invent him."

The Big Gods hypothesis has flaws. A notable one is that murder and crime in the Middle Ages were rampant despite near universal fear of God's retribution. But there's significant evidence—in the modern era as well—that corroborates Norenzayan's view that "watched people are nice people." If he's right, that's a crucial insight that can be used to deter abuses of power from those in authority.

So, what does the evidence show? Our impulse to hesitate about bad behavior when we're being watched begins early. Jared Piazza of the University of Kent in England set up an experiment in which children were left in a room with a tantalizing box and told not to look inside. Some of the children were left alone. Others were supervised by an adult who stayed in the room. But one group of children who were left alone were also told that the invisible force of "Princess Alice" would be checking to make sure they didn't open the box. The children in that group were then asked whether they believed that Alice was real. Everyone who said they believed in the princess refrained from peeking inside the forbidden box. The disbelieving children mostly opened the box. But even those kids ran their fingers across the chair where she supposedly lurked to verify that she didn't exist before breaking the rules. They were cautious, just in case.

Remarkably, when the researchers crunched the numbers, they found that the children who said they believed in Princess Alice behaved equally well as those who were in the physical presence of an adult. But abstractions are less effective than physical reminders of a watchful overlord. This explains why parents who found the threat of Santa Claus insufficient to turn their naughty children nice have innovated. Some now place a watchful Elf on a Shelf around Christmastime to extract slightly better behavior from their mischievous children.

Unfortunately, prison-guard abuse won't end with elves on the concrete shelves of jails, and the fear of divine retribution clearly isn't enough to stave off bad behavior from politicians and CEOs. But subtle reminders of being watched can nonetheless have potent effects. In one study by Newcastle University in England, people in a common work space were able to take refreshments, but were expected to pay for them using an "honesty box." In one version of the experiment, the honesty box had a poster above it with a picture of eyes glaring down. In the other version, the poster was just a picture of flowers. When the eyes were there, people gave three times more money than when daffodils were overseeing the box. (Several subsequent researchers haven't been able to replicate some of these findings, so they've claimed that the effects are overstated—and they're probably right.)

Nonetheless, the power of being watched versus feeling anonymous can also be shown if we return to the dictator game. Imagine you're paired up with another person. You're given $6 and told that you can keep all of it, or you can split some of it with the other person. Would your decision about how much to give away be remotely affected by what you were wearing at the time?

Researchers at the University of Toronto set up an experiment to test that question. They randomly altered one small detail about the experiment: some participants wore dark sunglasses; others wore clear eyeglasses. Remarkably, those who had the clear eyeglasses gave away an average of $2.71, compared to just $1.81 for those in dark sunglasses. That's a substantial difference, shifting behavior from a 55/45 split to a 70/30 division of the cash. The most plausible explanation was that wearing dark sunglasses primed people to feel more anonymous, thereby subconsciously tapping into their darker impulses. Thanks a lot, Ray·Ban.

These experiments point to the possibility that deterring bad behavior can hinge on tiny changes. Perhaps even subtle cues that remind people of being watched can have powerful effects. In one brilliantly designed experiment in Morocco, researchers approached shopkeepers and gave them a choice: either accept a cash gift or reject the cash so that it could be donated to charity instead. The only variation in the experiment was *when* they were being asked. Some shopkeepers were asked at random times throughout the day. A separate group was approached only while the call to prayer was being blared throughout the city—a visceral audio reminder of a deity above. In the randomized group, 60 percent of shopkeepers were generous (an encouraging finding about human nature)! But in the group that was asked during the call to prayer, *all* chose the charitable option. This study is particularly intriguing because it deals with both the carrot and the stick: the call to prayer should function as a reminder of the weight of responsibility to do good, but it simultaneously primes people to consider divine punishment when they indulge their bad side.

Still, these findings have limits. The belief in divine punishment from Big Gods may be the decisive factor guiding the behavior of some people in modern society, but it's certainly not what motivates everyone. Most people aren't devout enough to be constantly worrying about God as they ponder every bit of potentially devilish behavior, from speeding to stealing office supplies from work (you know who you are). And even if reminders work, it's not exactly a viable option to constantly pump the call to prayer or biblical hymns into corner offices throughout the headquarters of Fortune 500 companies or into the White House. Plus, even if plastering pictures of eyes throughout offices and police stations had any deterrent effect, it would only work for a little while before people just got used to them.

Thankfully, those impracticalities don't matter so much because modern governments and employers now provide the surveillance and punishment threats that were previously established by divine retribution and the specter of ordeals. Today's incarnation of Dennis (*Monty Python*'s suspiciously well-educated medieval peasant) would know—and fear—the intervention of the police or the IRS or their HR department. That doesn't affect the fundamental allure of religion in general, which remains strong for billions of people. But it does mean that, for many people, the social deterrence benefit from a divine gaze has been replaced by a mortal one.

There's evidence that watched people are more likely to behave better. It's clear that we no longer need to rely exclusively on gods to make people fear being caught and punished for bad behavior. But all these discussions are still a bit too abstract. How do we ensure that oversight will reduce abuses of power in the real world?

Lesson 8:
Focus Oversight on the Controllers,
Not the Controlled

Every day while commuting to my office, I walk past a corpse. I don't mean this figuratively. In a glass case at University College London lies the 189-year-old skeleton of Jeremy Bentham, the modern founder of utilitarianism—the philosophy that the most ethical choice is the one that will produce the greatest good for the greatest number of people. Bentham's body, or what's left of it, is dressed in his own clothes. Bentham intended for his head to be preserved along with the rest of his body. Some accounts suggest he even carried a set of glass eyes around in his pocket for the final ten years of his life so they'd be conveniently ready to go when he expired. However, when the desiccation took place to fulfill his wishes and preserve his head, it went "disastrously wrong, robbing the head of most of its facial expression, and leaving it decidedly unattractive." Its shriveled scowl is in the university museum instead, while a far more pleasing wax head sits in the glass case. (The oft-repeated story that Bentham's body is wheeled in to attend meetings of the College Council is, sadly, a myth, as is the fable that his head was stolen by rival universities and used in a football match.) It's fitting, however, that Bentham's corpse now lies in a fully glass box at the center of the University College London Student Centre, visible from all sides. His final resting place has ended up much like a surveillance system that he designed in life: the panopticon.

In 1785, Bentham designed a new kind of prison, aimed at ensuring that prisoners would comply with prison rules with minimal oversight. The idea was simple, sinister, and elegant. The prison would be circular, with cells occupying the circumference. In the center would be a single guard tower, designed to allow the guards to see the prisoners without the prisoners being able to see the guards. As a result, the panopticon would create what Bentham called an "invisible omnipresence," giving the impression that the guard *could* be watching at any moment. For the prisoner, however, it would be impossible to tell precisely when the guard was looking, forcing the prisoner to behave constantly. Over time, Bentham argued, the prisoners would simply conform—even without much intervention from the guards. In the idealized version of the panopticon, this would lead to self-reform, an enlightened transformation of the prisoner without the need for barking at prisoners or beating them. (The French philosopher Michel Foucault details the potentially sinister implications of this exercise of power in his book *Discipline and Punish*.) Bentham's idea was adopted all across the globe, from Stateville Prison in Illinois to the Round House in Australia and the Panoptico in Colombia. Several prisons still in use today were designed based on Bentham's principles.

But your office might be, too.

Bentham believed that his idea was "applicable, I think, without exception to all establishments whatsoever, in which within a space not too large to be covered or commanded by buildings, a number of persons are meant to be kept under inspections. No matter how different or even opposite the purpose." Plenty of companies have agreed with Bentham. They've made their offices into twenty-first-century versions of his panopticon prisons—albeit without the guard tower in the middle.

According to one 2014 study, nearly three-quarters of American offices are now designed to be "open plan," with low or no walls separating work spaces. If you're going to spend part of your working day on Twitter or chatting on the phone to family or friends, everybody will know—and you'll know that everyone will know. These office designs remain overwhelmingly popular despite consistent evidence that they have detrimental effects on employees. A 2011 review of a hundred different studies about open-plan offices found that they alienate employees, increase stress, and lower job satisfaction. Moreover, the entire point of the open-plan office was to encourage collaboration. Real-world data show that they do the opposite: there's 70 percent less social interaction in open-plan offices. Panopticon-style workplaces are great for surveillance, but terrible for the people who occupy them.

Furthermore, with the rise of digital technology, companies have an unprecedented ability to monitor *everything* about workers. The disturbing cornucopia of surveillance technology in the workplace continues to grow: always-on lapel microphones, microchipped ID badges, chair sensors to determine when you're at your desk, keystroke monitoring on your computer, software that takes pictures of you at your desk at regular intervals, and technology that routinely screenshots your computer screen to ensure that you're not looking at recipes when you should be trying to slay the ever-regenerating hydra that is the modern email in-box. Bentham would whistle in appreciation at all of these methods—if his newfound mouth weren't made of wax.

These dystopian systems are even worse in authoritarian countries. In China, for example, the "social credit system" aims to constantly monitor citizens and punish them for any "inappropriate" behaviors. The system, which currently exists as a series of pilot projects, is already ominous.

Thirteen million people have been blacklisted, making it impossible for them to book flights or buy train tickets. In some cities, if you jaywalk, facial-recognition software automatically identifies you. Your face is displayed on a giant billboard to shame you without delay. In other areas, anyone who breaks the rules set by the Communist Party is ostracized digitally, their faces flashed like mug shots to anyone using social media in the area. On the Chinese messaging app WeChat, people in the city of Shijiazhuang who are blacklisted are displayed on a map. The "telescreens" from George Orwell's imagined surveillance state in *1984* seem quaint and comforting by comparison.

Here's the problem: Our modern surveillance systems have everything backward. They should be inverted. We're watching the wrong people. The twenty-first-century panopticon should be turned inside out, so the people in power feel as if *they're* constantly being watched instead. When Enron imploded or Bernie Madoff's pyramid scheme collapsed, it wasn't because a junior employee stole a few paper clips or spent twenty minutes during the workday watching cat videos on YouTube. It was because those who controlled those junior employees were themselves behaving badly—and with much higher stakes.

According to various estimates, white-collar crime accounts for between $250 billion and $400 billion in losses or damages each year in the United States alone. Add up all the property crimes committed on American streets—burglaries, robberies, thefts, arson—and you're looking at just over $17 billion in damage, making white-collar crimes roughly fifteen to twenty-five times more costly. Conservative estimates similarly suggest that around three hundred thousand Americans die every year from corporate malfeasance, largely from toxic chemicals, faulty products, exposure to deadly waste or harmful pollutants, and addictive substances provided without rigorous checks. That's roughly twenty times higher than the number of homicides each year in the United States.

Yet, the most watched people in corporate headquarters are too often those who are least likely to do such serious damage. Corner offices and boardrooms remain opaque. Boardrooms aren't bugged for audio, board members aren't tracked with GPS software. CEOs who extol the virtues of open-plan design usually retreat behind closed doors to their corner office. You can be confident that the keystrokes of top-level executives aren't being logged and scrutinized to ensure that they're using their time "productively."

It's not that we should start implementing such draconian monitoring, but rather that any oversight should start at the top. China's corrupt Communist Party, not run-of-the-mill jaywalkers, deserves much more scrutiny. Those who control—not those *being* controlled—are the ones we need to worry about. (Japan provides an interesting example of reorienting a worker's physical space based on who can actually do damage in a company. Incompetent workers aren't fired in Japanese corporate culture, but rather become known as *madogiwa-zoku*, "window watchers." That's because they're moved to the periphery of the office. As they're demoted to work on insignificant projects, they can look out the window, as nobody need even bother watching them.)

In the modern era, we've largely replaced immortal omniscience with mortal surveillance. But today's watchers are the very people who *should* feel watched themselves. At least Big Gods are said to watch everyone equally. The world would be a better place if people in power worried more that their every corrupt move was being watched by someone lurking behind every rock and tree—or at least every rock.

That's a lesson that Anas Aremeyaw Anas has taken literally. As a pioneer of "undercover journalism" in Ghana, Anas has taken things a bit further than most in his profession. He is a master of disguise who uses elaborate costumes to ensure that people in power tell him secrets that they'd never disclose to a journalist. In some instances, he's even used a disguise to blend into his surroundings—by dressing up as a rock. (The costume is slightly amateurish and makes him look like a human-size lump of sandstone, with two comical eyeholes, but he says the disguise has been effective for blending in.) In addition to the rock, he's used prosthetic faces to pass as a priest in a Thai prison, as a police officer, as an inmate in a jail, as a patient in a psychiatric hospital, and, on several occasions, as a woman. His professional success relies on his being unrecognizable, so even though the name Anas is famous throughout West Africa, nobody knows what he looks like. Some call him the James Bond of journalism.

"My journalism has three purposes: name, shame, and jail the bad guys," Anas tells me when I speak to him over Skype. We've got our cameras switched on, but I can't see much. He's wearing a bucket hat with purple and gold beads draped over his face, obscuring everything but one ear. He tells me that he takes issue with what he calls parachute journalism, in which Western journalists drop into Ghana for a long weekend, interview people in power, write their stories, and take off. Such scrutiny, Anas argues, doesn't accomplish anything. Everything in Ghana is too opaque. Corruption never gets uncovered that way. "You cannot just fly in from London or the US and spend a week and think that you can uncover the truth better than us," he says, the beads swaying slightly from his breath as he speaks.

In various disguises, Anas has exposed powerful people across Africa. In Ghana, he broke a major soccer scandal, which involved kickbacks and mass corruption. He also posed undercover for years within the judicial system to get footage of more than thirty judges soliciting bribes. They received cash, goats, and sheep. In return, they allowed hardened criminals—including murderers, rapists, and drug traffickers—to go free. It blew up into one of the biggest scandals in the country's history and sparked mass reform of the judiciary.

Such work came at a cost. A member of parliament called for Anas to be identified and hanged for his undercover exposés. That MP managed to identify one of Anas's collaborators, Ahmed Hussein-Suale. The MP publicized Hussein-Suale's name and photo, along with information about where he lived. On January 16, 2019, Hussein-Suale was driving in a suburb of Ghana's capital, Accra. As he slowed at an intersection, two men who'd been loitering in the neighborhood for the previous week approached his car. They shot him at point-blank range, the first bullet hitting his neck, the second and third hitting his chest. As he bled to death, the gunmen turned to shocked witnesses, put a finger to their lips, smiled, and left.

That grisly murder only hardened Anas's resolve. Before his investigations, judges simply figured they could get away with blatant corruption. Politicians felt invincible. Bribes were just part of public life in Ghana. A culture of impunity allowed bad behavior to flourish. Everyone else was being watched, those in power believed, but nobody was watching them. Anas single-handedly flipped that expectation. Ghanaians in power started worrying that anyone around them—even rocks they didn't notice—could be watching. Because Anas never let anyone see his real face, *anyone* could be him. That was why it was so powerful.

Anas's work targeting corrupt top-level officials matters because taking down dishonest bigwigs is one of the only areas where "trickle down" principles actually seem to work. Adam Salisbury—one of my former students—conducted research at the University of Oxford into corruption in West Africa. He found that when a crooked official who led the customs union was taken out of power in Burkina Faso, the people that he previously controlled quickly cleaned up their act. Once underlings stopped getting corrupt cues from the top, they reformed themselves. Decapitating the head seems to work (welcome news for Jeremy Bentham). But Salisbury's finding adds further support to the notion that if we're going to put people under the microscope, we should focus our lens on those who are in charge. Their abuses are far more consequential, and cleaning up their act at the top is likely to make more people clean up their act at the bottom. It's hard to imagine the inverse happening: corrupt judges and CEOs aren't going to suddenly become squeaky-clean themselves if low-level clerks or secretaries behave better. Yet, because the powerful have positioned themselves as our modern-day Big Gods, we tend to focus our gaze on precisely the wrong people. As Juvenal, the Roman poet, famously put it, "Who will guard the guards themselves?"

Anas's brand of undercover journalism is pretty rare in Western societies, where it's deemed ethically dubious. That's a shame because it can be a potent way of not just exposing wrongdoing but also instilling a healthy bit of worry into those in power who are considering behaving badly. More important, journalism is in decline just about everywhere. Social media and falling advertising revenues online have taken a big chunk out of smaller outlets. As a result, there are just far fewer watchdogs out there. Big newspapers, such as the *Washington Post, Guardian, New York Times*, and *Le Monde*, continue to thrive. But the trend toward elite national newspapers while local and regional journalism gets hollowed out is likely to ensure that fewer people fear the fading oversight of a free press.

And the more that the press gets vacuumed up by powerful media conglomerates, the less that its gaze will be directed in the right places.

What happens without journalism? Uganda provides an instructive lesson. An audit of education spending in the East African nation discovered that up to $8 out of every $10 allocated to schools was being stolen. The money was funding corruption, not children. Journalists made the story front-page news. They exposed the gap between how much money had originally been allocated—and how much was actually spent on schools. Their reporting had an enormous effect. Soon, only $2 out of every $10 was being stolen. But here's the crucial bit: embezzlement decreased most in places that were near newspaper distributors. When corrupt officials were being exposed, it only mattered if people could actually read about it. If nobody writes the stories, or nobody reads them, the powerful will develop a sense of impunity and become even worse. Watching needs to be matched up with the right people *seeing*.

Technology can help, too. India, for example, has developed a clever system for targeting corruption. In India, ordinary people can report extortion via a website called I Paid a Bribe. Whenever a new report is filed anonymously, a new digital pin appears on a map. Over time, it quickly became clear where the crooked hot spots were—allowing reformers to focus on the worst areas.

In Bangalore, one reformer noticed something peculiar: lots and lots of little digital pins on the map at the driving-test center. It immediately clicked: officials who conducted driving tests were allowing bad drivers to pass in exchange for bribes. Not only was that corrupt, it was also dangerous. It would ensure that more people who shouldn't be on the roads were waved through, so long as they were willing to make their wallets a bit lighter. Researchers discovered a similar problem in New Delhi when they offered a cash reward to any drivers who could quickly pass their driving test. Most passed almost immediately and claimed the reward. But when those who passed were subsequently given a surprise driving test by a squeaky-clean instructor who refused bribes, 74 percent admitted that they hadn't bothered to learn how to drive. The majority failed the clean test. They'd paid their way onto the roads. The entire system was corrupt.

To stop such deadly kickbacks, the local government in Bangalore changed the driving test so that it was littered with electronic sensors. The entire test was also videotaped. Overnight, bribery in Bangalore's automotive test centers plummeted. But it didn't take keystroke logging or GPS monitoring of driving instructors. The problem was pinpointed and fixed with the least invasive oversight necessary to be effective. It worked. We may not all face corrupt driving examiners, but the lessons of that successful intervention are universal.

From Anas's undercover journalism to driving tests in India to panopticon prisons, it's clear: you don't have to constantly watch people. In fact, constantly watching people—especially those who aren't in power—is a pretty good recipe for a dystopia. But to inch toward a utopia instead, we should make people in authority think that they *could* be watched at any time. That provides a middle ground that allows us to avoid constant invasions of privacy while still making those in charge think twice before they abuse their power.

Lesson 9:
Exploit Randomness to Maximize Deterrence While Minimizing Invasions of Privacy

It's December 2013, a few days before Christmas, and the sun-baked cobblestones of Madagascar's capital radiate heat, intensifying the smells of street food and sewage. Our convoy of 4x4s rumbles through the crumbling roads of the city, honking whenever a zebu, or humped cow, walks into the road. With our noisy engines, we're not exactly a subtle group. To make sure we don't blend in, our dorky blue canvas vests are emblazoned with ELECTION OBSERVER in bold white letters on the back. We're the watchers—deployed to ensure that there's no funny business. It's election day.

When we arrive, we go through our checklists. Ballot box sealed with its original zip tie? No soldiers intimidating voters? Voters being asked to produce proof of registration? We tick the boxes. Everything seems to be in order. Maybe the election is clean after all. Or maybe, just maybe, the poll workers have been warned that we're coming. Either way, with the job done, we pile back into our convey and set off down the road. It's a straight shot to the next polling location, a half mile away. There's nothing stopping the poll workers at the last location from calling people at the next one and telling them we're on our way, a warning that gives them precious minutes to hide any fraud.

Sometimes, oversight doesn't end bad behavior, it just displaces it.

Election monitoring is like a game of Whac-A-Mole. When you suppress vote rigging in one place, it's more likely to pop up elsewhere. Henchmen are rarely stupid enough to stuff fistfuls of ballots into ballot boxes when foreigners in official vests are watching. But researchers have found that when election observers are deployed, rigging usually spikes in nearby precincts that aren't monitored. If you're not careful, election observation can be a waste of time, only creating a minor inconvenience for those who are rigging the election. In that way, badly designed monitoring doesn't deter, it simply forces innovation. Thankfully, there's a simple, elegant solution: randomness. Henchmen and crooks have a harder time getting away with fraud if they never know when or where you'll be watching.

The NYPD can show us how it's done.

It's a routine drugs bust in northwest Manhattan. The Drug Enforcement Administration (DEA) has found the drug lair of a dealer. He's reasonably small fry, a local kingpin at best. But there's a problem: the warrant to conduct a thorough search of his apartment is being held up. Typical of the paper pushers. So the DEA agents call the NYPD and ask a cop from Washington Heights—a place that used to be known as the "crack capital of America"—to babysit the place. Make sure nobody comes in or out. There's probably a lot of drugs and plenty of cash inside, they tell the cop. They can't take the chance that someone in the gang will find out the dealer has been made and try to clean up the mess.

The NYPD cop agrees to babysit the spot. He rolls up to the building, climbs up the stairs to the apartment, and lets himself in. Sure enough, bags of heroin are littered across the place. Then he spots it: $20,000 in cash, tightly wound into fat rolls. He's alone in the apartment. It's drug money. Nobody from law enforcement has been inside. Who knows how much money is there? Who's going to miss it? If the perp complains that some of the rolls have gone missing, it's the word of someone with a badge against someone with a rap sheet. Everyone knows how that story ends. The cop peels off $6,000, leaving enough so it still looks right. He stuffs the wad of cash under his protective vest and waits for the DEA to arrive with the warrant.

When they arrive, they thank him for his help. He takes off, going about his day as if nothing has happened. His shift ends. But when he tries to go home with his illicit score, he's arrested.

The "DEA agents" were undercover Internal Affairs cops at NYPD. The bags of "heroin" were actually filled with pancake mix. The "drug lair" was an apartment rented by the city police department. The entire place was wired like Fort Knox, with bugs and cameras capturing every move. The cop, who had been suspected of police corruption and illegal activity, had just failed an integrity test.

"Those tests made it much more difficult—not impossible—but much more difficult to steal," Charles Campisi tells me. Campisi was the head of the NYPD Internal Affairs Bureau from 1996 through 2014, and he almost single-handedly helped clean up the department. It started small. "We had a policy here that you couldn't walk into a store and get free coffee," Campisi says. "It was at the very bottom of the corruption level. But the idea was, if you didn't start at the bottom, you'd never get to the top." Such policies were reinforced by integrity tests, or stings—by cops, for cops.

Sometimes the tests were targeted. When Internal Affairs got a tip from either a fellow cop or a member of the public, they'd put the suspected officer under surveillance and give them an easy opportunity to behave badly. They never pressured anyone in uniform to commit a crime, but often manufactured a situation in which a quick and seemingly undetectable payoff was waiting, such as a wallet turned in that was chock-full of cash. Other times, undercover officers posed as crooks. During an interrogation or an arrest, the fake criminals would insult their coworker cops to see if they got rough and used violence. If the cop pocketed the money or threw a punch, they were put in handcuffs.

But Campisi's most effective innovation was randomizing the integrity tests. After years under his watch, the NYPD had already considerably improved. In 2012, for example, Campisi helped organize 530 integrity tests. There were dozens of procedural failures. But only six cops took the money or stole planted drugs. And here's the crucial insight that Campisi noticed. If you do five hundred random integrity tests a year, *thousands* of cops are going to think they've been tested. After all, members of the public *do* turn in wallets, and drug busts often involve cash on tables. There are going to be plenty of false positives, real situations that officers incorrectly believe are staged to test them.

Sure enough, in the late 1990s, one researcher surveyed NYPD officers and asked them whether they'd personally been targeted by an Internal Affairs operation in the past year. Based on the answers, the researcher predicted that about six thousand integrity tests were being carried out each year—twelve times more than the reality. And beyond the cops that personally felt that they'd been targeted, the remainder of the force knew they *could* be under surveillance at any moment. Any drugs bust or routine traffic stop could be an elaborate test. With that healthy dose of fear, fewer officers skimmed cash or stole drugs or beat up insolent criminals.

The lesson here isn't to start baiting employees by planting pieces of cake in the break-room fridge with enough hidden cameras to catch the person who snatches it. Nobody wants to live in a society like that, where everyone is under suspicion and social trust is absent. Instead, we should make sure that only people who are in uniquely consequential positions of authority worry about being watched. Constant surveillance for anyone is unhealthy. Constant surveillance for run-of-the-mill workers is downright unacceptable. But randomized integrity testing for those who have plenty of opportunity to cause serious harm is usually justified. That, combined with more robust oversight from nosy journalists such as Anas, can go a long way in deterring the worst avoidable abuses in our societies. Careful scrutiny can play the role that Big Gods played before we developed such robust mortal oversight. But lest we end up creating Orwell's *1984*, any human surveillance should be as limited as possible, target those in power most, and, when feasible, use randomization rather than constant monitoring. We must not sacrifice our freedoms on the altar of deterrence.

Finally, it doesn't have to be all stick and no carrot. Well-designed randomized systems should encourage good behavior, too. In Sweden, for example, one anti-speeding effort used a two-tier process. As you might expect, those who were speeding were fined. But those who were driving *below* the speed limit were randomly entered into a lottery. The fines paid by the speeders were used as a prize for random winners from the law-abiding drivers. It punished bad behavior at the same time that it created incentives for good behavior. Just as randomization—sortition—can be useful to select people for power, it can also be a useful tool to hold people in power accountable for their actions. The power of randomness should be used more often in the fight against the corruptible people who too often end up in charge.

Whatever methods we use, we must swing the pendulum back toward watching those in power rather than ordinary workers or citizens. And that's because of Norenzayan's simple truth, present from ancient Egypt until today: watched people are nice people.

XIII

WAITING FOR CINCINNATUS

Lesson 10: Stop Waiting for Principled Saviors. Make Them Instead

In 458 BC, the Aequi, a tribe from the Apennine Mountains east of Rome, besieged a Roman army. As Livy tells it, only "five mounted men got through the enemies' outposts and brought to Rome the news that the consul and his army were blockaded." In the "panic and confusion" that followed, Romans gave in to their Stone Age brains: they sought a strong leader to give them confidence in the face of crisis. They agreed on Lucius Quinctius Cincinnatus.

When the Romans approached Cincinnatus, he was plowing his field, fully "intent on his husbandry." Far removed from the power struggles in the city, he was surprised to find that he'd been named dictator. But he reluctantly agreed to take on the responsibility and to lead the Romans. It was his duty. His term was to last at least six months. Instead, after leading an army and defeating the Aequi in battle, Cincinnatus "resigned on the sixteenth day [of] the dictatorship." He returned to his farm.

Two decades later, the Romans again called on Cincinnatus. This time, they asked him to see off the threat of a rich populist named Spurius Maelius, who was trying to seize power by buying the support of the population. It was a classic example not just of a scheming power-hungry usurper, but also of the masses being tempted by a would-be demagogue. Cincinnatus saw off the threat. Then, again, he relinquished power. He'd only spent twenty-one days in control.

The legend of Cincinnatus (and some historians suggest it's more legend than history) offers a crucial and complex parable for humanity. Cincinnatus was revered as an exemplar of leadership, a man who didn't seek power but grudgingly accepted it to serve others. Perhaps it was because he didn't want power that he was able to wield it justly. The Greek historian Dionysius of Halicarnassus fawned over Cincinnatus and others who followed his example because "they worked with their own hands, led frugal lives, did not chafe under honorable poverty, and, far from aiming at positions of royal power, actually refused them when offered." Dionysius lamented how unusual that form of leadership had become, as his contemporaries "follow the very opposite practices in everything." We can relate.

More than two thousand years after Cincinnatus defeated the Aequi, George Washington became known as the American Cincinnatus. The parallels seemed striking: another patriot-farmer who served his country, was asked to become monarch, and refused after serving two terms as president. These were, it seemed, the exceptions that prove the rule: power attracts the worst people and power corrupts even the best people, but Cincinnatus and George Washington were somehow immune from both effects. They neither sought power nor were worsened by its seductive allure. They weren't corruptible.

To honor both men, the Society of the Cincinnati was formed in Washingtonian America. Its motto highlighted its ethos of public service: *Omnia reliquit servare rempublicam*—"He relinquished everything to save the Republic." George Washington was made the society's first honorary president. But soon, the society faced criticism. Benjamin Franklin worried that it would create a new American nobility, an "Order of hereditary Knights." Franklin was concerned by the society's membership rules, which operated on the principle of primogeniture—meaning the elite would replicate itself, passing membership from father to son. Power would flow not through merit, but through veins. Washington, ever the principled revolutionary, threatened to step down from his post unless the hereditary clause was removed. The society agreed. But when nobody was looking, they reinstated it. To this day, Cincinnati membership is tied to bloodlines. Here was a striking irony: a society dedicated to the legacy of scrupulously relinquishing status to serve others behaved unscrupulously to cling to status while serving themselves. They invoked the name of Cincinnatus, but didn't live up to it, an all-too-common occurrence.

The lesson is this: we need a better strategy than waiting for a modern-day Cincinnatus to save us. Most of the time, that wait will end in disappointment, our hopes dashed. That's because too many of our current systems disproportionately attract and then sort corruptible people into power. Once there, power changes them—for the worse. There will be principled exceptions. The world is mostly full of good, decent people. Many are our coaches, our bosses, our neighborhood cops. Nonetheless, a small but influential group of malicious people have inflicted enormous damage with the power they wield. Instead of waiting for our principled saviors to leave their farms, a more realistic goal is to change our systems to make more ordinary people *behave* like Cincinnatus: answering the call to power rather than seeking it, and relinquishing control rather than relishing its intoxicating effects as it corrupts.

We've come a long way. From chimpanzees to CEOs, our evolution—from primate despotism, to bands of hunter-gatherers, to the most sophisticated hierarchies ever created—took hundreds of thousands of years. But in a comparatively short time since, we've made a mess of things. Despite enormous progress that's made the world immeasurably better over the last several centuries, we're still consistently disappointed by those in charge. It's why Lord Acton's aphorism—that power corrupts—is widely accepted as not just true, but obvious. So many people in positions of authority are awful. They don't have to be. But to fix a problem, first we must understand it.

A psychopathic custodian showed us that people most attracted to power are often those least suited for it. Military madness in local police departments taught us that bad recruitment strategies compound that problem, luring in the most power-hungry among us. An Arizona autocrat who ruled over ninety-nine homes like his personal fiefdom made clear that competition is crucial to keeping such corruptible figures at bay. But even with competition, white guys in ties, children picking ship captains, sneezing dogs, and a Prussian king's obsession with tall soldiers demonstrated that our Stone Age brains continue to delude us into picking the wrong leaders for the wrong reasons. If we overcome those cognitive biases, solo sippers in Starbucks, double-parking diplomats, and the viceroy of Vermont underscored how much we still need to reform systems if we want to affect the behavior of those in charge. A Thai prime minister who got his hands dirty, a thief who was a lifelong learner, and a doctor who killed people as floodwaters rose each helped explain why power might not corrupt quite as much as we think. But lest we get too optimistic, a cult-leader bioterrorist and badly behaved BMW drivers revealed that Lord Acton's maxim is, sadly, accurate. Coked-up monkeys, blow-darted baboons, and rapidly aging executives proved how power without a sense of control can cause physiological stress that takes quite a toll on us.

None of these dynamics are set in stone, however. Better people can lead us. We can recruit smarter, use sortition to second-guess powerful people, and improve oversight. We can remind leaders of the weight of their responsibility. We can make them see people as human beings, not abstractions, before the powerful turn them into victims. We can rotate personnel to deter and detect abuse. We can use randomized integrity tests to catch bad apples. And if we're going to watch people, we can focus on those at the top who do the *real* damage, not the rank and file.

Yes, there *is* a better way. And we *can* make a better world. With concerted effort and the right reforms, we can swing the pendulum back, pushing away corruptible people who seek and abuse power and inviting others to take their place. Then, finally, we can experience what it's like to live in a society in which the powerful and the incorruptible are one and the same.

ACKNOWLEDGMENTS

I wrote much of this book while sitting in a portable camping chair that I carried in panniers on my bike to a vast expanse of empty beach on England's south coast, taking social distancing to absurd extremes during a global pandemic. But a book—and especially a book like this one—is the intellectual opposite of social distancing. It's the culmination of years and years of an author's brain being piqued by intriguing ideas proposed by others, seemingly trivial encounters that linger in one's thoughts for years, and little asides made by smart people in casual conversation. I am indebted to many of those smart people who were kind enough to share their insights about the maddening complexities of power, hierarchy, and status—and to many awful people who told me how they successfully climbed to the top, and why they tore others down.

I'm also indebted to Anthony Mattero, my agent, who always wields his power justly, and who believed in this idea from the beginning. If he were a meerkat, his "move call" would always be worth following. Rick Horgan, my US editor, is a true guru of publishing. Like Bhagwan Shree Rajneesh, he has a devoted cult—of grateful authors who have benefitted from his wisdom. I've happily joined it. But I'm confident that he will never abuse that authority to poison salad bars with salmonella. Joe Zigmond, my UK editor, steered me away from my boring ideas and made the book much better. I am very happy to have chosen him—and Caspian

Dennis, my UK agent—to captain this ship in British waters (a selection based on their smart guidance rather than seeing their faces in a computer simulation). Thanks are also due to the careful attention of Beckett Rueda, Olivia Bernhard, Dan Cuddy, and Steve Boldt.

This book couldn't have been written without the hospitality and kindness of people who helped me understand broken people and broken systems of power as I conducted research across the globe, including in Madagascar, Thailand, Zambia, Belarus, Côte d'Ivoire, Tunisia, France, Latvia, the United Kingdom, India, Switzerland, the United States, and Togo. And thanks, sort of, to the countless people I don't admire—violent rebels in West Africa, coup generals in Southeast Asia, corrupt CEOs in Eastern Europe, torturers in North Africa—who helped me understand how they got to where they are today. I hope this book helps block those paths to other similarly corruptible people in the future.

Many thanks also to a small cohort of enthusiastic undergraduates at University College London who gave up part of their summer in lockdown to help me read about hyenas, hierarchies, and homeowners associations: Antoni Mikocki, Daniella Sims, Edu Kenedi, Emilie Cunning, Hannah White, Maria Kareeva, and Tara De Klerk. Consider this my enthusiastic letter of recommendation. Just attach this acknowledgements section in grad school applications or show it to prospective employers. If you're reading this for that reason, admit them or hire them. They're phenomenal.

I'm also grateful to several people I interviewed but didn't directly include in the text. Their ideas percolated through my thinking as I wrote each chapter. To name a few: Ambassador Samantha Power, Shane Bauer, Erica Chenoweth, Marco Villafaña, Laura Kray, Bernardo Zacka, Danni Wang, David Skarbek, Leigh Goodmark, Lord Peter Mandelson, Zoe Billingham, John Tully, Prime Minister Anand Panyarachun, Dane Morriseau, Omar McDoom, Simon Mann, Jean-Francois Bonnefon, Dennis Tourish, and Kristof Titeca.

Finally, the biggest thanks goes to my family. They taught me everything important I know—and that the greatest power of all is to be able to spend time with wonderful people who love you.

Notes

Chapter 1: Introduction

1   **fortune in silver coins:** Roger W. Byard, "The Brutal Events on Houtman Abrolhos following the Wreck of the *Batavia* in 1629," *Forensic Science, Medicine, and Pathology,* 2020.

1   **"spartan as one moved toward the bow":** Mike Dash, *Batavia's Graveyard* (New York: Crown, 2002), 82.

2   **personal calamities:** Ibid.

3   **"escape *Batavia* alive":** Ibid., 150. See also E .D. Drake-Brockman, *Voyage to Disaster: The Life of Francisco Pelsaert* (Sydney: Angus & Robertson, 1963).

3   **"that survived on the island as well":** Mike Dash, author of *Batavia's Graveyard,* personal interview, 25 May 2020.

3   **"suchlike adornments":** The *Batavia* journals, as quoted in Dash, *Batavia's Graveyard,* 216.

4   **rest for the night:** "Six Tongan Castaways in 'Ata Island," Australia Channel 7 documentary, first broadcast in 1966. Available from https://www.youtube.com/watch?v=qHO_RlJxnVI.

4   **seabird blood:** Ibid.

5   **collect rainwater:** Ibid. See also Rutger Bregman, *Humankind: A Hopeful History* (London: Bloomsbury, 2020).

5   **simply move apart:** Rutger Bregman, "The Real Lord of the
     Flies: What Happened When Six Boys Were Shipwrecked
     for 15 Months," *Guardian*, 9 May 2020. See also Bregman,
     Humankind.

5   **"in that humid atmosphere":** Peter Warner, fisherman who
     rescued the boys, phone interview, 3 June 2020.

6   **"no haircut":** Ibid.

6   **"Perhaps they won't remember?":** "Six Tongan Castaways
     in 'Ata Island.'"

8–9 **sky-high economic growth:** World Bank Data, "Madagas-
     car: GDP Growth (Annual %), https://data.worldbank.org
     /indicator/NY.GDP.MKTP.KD.ZG?locations=MG.

9   **"make important decisions":** Marc Ravalomanana, former
     president of Madagascar, personal interview, 9 May 2016,
     Antananarivo, Madagascar.

10   **register his candidacy:** See Brian Klaas, "A Cosmetic End
     to Madagascar's Crisis?," International Crisis Group, Africa
     Report No. 218, May 2014.

10   **Air Force Two:** "Madagascar : Air Force Two s'envole vers les
     Etats-Unis," Radio France Internationale, 23 November 2012.

11   **radio DJ in power:** Brian Klaas, "Bullets over Ballots: How
     Electoral Exclusion Increases the Risk of Coups d'État and
     Civil Wars" (DPhil thesis, University of Oxford, 2015).

12   **shadows of their former selves:** The original Stanford
     Prison Experiment is outlined in a series of articles, notably
     Craig Haney, Curtis Banks, and Philip Zimbardo, "Study of
     Prisoners and Guards in a Simulated Prison," *Naval Research
     Reviews* 9:1–17 (Washington, DC: Office of Naval Research).
     See also Craig Haney and Philip Zimbardo, "Social Roles and
     Role-Playing: Observations from the Stanford Prison Study,"
     in *Current Perspectives in Social Psychology*, 4th ed., ed. E. P.

Hollander and R. G. Hunt (New York: Oxford University Press, 1976), 266–74.

12 **putting on a performance:** Ben Blum, "The Lifespan of a Lie," Medium, 7 June 2018.

12 **audio recording of the experiment's:** Brian Resnick, "The Stanford Prison Experiment Is Based on Lies. Hear Them for Yourself," Vox, 14 June 2018.

13 **researchers at Western Kentucky University:** Thomas Carnahan and Sam McFarland, "Revisiting the Stanford Prison Experiment: Could Participant Self-Selection Have Led to the Cruelty?," *Personality and Social Psychology Bulletin* 33 (5) (2007): 603–14.

13 **"empathy and altruism":** Ibid., 608.

14 **researchers in Switzerland:** John Antonakis and Olaf Dalgas, "Predicting Elections: Child's Play!," *Science* 323 (5918): (2009): 1183.

14 **nearly identical results:** Ibid.

15 **study conducted in Bangalore:** Rema Hanna and Shing-Yi Wang, "Dishonesty and Selection into Public Service: Evidence from India," *American Economic Journal: Economic Policy* 9 (3) (2017): 262–90.

16 **similar experiment in Denmark:** S. Barfort et al., "Sustaining Honesty in Public Service: The Role of Selection," *American Economic Journal: Economic Policy* 11 (4) (2019): 96–123. See also Ray Fisman and Miriam A. Golden, *Corruption: What Everyone Needs to Know* (Oxford: Oxford University Press, 2017).

Chapter II: The Evolution of Power

18 **Last Universal Common Ancestor:** See M. C. Weiss et al., "The Physiology and Habitat of the Last Universal Common Ancestor," *Nature Microbiology* 1 (9) (2016): 1–8.

18   **Chimpanzee-Human Last Common Ancestor:** See P. Duda and J. Zrzavý, "Evolution of Life History and Behavior in Hominidae: Towards Phylogenetic Reconstruction of the Chimpanzee-Human Last Common Ancestor," *Journal of Human Evolution* 65 (4) (2013): 424–46.

18   **DNA with chimps:** R. Waterson, E. Lander, and R. Wilson, "Initial Sequence of the Chimpanzee Genome and Comparison with the Human Genome," *Nature* 437 (2005): 69–87.

19   ***Chimpanzee Politics:*** Frans de Waal, *Chimpanzee Politics: Power and Sex among Apes* (New York: Harper & Row, 1982).

19   **"very much into power":** Frans de Waal, Emory University primatologist, phone interview, 25 March 2020.

19   **"position number three":** Ibid.

20   **1964 study:** E. W. Menzel, "Patterns of Responsiveness in Chimpanzees Reared through Infancy under Conditions of Environmental Restriction," *Psychologische Forschung* 27 (4) (1964): 337–65. See also W. A. Mason, "Sociability and Social Organization in Monkeys and Apes," in *Advances in Experimental Social Psychology*, ed. L. Berkowitz (New York: Academic Press, 1964), 1:277–305.

20   **evolved from our primate ancestors:** Katherine S. Pollard, "What Makes Us Different?," *Scientific American*, 1 November 2012.

21   **human accelerated region:** Ibid.

21   **"lucky" child or an "unlucky" child:** K. Hamann et al., "Collaboration Encourages Equal Sharing in Children but Not in Chimpanzees," *Nature* 476 (7360) (2011): 328–31.

22   **"learned from their parents":** Michael Tomasello, developmental psychologist at Duke University, email interview, 23 May 2020.

22   **Collaboration was irrelevant:** Hamann et al., "Collaboration Encourages Equal Sharing."

23　**prehistoric way of life:** See J. D. Lewis-Williams and M. Biesele, "Eland Hunting Rituals among Northern and Southern San Groups: Striking Similarities," *Africa*, 1978, 117–34.

23　**"insulting the meat":** See R. B. Lee and I. DeVore, eds., *Kalahari Hunter-Gatherers: Studies of the !Kung San and Their Neighbors* (Cambridge, MA: Harvard University Press, 1976).

23　**"pile of bones?":** Richard B. Lee, "Eating Christmas in the Kalahari," *Natural History*, December 1969, 224. See also Christopher Boehm, *Hierarchy in the Forest: The Evolution of Egalitarian Behavior* (Cambridge, MA: Harvard University Press, 2009).

23　**"make him gentle":** Lee, "Eating Christmas," 225.

23　**owner of the arrowhead:** See Polly Wiessner, "Leveling the Hunter," in *Food and the Status Quest: An Interdisciplinary Perspective*, ed. P. Wiessner and W. Schiefenhövel (Oxford: Berghan Books, 1996).

24　**part of our primate legacy:** Mark van Vugt, evolutionary psychologist, Vrije Universiteit Amsterdam, phone interview, 8 May 2020.

24　**"Humans are the only species":** Neil Thomas Roach, "The Evolution of High-Speed Throwing," Harvard University research summary, https://scholar.harvard.edu/ntroach/evolution-throwing.

24　**evolutionary cosmetic surgery:** Neil Thomas Roach, "The Biomechanics and Evolution of High-Speed Throwing" (PhD diss., Harvard University, 2012).

25　**Clacton Spear:** L. Allington-Jones, "The Clacton Spear: The Last One Hundred Years," *Archaeological Journal* 172 (2) (2015): 273–96.

25　**Green Beret named Richard Flaherty:** David Yuzuk, *The Giant Killer: American Hero, Mercenary, Spy . . . The In-*

credible True Story of the Smallest Man to Serve in the U.S. Military—Green Beret Captain Richard Flaherty (New York: Mission Point Press, 2020).

25 **shot by a toddler:** Christopher Ingraham, "American Toddlers Are Still Shooting People on a Weekly Basis This Year," *Washington Post*, 29 September 2017.

25 **physical size differences between males and females:** Peter Turchin, *Ultrasociety: How 10,000 Years of War Made Humans the Greatest Cooperators on Earth* (Chaplin, CT: Beresta Books, 2016), 106.

26 *reverse dominance hierarchy:* Boehm, *Hierarchy in the Forest.*

27 **"All men seek to rule":** Ibid., 105.

27 **differentiation within graves:** See E. A. Cashdan, "Egalitarianism among Hunters and Gatherers," *American Anthropologist* 82 (1) (1980): 116–20.

28 **much more diversity in the structure of prehistoric societies:** "Human social organization during the Late Pleistocene: Challenging the nomadic-egalitarian model" by Manvir Singh and Luke Glowacki, 2021.

28 **with regard to the sexes:** Some research has argued that hunter-gatherer societies treated women more as equals; other research suggests the opposite. See John D. Speth, "Seasonality, Resource Stress, and Food Sharing in So-Called 'Egalitarian' Foraging Societies," *Journal of Anthropological Archaeology* 9 (1990): 148–88.

28 **ostracism meant social death:** Boehm, *Hierarchy in the Forest.*

28 **recent study by Spanish researchers:** J. Gómez et al., "The Phylogenetic Roots of Human Lethal Violence," *Nature* 538 (7624) (2016): 233–37.

28 **cuddly Madagascan lemurs:** Ibid.

29 **"problem personalities were males":** Boehm, *Hierarchy*

in the Forest, 7–8; and phone interview with Christopher Boehm, 29 May 2020.

29 **Valentin Turchin:** Peter Turchin, scientist/professor at University of Connecticut, phone interview, 7 April 2020.

32 **mathematical logic:** This mathematic relationship was identified by Frederick Lanchester, an engineer who was also a pioneer of the British car industry in the early 1900s. The magnified advantage for larger armies with ranged warfare was named Lanchester's square law.

33 **ironclad rule of history:** Turchin, phone interview.

33 **"set themselves up as chiefs":** Ibid.

33 **Neolithic Revolution:** See J. L. Weisdorf, "From Foraging to Farming: Explaining the Neolithic Revolution," *Journal of Economic Surveys* 19 (4) (2005): 561–86; and Jared Diamond, "The Worst Mistake in the History of the Human Race," *Discover*, 1 May 1999.

34 **environmental circumscription:** R. L. Carneiro, "A Theory of the Origin of the State: Traditional Theories of State Origins Are Considered and Rejected in Favor of a New Ecological Hypothesis," *Science* 169 (3947) (1970): 733–38.

35 **tens of millions:** Turchin, *Ultrasociety*.

35 **10 percent in some of our darkest eras:** Gómez et al., "Phylogenetic Roots."

35 **die at the hands of another human being:** Ibid.

36 **"cook food or to burn people":** Turchin, phone interview.

Chapter III: Moths to a Flame

37 **son of a kosher baker:** For a discussion of Wald's life, see Jordan Ellenberg, *How Not to Be Wrong* (New York: Penguin, 2014).

38 **"frequently things happened":** W. Allan Wallis, "The Sta-

tistical Research Group, 1942–1945," *Journal of the American Statistical Association* 75 (370) (1980): 322.

40 **Nilgiri Mountains:** Oskar Morgenstern, "Abraham Wald, 1902–1950," *Econometrica* 19 (4) (1951): 361–67.

42 **designer glasses and bright red lipstick:** Marie-France Bokassa, interview, 30 September 2019, Paris, France.

42 **He was coronated:** J. H. Crabb, "The Coronation of Emperor Bokassa," *Africa Today* 25 (3) (1978): 25–44. See also "The Coronation of Jean-Bedel Bokassa," BBC World Service, 4 December 2018.

42 **bespoke twelve-foot-tall bronze statue:** Brian Tetley, *Dark Age: The Political Odyssey of Emperor Bokassa* (Montreal: McGill-Queen's Press, 2002).

43 **Nile crocodiles:** Ibid. See also "In Pictures: Bokassa's Ruined Palace in CAR," BBC News, 8 February 2014.

43 **served it to visiting dignitaries:** Scott Kraft, "Ex-Emperor's Reign of Terror Relived: Bokassa Trial: Lurid Tales of Cannibalism, Torture," *Los Angeles Times*, 15 March 1987.

43 **"you ate human flesh":** "Nostalgia for a Nightmare," *Economist*, 25 August 2016.

43 **fraud or drug abuse:** Jeremy Luedi, "The Vietnamese Daughters of an African Emperor," Asia by Africa, 13 May 2018. For more on Bokassa's family, see also Jay Nordlinger, *Children of Monsters* (New York: Encounter Books, 2015).

44 **part of the Bokassa brand:** Bokassa, interview. See also Marie-France Bokassa, *Au château de l'ogre* (Paris: Flammarion, 2019).

46 **Minnesota Twin study:** R. D. Arvey et al., "The Determinants of Leadership Role Occupancy: Genetic and Personality Factors," *Leadership Quarterly* 17 (1) (2006): 1–20.

46 **born to lead or born to follow?:** J.-E. De Neve et al., "Born to Lead? A Twin Design and Genetic Association Study of

Leadership Role Occupancy," *Leadership Quarterly* 24 (1) (2013): 45–60.

48 **baby hyena . . . leader of the pack:** M. L. East et al., "Maternal Effects on Offspring Social Status in Spotted Hyenas," *Behavioral Ecology* 20 (3) (2009): 478–83; and K. E. Holekamp and L. Smale, "Dominance Acquisition during Mammalian Social Development: The 'Inheritance' of Maternal Rank," *American Zoologist* 31 (2) (1991): 306–17.

48 **gene of interest . . . SLC6A4:** M. A. van der Kooij and C. Sandi, "The Genetics of Social Hierarchies," *Current Opinion in Behavioral Sciences* 2 (2015): 52–57.

48 **zebra fish . . . social status of the father:** S. Zajitschek et al., "Paternal Personality and Social Status Influence Offspring Activity in Zebrafish," *BMC Evolutionary Biology* 17 (1) (2017): 1–10.

48 **7 percent wanted a top-level leadership position:** Nicole Torres, "Most People Don't Want to Be Managers," *Harvard Business Review*, 18 September 2014.

49 **"need for power":** D. C. McClelland, C. Alexander, and E. Marks, "The Need for Power, Stress, Immune Function, and Illness among Male Prisoners," *Journal of Abnormal Psychology* 91 (1) (1982): 61.

49 **Social Dominance Orientation:** F. Pratto et al., "Social Dominance Orientation: A Personality Variable Predicting Social and Political Attitudes," *Journal of Personality and Social Psychology* 67 (4) (1994): 741.

50 **recruiting video on the department's website:** Radley Balko, "Tiny Georgia Police Department Posts Terrifying SWAT Video," *Washington Post*, 13 August 2014.

51 **surplus military equipment:** C. Delehanty et al., "Militarization and Police Violence: The Case of the 1033 Program," *Research & Politics* 4 (2) (2017): 1–7.

51 **Thetford Township, Michigan:** Francis X. Donnelly, "Michigan Town's Feud over Military Gear Gets Ugly," *Detroit News*, 17 April 2018. It's worth noting that the police chief has recently been indicted for embezzlement related to the military-surplus equipment.

51 **amphibious assault boat:** Radley Balko, "Overkill: The Rise of Paramilitary Police Raids in America," *CATO Institute*, 25 March 2014, 8.

51 **Lebanon, Tennessee:** Lorenzo Franceschi-Bicchierai, "Small-Town Cops Pile Up on Useless Military Gear," *Wired*, 26 June 2012.

51 **"a bully, a bigot, or a sexual predator":** Helen King, former assistant commissioner of the London Metropolitan Police, interview, 11 February 2020, London, United Kingdom.

52 **Marshall Project:** Simone Weichselbaum and Beth Schwartzapfel, "When Warriors Put on the Badge," Marshall Project, 30 March 2017.

52 ***after* the military equipment arrived:** Delehanty et al., "Militarization and Police Violence."

53 **"Do you care enough to be a cop?":** "Freeze! NZ Police's Most Entertaining Recruitment Video, Yet!," NZPoliceRecruitment, 26 November 2017, https://www.youtube.com/watch?v=f9psILoYmCc.

53 **"We take policing seriously":** Kaye Ryan, deputy chief executive for people, New Zealand police, phone interview, 12 May 2020.

53 **"Hungry Boy":** "Hungry Boy 45 Sec—'Do You Care Enough to Be a Cop?,'" NZPoliceRecruitment, 30 March 2016, https://www.youtube.com/watch?v=6pz42UqcmzQ.

54 **"just that they come anyway":** Ryan, interview.

54 **applications are up 24 percent:** Data for this section was provided by New Zealand police via email, 12 June 2020.

55 **0.8 deaths per year:** Freedom of Information request to the New Zealand government, 29 October 2015, https://fyi.org .nz/request/3174/response/10477/attach/html/3/rakete%20 emma%2015%2017696%201%20signed%20reply.pdf.html.

55 **1,146 civilians:** "The Counted," *Guardian*, 2016 data, https:// www.theguardian.com/us-news/ng-interactive/2015/jun/01 /the-counted-police-killings-us-database.

56 **"the Cannon because I hit hard":** Roger Torres, former MMA fighter, email, 5 September 2020.

56 **40 million do:** "National and State Statistical Review for 2017," Community Associations Institute, 2017, https://foundation .caionline.org/wp-content/uploads/2018/06/2017StatsReview .pdf.

56 **"apathy was rampant":** Roger Torres, phone interview, 13 May 2020.

Chapter IV: The Power Delusion

61 **edition of *Cosmopolitan* magazine:** Mitch Moxley, *Apologies to My Censor* (New York: Harper Perennial, 2013).

62 **"some kind of ceremony":** Mitch Moxley, journalist, phone interview, 27 April 2020.

62 **"DOLOE & GOB8ANA":** Moxley, *Apologies to My Censor*, 261.

63 **"looked the oldest":** Moxley, phone interview.

63 **"music band called Traveller":** Alice Yan, "Inside China's Booming 'Rent a Foreigner' Industry," *South China Morning Post*, 12 June 2017.

63 **"didn't speak English":** Ibid.

63 **468 are run by a man:** The data in this section, from publicly available sources, was compiled for me by Maria Kareeva.

64 **Alexa and Siri:** Christopher Zara, "People Were Asked to Name Women Tech Leaders. They said 'Alexa' and 'Siri,'" *Fast Company*, 20 March 2018.

65 **Snowy Peaks and Vanilla Boys:** "Black bosses 'shut out' by 'vanilla boys' club,'" BBC News, 3 February 2021, https://www.bbc.co.uk/news/business-55910874

65 **8 percent of the total:** This is from publicly available data, compiled for me by Daniella Sims.

65 **one in four:** Data in this section is from "Women in Parliaments," Inter-Parliamentary Union, https://data.ipu.org/women-ranking?month=10&year=2020.

65 **rubber-stamp his agenda:** See Brian Klaas, *The Despot's Accomplice: How the West Is Aiding & Abetting the Decline of Democracy* (Oxford: Oxford University Press, 2017).

66 **"have no followers":** Frans de Waal, primatologist at Emory University, phone interview, 25 March 2020.

66 **stotting or pronking:** C. D. FitzGibbon and J. H. Fanshawe, "Stotting in Thomson's Gazelles: An Honest Signal of Condition," *Behavioral Ecology and Sociobiology* 23 (2) (1988): 69–74.

67 **evolved to quickly convey information:** See S. R. X. Dall et al., "Information and Its Use by Animals in Evolutionary Ecology," *Trends in Ecology & Evolution* 20 (4) (2005): 187–93.

67 **fiddler crab:** Simon P. Lailvaux, Leeann T. Reaney, and Patricia R. Y. Backwell, "Dishonest Signalling of Fighting Ability and Multiple Performance Traits in the Fiddler Crab, *Uca mjoebergi*," *Functional Ecology* 23 (2) (2009): 359–66.

68 **power pose:** D. R. Carney, A. J. Cuddy, and A. J. Yap, "Power Posing: Brief Nonverbal Displays Affect Neuroendocrine Levels and Risk Tolerance," *Psychological Science* 21 (10) (2010): 1363–68.

68   **TED talk:** Amy Cuddy, "Your Body Language May Shape Who You Are," https://www.ted.com/talks/amy_cuddy_your _body_language_may_shape_who_you_are?language=en.

68   **"effects are real":** Maquita Peters, "Power Poses Co-author: 'I Do Not Believe the Effects Are Real,'" *NPR Weekend Edition Saturday*, 1 October 2016.

68   **other research:** See, for example: L. ten Brinke, K. D. Vohs, and D. R. Carney, "Can Ordinary People Detect Deception After All?," *Trends in Cognitive Sciences* 20 (8) (2016): 579–88.

69   **"potlatch" ceremonies:** R. Bliege Bird et al., "Signaling Theory, Strategic Interaction, and Symbolic Capital," *Current Anthropology* 46 (2) (2005): 221–48.

69   **"conspicuous consumption":** Thorstein Veblen, *The Theory of the Leisure Class* (New York: MacMillan, 1899).

70   **money into social capital:** A. B. Trigg, "Veblen, Bourdieu, and Conspicuous Consumption," *Journal of Economic Issues* 35 (1) (2001): 99–115.

70   **empty their pockets:** M. Van Vugt and W. Iredale, "Men Behaving Nicely: Public Goods as Peacock Tails," *British Journal of Psychology* 104 (1) (2013): 3–13.

70   **lace became meaningless:** See, for example, P. Blumberg, "The Decline and Fall of the Status Symbol: Some Thoughts on Status in a Post-Industrial Society," *Social Problems* 21 (4) (1974): 480–98.

71   **life of leisure indoors:** Amanda Riley-Jones, "The Evolution of Tanning," *Reader's Digest*, https://www.readersdigest .co.uk/health/health-conditions/the-evolution-of-tanning.

71   **stayed the same size:** R. I. Dunbar, "The Social Brain Hypothesis and Its Implications for Social Evolution," *Annals of Human Biology* 36 (5) (2009): 562–72. See also R. Giphart and M. van Vugt, *Mismatch: How Our Stone Age Brain Deceives*

Us Every Day (and What We Can Do about It) (London: Hachette, 2018).

71 **"house a Stone Age mind":** Leda Cosmides and John Tooby, "Evolutionary Psychology: A Primer," UC–Santa Barbara Center for Evolutionary Psychology, 1997, https://www.cep.ucsb.edu/primer.html.

72 **sweet as a carrot:** Daniel Lieberman, "Evolution's Sweet Tooth," *New York Times*, 5 June 2012.

72 **"evolutionary mismatch":** N. P. Li, M. van Vugt, and S. M. Colarelli, "The Evolutionary Mismatch Hypothesis: Implications for Psychological Science," *Current Directions in Psychological Science* 27 (1) (2018): 38–44.

72 **snakes and spiders:** A. Ahuja and M. van Vugt, *Selected: Why Some People Lead, Why Others Follow, and Why It Matters* (London: Profile Books, 2010).

73 **"an imposing physique":** M. van Vugt and R. Ronay, "The Evolutionary Psychology of Leadership: Theory, Review, and Roadmap," *Organizational Psychology Review* 4 (1) (2014): 74–95.

73 **evolutionary leadership theory:** Ibid.

74 **"forward in science careers":** Corinne Moss-Racusin, associate professor of psychology at Skidmore College, phone interview, 23 April 2020.

74 **higher potential starting salary:** C. A. Moss-Racusin et al., "Science Faculty's Subtle Gender Biases Favor Male Students," *Proceedings of the National Academy of Sciences* 109 (41) (2012): 16474–79.

75 ***Herland:*** C. P. Gilman, *Herland* (1915; repr., New York: Pantheon, 2010).

75 **eager to rule by democratic means:** A. H. Eagly and B. T. Johnson, "Gender and Leadership Style: A Meta-Analysis," *Psychological Bulletin* 108 (2) (1990): 233.

76 **effect of masculinity is magnified:** M. van Vugt et al., "Evolution and the Social Psychology of Leadership: The Mismatch Hypothesis," *Leadership at the Crossroads* 1 (2008): 267–82. See also Ahuja and van Vugt, *Selected.*

77 **"in times of war":** Ahuja and van Vugt, *Selected,* 164.

77 **taller aide was the king:** J. M. O'Brien, *Alexander the Great: The Invisible Enemy, a Biography* (London: Routledge, 2003), 56.

77 **"they are my weakness":** Stephen S. Hall, *Size Matters: How Height Affects the Health, Happiness, and Success of Boys— and the Men They Become* (Boston: Houghton Mifflin, 2006).

77 **Irish giant on the streets of London:** Nancy Mitford, *Frederick the Great* (1970; repr., London: Vintage, 2011).

78 **long arm span:** Ibid.

78 **men of their time:** G. Stulp et al., "Tall Claims? Sense and Nonsense about the Importance of Height of US Presidents," *Leadership Quarterly* 24 (1) (2013): 159–71.

78 **shorter opponent(s):** Ibid.

78 **perceived as more leader-like:** N. M. Blaker et al., "The Height Leadership Advantage in Men and Women: Testing Evolutionary Psychology Predictions about the Perceptions of Tall Leaders," *Group Processes & Intergroup Relations* 16 (1) (2013): 17–27.

78 **Hajnal Ban:** Marissa Calligeros, "Queensland Councillor Has Legs Broken to Gain Height," *Sydney Morning Herald,* 29 April 2009.

79 **eighteenth-century Germany:** J. Komlos, "Height and Social Status in Eighteenth-Century Germany," *Journal of Interdisciplinary History* 20 (4) (1990): 607–21.

79 **additional lifetime earnings:** A. Case and C. Paxson, "Stature and Status: Height, Ability, and Labor Market Outcomes,"

Journal of Political Economy 116 (3) (2008): 499–532. See also N. Persico, A. Postlewaite, and D. Silverman, "The Effect of Adolescent Experience on Labor Market Outcomes: The Case of Height," *Journal of Political Economy* 112 (5) (2004): 1019–53.

80 **Manchester United jersey:** M. Levine et al., "Identity and Emergency Intervention: How Social Group Membership and Inclusiveness of Group Boundaries Shape Helping Behavior," *Personality and Social Psychology Bulletin* 31 (4) (2005): 443–53.

81 **from their own school:** See Ahuja and van Vugt, *Selected*, "Chapter 6: The Mismatch Hypothesis."

81 **baby-faced defendants:** See D. S. Berry and L. Zebrowitz-McArthur, "What's in a Face? Facial Maturity and the Attribution of Legal Responsibility," *Personality and Social Psychology Bulletin* 14 (1) (1988): 23–33; D. S. Berry and L. Z. McArthur, "Some Components and Consequences of a Babyface," *Journal of Personality and Social Psychology* 48 (1985): 312–23; and D. J. Shoemaker, P. R. South, and J. Lowe, "Facial Stereotypes of Deviants and Judgments of Guilt or Innocence," *Social Forces* 51 (1973): 427–33.

81 **than less baby-faced black people:** R. W. Livingston and N. A. Pearce, "The Teddy-Bear Effect: Does Having a Baby Face Benefit Black Chief Executive Officers?," *Psychological Science* 20 (10) (2009): 1229–36.

Chapter V: Petty Tyrants and Psychopaths

85 **"little thermometer":** Rich Agnello, special education teacher in Schenectady, phone interview, 18 March 2020.

85 **"crime against humanity":** Ibid.

85 **"veins on his head throbbing":** "Petty Tyrant," *This American Life*, 12 November 2010.

86 **Lou Semione:** Steven Cook, "Day 8: Workers Cite Raucci Abuse," *Schenectady Daily Gazette*, 11 March 2010.

86 **manipulating the software:** "Petty Tyrant," *This American Life*.

87 **"fu**ing with you":** Steven Cook, "Day 7: Witnesses Recall Raucci's Drive for Power in School District," *Schenectady Daily Gazette*, 10 March 2010.

87 **"her type":** "Petty Tyrant," *This American Life*.

87 **"will be the fixer":** Kathy Garrison, under cross-examination, trial of Steve Raucci, 8 March 2010.

87 **anonymous letter:** Anonymous letter to CSEA president Kathy Garrison, undated.

88 **big letters across their house:** Steve Cook, "Day 10: At Raucci Trial, Victim Tells of Threats, Damage," *Schenectady Daily Gazette*, 16 March 2010.

88 **while on the clock:** "Petty Tyrant," *This American Life*.

88 **"trucky truck":** Transcript of secret audio recordings of Steve Raucci submitted as evidence in his trial.

88 *The Godfather:* Kathleen Moore, "Emails Show How Raucci Complaints Went Nowhere," *Schenectady Daily Gazette*, 22 July 2011.

88 **gave him a loan:** Cook, "Day 7."

89 **DNA were on the cigarette:** Steven Cook, "DNA Test Links Explosive to Raucci," *Schenectady Daily Gazette*, 12 May 2009.

89 **the Peter Pause:** Steven Cook, "Friend-Turned-Informant Provided Crucial Evidence in Raucci Case," *Schenectady Daily Gazette*, 7 June 2010.

89 **"narcissistic liar" . . . "sick ego":** Ron Kriss, former Schenectady district employee, email interview, 10 March 2020.

89   **"what Steve did"**: Transcript of secret audio recordings of Steve Raucci submitted as evidence in his trial.

89   **"they got a Steve"**: Ibid.

90   **the dark triad:** D. L. Paulhus and K. M. Williams, "The Dark Triad of Personality: Narcissism, Machiavellianism, and Psychopathy," *Journal of Research in Personality* 36 (6) (2002): 556–63.

90   **the Dirty Dozen:** P. K. Jonason and G. D. Webster, "The Dirty Dozen: A Concise Measure of the Dark Triad," *Psychological Assessment* 22 (2) (2010): 420.

91   **subject isn't lying:** Caoimhe Mcanena, forensic clinical psychologist, phone interview, 24 February 2020.

91   *Myrmarachne melanotarsa:* Ed Yong, "Spiders Gather in Groups to Impersonate Ants," *National Geographic*, 3 June 2009.

91   **"silken apartments":** Ed Yong, "Spider Mimics Ant to Eat Spiders and Avoid Being Eaten by Spiders," *National Geographic*, 1 July 2009.

91   **"Oscar-worthy performance":** Ximena Nelson, "The Spider's Charade," *Scientific American* 311 (6) (December 2014): 86–91.

92   **"can eat spiders":** Yong, "Spider Mimics Ant."

92   **kicked a dog to death:** Kevin Dutton, *The Wisdom of Psychopaths* (London: Random House, 2012).

92   *manie sans delire:* Y. Trichet, "Genèse et évolution de la manie sans délire chez Philippe Pinel. Contribution à l'étude des fondements psychopathologiques de la notion de passage à l'acte," *L'Évolution psychiatrique* 79 (2) (2014): 207–24.

92   **theory of mind:** M. Dolan and R. Fullam, "Theory of Mind and Mentalizing Ability in Antisocial Personality Disorders with and without Psychopathy," *Psychological Medicine* 34 (2004): 1093–102.

92 **"mirror neuron system"**: G. Rizzolatti and L. Craighero, "The Mirror-Neuron System," *Annual Review of Neuroscience* 27 (2004): 169–92.

92 **smelled something awful:** K. Jankowiak-Siuda, K. Rymarczyk, and A. Grabowska, "How We Empathize with Others: A Neurobiological Perspective," *Medical Science Monitor* 17 (1) (2011): RA18.

93 **empathy that mimicked that of normal people:** H. Meffert et al., "Reduced Spontaneous but Relatively Normal Deliberate Vicarious Representations in Psychopathy," *Brain* 136 (8) (2013): 2550–62.

94 **"noninvasive brain stimulation":** Nicholas Cooper, psychologist at University of Essex, phone interview, 20 May 2020. See also C. C. Yang, N. Khalifa, and B. Völlm, "The Effects of Repetitive Transcranial Magnetic Stimulation on Empathy: A Systematic Review and Meta-Analysis," *Psychological Medicine* 48 (5) (2018): 737–50.

94 **"snakes in suits":** P. Babiak, R. D. Hare, and T. McLaren, *Snakes in Suits: When Psychopaths Go to Work* (New York: Regan Books, 2006).

95 **"impression management":** N. Roulin and J. S. Bourdage, "Once an Impression Manager, Always an Impression Manager? Antecedents of Honest and Deceptive Impression Management Use and Variability across Multiple Job Interviews," *Frontiers in Psychology* 8 (2017): 29.

96 **climbing the corporate ladder:** J. Volmer, I. K. Koch, and A. S. Göritz, "The Bright and Dark Sides of Leaders' Dark Triad Traits: Effects on Subordinates' Career Success and Well-Being," *Personality and Individual Differences* 101 (2016): 413–18.

96 **professionals from seven companies:** P. Babiak, C. S. Neumann, and R. D. Hare, "Corporate Psychopathy: Talking the Walk," *Behavioral Sciences & the Law* 28 (2) (2010): 174–93.

97 **one in a hundred people are psychopaths:** See G. Morse, "Executive Psychopaths," *Harvard Business Review* 82 (10) (2004): 20–21.

97 **"other management position":** Babiak, Neumann, and Hare, "Corporate Psychopathy."

97 **Japanese researchers . . . the ultimatum game:** T. Osumi and H. Ohira, "The Positive Side of Psychopathy: Emotional Detachment in Psychopathy and Rational Decision-Making in the Ultimatum Game," *Personality and Individual Differences* 49 (5) (2010): 451–56.

98 **how the world *should* be:** J. B. Vieira et al., "Distinct Neural Activation Patterns Underlie Economic Decisions in High and Low Psychopathy Scorers," *Social Cognitive and Affective Neuroscience* 9 (8) (2014): 1099–107.

99 **chefs, and civil servants:** Dutton, *Wisdom of Psychopaths.*

99 **region in the United States:** Ryan Murphy, "Psychopathy by US State," SSRN, 26 May 2018, https://ssrn.com/abstract=3185182.

100 **psychopaths are less torn:** M. Cima, F. Tonnaer, and M. D. Hauser, "Psychopaths Know Right from Wrong but Don't Care," *Social Cognitive and Affective Neuroscience* 5 (1) (2010): 59–67.

100 **"fewer psychopathic traits":** Leanne ten Brinke, psychologist, University of British Columbia, phone interview, 12 February 2020.

100 **101 hedge fund managers:** L. ten Brinke, A. Kish, and D. Keltner, "Hedge Fund Managers with Psychopathic Tendencies Make for Worse Investors," *Personality and Social Psychology Bulletin* 44 (2) (2018): 214–23.

101 **rotting in a jail cell or executed:** See Brian Klaas, *The Despot's Accomplice* (Oxford: Oxford University Press, 2017).

101 **"torn to pieces":** H. M. Lentz, ed., *Heads of States and Governments since 1945* (London: Routledge, 2014).

102 **based on irrational emotions:** J. J. Ray and J. A. B. Ray, "Some Apparent Advantages of Subclinical Psychopathy," *Journal of Social Psychology* 117 (1) (1982): 135–42.

102 **highly stressful situations:** Ibid. See also Dutton, *Wisdom of Psychopaths.*

103 **"move call":** G. E. Gall et al., "As Dusk Falls: Collective Decisions about the Return to Sleeping Sites in Meerkats," *Animal Behaviour* 132 (2017): 91–99. See also Elizabeth Preston, "Sneezing Dogs, Dancing Bees: How Animals Vote," *New York Times*, 2 March 2020.

103 **wild dogs:** Preston, "Sneezing Dogs."

104 **help humans survive:** D. D. Johnson and J. H. Fowler, "The Evolution of Overconfidence," *Nature* 477 (7364) (2011): 317–20.

104 **Bill & Melinda Gates Foundation:** J. Kolev, Y. Fuentes-Medel, and F. Murray, "Is Blinded Review Enough? How Gendered Outcomes Arise Even under Anonymous Evaluation," National Bureau of Economic Research, 2019, https://www.nber.org/papers/w25759?utm_campaign=ntwh&utm_medium=email&utm_source=ntwg16.

Chapter VI: Bad Systems or Bad People?

107 **various Starbucks locations:** T. Talhelm et al., "Large-Scale Psychological Differences within China Explained by Rice versus Wheat Agriculture," *Science* 344 (6184) (2014): 603–8. See also Michaeleen Doucleff, "Rice Theory: Why Eastern Cultures Are More Cooperative," National Public Radio, 8 May 2014.

107 **"chair test":** T. Talhelm, X. Zhang, and S. Oishi, "Moving Chairs in Starbucks: Observational Studies Find Rice-Wheat Cultural Differences in Daily Life in China," *Science Advances* 4 (4) (2018).

109 **"holistic" thinker:** David Biello, "Does Rice Farming Lead to Collectivist Thinking?," *Scientific American*, 12 May 2014.

110 **"fundamental attribution error":** See, for example, S. Maruna and R. E. Mann, "A Fundamental Attribution Error? Rethinking Cognitive Distortions," *Legal and Criminological Psychology* 11 (2) (2006): 155–77.

111 **tested in Austria:** S. Kaiser, G. Furian, and C. Schlembach, "Aggressive Behaviour in Road Traffic—Findings from Austria," *Transportation Research Procedia*, 14 (2016): 4384–92.

112 **150,000 parking tickets:** R. Fisman and E. Miguel, "Corruption, Norms, and Legal Enforcement: Evidence from Diplomatic Parking Tickets," *Journal of Political Economy* 115 (6) (2007): 1020–48.

113 **Andrea Ichino and Giovanni Maggi:** A. Ichino and G. Maggi, "Work Environment and Individual Background: Explaining Regional Shirking Differentials in a Large Italian Firm," *Quarterly Journal of Economics* 115 (3) (2000): 1057–90.

115 **what is best for the hive:** Francis Ratnieks, professor of apiculture at the University of Sussex, phone interview, 1 April 2020.

115 **excess queens *lower* productivity:** F. L. Ratnieks and T. Wenseleers, "Policing Insect Societies," *Science* 307 (5706) (2005): 54–56.

115 **"brood comb":** Ibid.

115 **"good of yourself":** Ratnieks, phone interview.

116 *Melipona* **bees:** See T. Wenseleers and F. L. Ratnieks, "Trag-

edy of the Commons in *Melipona* Bees," *Proceedings of the Royal Society of London. Series B: Biological Sciences* 271 (2004): S310–12; and T. Wenseleers, A. G. Hart, and F. L. Ratnieks, "When Resistance Is Useless: Policing and the Evolution of Reproductive Acquiescence in Insect Societies," *American Naturalist* 164 (6) (2004): E154–67.

116 **policing is ineffective:** Ratnieks, phone interview.

117 **the Builder King:** Most of the research from this section comes from Adam Hochschild, *King Leopold's Ghost: A Story of Greed, Terror, and Heroism in Colonial Africa* (London: Houghton Mifflin Harcourt, 1999).

117 ***"petit pays, petits gens":*** Ibid., 36.

117 **"make her learn":** N. Ascherson, *The King Incorporated: Leopold the Second and the Congo* (London: Granta Books, 1999).

117 **"African cake":** Hochschild, *King Leopold's Ghost.* See also "Léopold II à Solvyns, 17 Novembre 1877," in P. van Zuylen, *L'échiquier congolais, ou le secret du Roi* (Brussels: Dessart, 1959), 43.

118 **sulfur into melted rubber:** C. Guise-Richardson, "Redefining Vulcanization: Charles Goodyear, Patents, and Industrial Control, 1834–1865," *Technology and Culture* 51 (2) (2010): 357–87.

118 **$200,000 in debt:** G. B. Kauffman, "Charles Goodyear (1800–1860), American Inventor, on the Bicentennial of His Birth," *Chemical Educator* 6 (1) (2001): 50–54.

118 **coast over bumps in the road:** "How Scot John Boyd Dunlop Gave the World the Pneumatic Tyre," *Scotsman*, 5 February 2016.

118 **"bicycle boom":** G. A. Tobin, "The Bicycle Boom of the 1890's: The Development of Private Transportation and the Birth of the Modern Tourist," *Journal of Popular Culture* 7 (4) (1974): 838.

118 **E. D. Morel:** Hochschild, *King Leopold's Ghost.* See also C. A. Cline, "ED Morel and the Crusade against the Foreign Office," *Journal of Modern History* 39 (2) (1967): 126–37.

119 **was peeled off:** Hochschild, *King Leopold's Ghost.*

119 **"couple of goats apiece":** Ibid., 161.

119 **twenty human heads:** B. B. de Mesquita, "Leopold II and the Selectorate: An Account in Contrast to a Racial Explanation," *Historical Social Research / Historische Sozialforschung,* 2007, 203–21.

120 **THE BLACKS ARE FED BY THE ORGANIZING COMMITTEE:** Hochschild, *King Leopold's Ghost.* See also Joanna Kakissis, "Where 'Human Zoos' Once Stood, a Belgian Museum Now Faces Its Colonial Past," National Public Radio, 26 September 2018.

120 *crimes against humanity:* N. Geras, *Crimes against Humanity: Birth of a Concept* (Manchester, United Kingdom: Manchester University Press, 2013).

120 **$1.1 billion in today's value:** Belgian scholar Jules Marchal, in correspondence with Hochschild, *King Leopold's Ghost,* 277.

120 **world's worst natural experiment:** De Mesquita, "Leopold II and the Selectorate."

120 **"park bench and a ski instructor":** L. Paul Bremer III, diplomat, interview, 2 February 2020, Vermont.

121 **ten thousand grams of gold:** "Bin Laden Said to Offer Gold to Killers," Associated Press, 7 May 2004.

121 **massive casualties is growing:** *Report of the National Commission on Terrorism,* 6 June 2000, pursuant to Public Law 105-277.

122 **"a big job":** Bremer, interview.

122 **Timberland combat-style boots:** L. P. Bremer, *My Year*

in Iraq: The Struggle to Build a Future of Hope (New York: Simon & Schuster, 2006).

122 **ran a story about it:** Patrick E. Tyler, "New Policy in Iraq to Authorize GI's to Shoot Looters," *New York Times*, 14 May 2003.

123 **Dia Jabar:** Valentinas Mite, "Disappointing Some Iraqis, U.S. Says It Won't Shoot Looters," Radio Free Europe / Radio Liberty, 16 May 2003.

123 **"different from what you do in the United States":** Bremer, interview.

124 **told PBS News:** "Closure of Shiite Newspaper in Baghdad Sparks Protests," *PBS News*, 29 March 2004.

124 **"could make it happen":** Bremer, interview.

Chapter VII: Why It Appears That Power Corrupts

127 **"read these books myself":** J. J. Martin, "Tortured Testimonies," *Acta Histriae* 19 (2011): 375–92.

127 **strappado:** R. E. Hassner, "The Cost of Torture: Evidence from the Spanish Inquisition," *Security Studies* 29 (3) (2020): 1–36.

127 **Mandell Creighton:** F. E. de Janösi, "The Correspondence between Lord Acton and Bishop Creighton," *Cambridge Historical Journal* 6 (3) (1940): 307–21.

128 **"white gloves":** Sydney E. Ahlstrom, "Lord Acton's Famous Remark," *New York Times*, 13 March 1974.

128 **"almost always bad men":** de Janösi, "Correspondence between Lord Acton."

129 **"thought you'd be older":** Abhisit Vejjajiva, former prime minister of Thailand, interview, 25 March 2016, Bangkok, Thailand.

130 **"changes to the country"**: Ibid.

130 *Tasting, Grumbling:* Ian MacKinnon, "Court Rules Thai Prime Minister Must Resign over Cookery Show," *Guardian,* 9 September 2008.

130 **"I hope I've succeeded"**: Abhisit Vejjajiva, interview, 5 November 2019, Bangkok, Thailand.

131 **thousand others were injured:** "Descent into Chaos: Thailand's 2010 Red Shirt Protests and the Government Crackdown," Human Rights Watch, 2 May 2011.

131 **"three or four hours of sleep"**: Abhisit, interview, 5 November 2019.

131 **"live-fire" zones:** "Thailand PM Abhisit in Pledge to End Bangkok Protest," BBC News, 15 May 2010.

132 **murder charges were dropped:** "Thailand Ex-PM Abhisit Murder Charge Dismissed," BBC News, 28 August 2014.

132 **"my time in office"**: Abhisit, interview, 5 November 2019.

132 **"bloody civil war"**: Major General Werachon Sukondhapatipak, Thai military, interview, 18 December 2014, Bangkok, Thailand.

133 **"govern innocently?"**: See M. Walzer, "Political Action: The Problem of Dirty Hands," *Philosophy & Public Affairs* 2 (2) (Winter 1973): 160–80.

133 **"often right to do so"**: Ibid.

134 **"unprincipled acts"**: R. Bellamy, "Dirty Hands and Clean Gloves: Liberal Ideals and Real Politics," *European Journal of Political Theory* 9 (4) (2010): 412–30.

134 **put their vessels at risk:** "Churchill's HMAS *Sydney* Mystery," *Daily Telegraph,* 17 November 2011.

135 **"purest man in America"**: James Scovel, "Thaddeus Stevens," *Lippincott's Monthly Magazine,* April 1898, 548–50.

135 **"time when I didn't steal":** Eric Allison, former thief, phone interview, 20 May 2020. All of Allison's quotes from this section are from this interview.

139 **authoritarian learning:** S. G. Hall and T. Ambrosio, "Authoritarian Learning: A Conceptual Overview," *East European Politics* 33 (2) (2017): 143–61.

139 **Nikita Khrushchev in a swimming pool:** Mike Dash, "Khrushchev in Water Wings: On Mao, Humiliation and the Sino-Soviet Split," *Smithsonian Magazine*, 4 May 2012.

139 **disappearing ink:** Nic Cheeseman and Brian Klaas, *How to Rig an Election* (New Haven, CT: Yale University Press, 2018).

139 **"very early in the morning to beat us":** Ibid.

140 **"double bread with meat":** Zack Beauchamp, "Juche, the State Ideology That Makes North Koreans Revere Kim Jong Un, Explained," Vox, 18 June 2018.

141 **ratcheting effect:** C. Crabtree, H. L. Kern, and D. A. Siegel, "Cults of Personality, Preference Falsification, and the Dictator's Dilemma," *Journal of Theoretical Politics* 32 (3) (2020): 409–34.

142 **battlefield injuries were treated:** I. Robertson-Steel, "Evolution of Triage Systems," *Emergency Medicine Journal* 23 (2) (2006): 154–55.

143 **manually pump air:** Sheri Fink, "The Deadly Choices at Memorial," *New York Times*, 25 August 2009.

143 **"first for evacuation":** Ibid.

144 **"too many witnesses":** Ibid. See also Sheri Fink, *Five Days at Memorial: Life and Death in a Storm-Ravaged Hospital* (New York: Atlantic Books, 2013).

144 **"benzodiazepine sedative":** Fink, "Deadly Choices at Memorial."

144 **"rock and roll?":** Ibid.

145 **"beyond coincidence"**: Sheri Fink, "The Deadly Choices at Memorial," *New York Times Magazine*, 11 September 2009.

146 **since the 1970s:** Dominic Rushe, "Bernard Madoff Fraud 'Began 20 Years Earlier than Admitted,'" *Guardian*, 18 November 2011.

147 **"my niece even married one"**: Brian Ross and Joseph Rhee, "SEC Official Married into Madoff Family," ABC News, 16 December 2008, https://abcnews.go.com/Blotter/WallStreet/story?id=6471863&page=1.

147 **potential conflict of interest:** "Investigation of Failure of the SEC to Uncover Bernard Madoff's Ponzi Scheme," public report, US Securities and Exchange Commission, 31 August 2009, https://www.sec.gov/files/oig-509-exec-summary.pdf.

147 **"biggest Ponzi scheme ever"**: Ibid.

147 **between 2001 and 2005:** See Harry Markopolos, *No One Would Listen: A True Financial Thriller* (Hoboken, NJ: John Wiley & Sons, 2011).

147 **Seven million people disappeared:** "The IRS' Case of Missing Children," *Los Angeles Times*, 11 December 1989.

Chapter VIII: Power Corrupts

149 **opportunities that most Indians didn't:** See Manbeena Sandhu, *Nothing to Lose: The Authorized Biography of Ma Anand Sheela* (New Delhi: Harper Collins India, 2020).

149 **"artist of how to live life!"**: Sheela Birnstiel, also known as Ma Anand Sheela, email interview, 7 August 2020.

150 **sexual abuse:** Win McCormack, "Bhagwan's Sexism," *New Republic*, 12 April 2018. See also Win McCormack, *The Rajneesh Chronicles: The True Story of the Cult That Unleashed the First Act of Bioterrorism on US Soil* (Portland, OR: Tin House Books, 2010).

150 **"I didn't know what I was doing"**: Ma Anand Sheela, interview, 6 October 2018, Switzerland.

150 **Rancho Rajneesh**: Win McCormack, "Range War: The Disciples Come to Antelope," *Oregon Magazine*, November 1981.

151 **took over the Antelope city council**: See Frances FitzGerald, "Rajneeshpuram," *New Yorker*, 15 September 1986.

151 **alfalfa-sprout sandwiches**: Ibid.

151 **"very cheap DC-3"**: Ma Anand Sheela, phone interview, 12 February 2020.

151 **supplied 90 percent of their food**: FitzGerald, "Rajneeshpuram."

152 **"haven't learned their lesson"**: FitzGerald, "Rajneeshpuram."

153 **"unbearable stomach pain"**: Les Zaitz, "Rajneeshee Leaders Take Revenge on the Dalles' with Poison, Homeless," *Oregonian*, republished 14 April 2011.

153 **"the enlightened master"**: Frances FitzGerald, "Rajneeshpuram II," *New Yorker*, 29 September 1986.

153 **"samples of sick people"**: Barry Sheldahl, former prosecutor, phone interview, 11 October 2018.

153 **pureeing beavers**: McCormack, *Rajneesh Chronicles*.

153 **weaponizing HIV**: Ibid.

154 *The Perfect Crime:* Ibid.

155 **"have you had a snack?"**: Dacher Keltner, psychologist at UC-Berkeley, interview, Berkeley, CA, 27 January 2020.

156 **Power Approach and Inhibition Theory**: D. Keltner, D. H. Gruenfeld, and C. Anderson, "Power, Approach, and Inhibition," *Psychological Review* 110 (2) (2003): 265.

156 **"I swear more"**: Keltner, interview.

157 **"drive through the pedestrian zone"**: "Who Gets Power—

and Why It Can Corrupt Even the Best of Us," *The Hidden Brain*, National Public Radio, 29 June 2018.

157 **"actually the worst"**: Ibid.

157 **"disrespectful ways"**: D. Keltner, *The Power Paradox: How We Gain and Lose Influence* (New York: Penguin, 2016).

158 **"biased by our samples"**: Keltner, interview.

159 **"outside of the West"**: J. Henrich, S. J. Heine, and A. Norenzayan, "The Weirdest People in the World?," *Behavioral and Brain Sciences* 33 (2–3) (2010): 61–83.

160 **one 2015 study:** S. Bendahan et al., "Leader Corruption Depends on Power and Testosterone," *Leadership Quarterly* 26 (2) (2015): 101–22.

161 **narcissistic abuse:** N. L. Mead et al., "Power Increases the Socially Toxic Component of Narcissism among Individuals with High Baseline Testosterone," *Journal of Experimental Psychology: General* 147 (4) (2018): 591.

161 **talapoin monkeys:** A. F. Dixson and J. Herbert, "Testosterone, Aggressive Behavior and Dominance Rank in Captive Adult Male Talapoin Monkeys (*Miopithecus talapoin*)," *Physiology & Behavior* 18 (3) (1977): 539–43.

161 **illusory control:** N. J. Fast et al., "Illusory Control: A Generative Force behind Power's Far-Reaching Effects," *Psychological Science* 20 (4) (2009): 502–8.

162 **2008 experiment:** G. A. Van Kleef et al., "Power, Distress, and Compassion: Turning a Blind Eye to the Suffering of Others," *Psychological Science* 19 (12) (2008): 1315–22.

162 **master and a slave:** See N. Harding, "Reading Leadership through Hegel's Master/Slave Dialectic: Towards a Theory of the Powerlessness of the Powerful," *Leadership* 10 (4) (2014): 391–411.

162 **interrupt others more:** See Keltner, *Power Paradox*, for an overview of research on the corrosive effects of power.

Chapter IX: How Power Changes Your Body

165 **major busts are burned:** Kelcie Grega, "What Happens to Drugs, Property and Other Assets Seized by Law Enforcement?," *Las Vegas Sun*, 14 February 2020.

165 **"schedule II license":** Dr. Michael Nader, professor of physiology and pharmacology at Wake Forest University, phone interview, 14 May 2020.

166 **work with closely:** Ibid.

167 **number of dopamine receptors:** See M. A. Nader et al., "PET Imaging of Dopamine D2 Receptors during Chronic Cocaine Self-Administration in Monkeys," *Nature Neuroscience* 9 (8) (2006): 1050–56.

167 **not that reinforcing:** Nader, phone interview.

167 **dominant monkeys chose food:** D. Morgan et al., "Social Dominance in Monkeys: Dopamine D-2 Receptors and Cocaine Self-Administration," *Nature Neuroscience* 5 (2) (2002): 169–74.

167 **food over the cocaine:** R. W. Gould et al., "Social Status in Monkeys: Effects of Social Confrontation on Brain Function and Cocaine Self-Administration," *Neuropsychopharmacology* 42 (5) (2017): 1093–102.

168 **"well taken care of":** Nader, phone interview.

169 **Whitehall II Study:** M. G. Marmot et al., "Health Inequalities among British Civil Servants: The Whitehall II Study," *Lancet* 337 (8754) (1991): 1387–93.

169 **better than the average or worse:** Sir Michael Marmot, professor of epidemiology at University College London, phone interview, 6 May 2020.

170 **the Status Syndrome:** See Michael Marmot, *The Status Syndrome: How Social Standing Affects Our Health and Longevity* (New York, Times Books, 2004).

170   "explains everything in our data": Marmot, phone interview.

170   crucial tool in survival: Robert Sapolsky, *Why Zebras Don't Get Ulcers: The Acclaimed Guide to Stress, Stress-Related Diseases, and Coping* (New York: W. H. Freeman, 1998).

171   when we're nervous: Robert Sapolsky, "The Physiology and Pathophysiology of Unhappiness," in *Well-Being: Foundations of Hedonic Psychology*, ed. D. Kahneman, E. Diener, and N. Schwarz (New York: Russell Sage Foundation, 1999).

171   short-term emergency one: See Marmot, *Status Syndrome*, "Chapter 5: Who's in Charge?"

172   "get the hang of it after a while": Jordan Anderson, doctoral student, Duke University, phone interview, 21 April 2020.

172   keel over and sleep: Jenny Tung, evolutionary anthropologist and geneticist at Duke University, phone interview, 21 April 2020.

173   "metaphysics than Locke": D. L. Cheney and R. M. Seyfarth, *Baboon Metaphysics: The Evolution of a Social Mind* (Chicago: University of Chicago Press, 2008).

173   "a little chemical mark": Tung, phone interview.

173   birthdays we've celebrated: Ibid.

174   aged much faster: J. Tung et al., "The Costs of Competition: High Social Status Males Experience Accelerated Epigenetic Aging in Wild Baboons," *bioRxiv*, 2020, https://www.biorxiv.org/content/biorxiv/early/2020/02/24/2020.02.22.961052.full.pdf.

174   Stanford's Robert Sapolsky: See R. M. Sapolsky, "The Influence of Social Hierarchy on Primate Health," *Science* 308 (5722) (2005): 648–52.

174   bolstered by a 2011 study: L. R. Gesquiere et al., "Life at

the Top: Rank and Stress in Wild Male Baboons," *Science* 333 (6040) (2011): 357–60.

175 **Led by Mark Borgschulte:** Mark Borgschulte et al., "CEO Stress, Aging, and Death," working paper, 19 July 2020, https://eml.berkeley.edu/~ulrike/Papers/CEO_Stress.pdf.

175 **"CEO two years younger":** Ibid.

176 **included seventeen countries:** A. R. Olenski, M. V. Abola, and A. B. Jena, "Do Heads of Government Age More Quickly? Observational Study Comparing Mortality between Elected Leaders and Runners-Up in National Elections of 17 Countries," *British Medical Journal*, 2015, 351.

176 **aged a full year faster:** Borgschulte et al., "CEO Stress and Life Expectancy: The Role of Corporate Governance and Financial Distress," 1 September 2019, https://eml.berke ley.edu/~ulrike/Papers/CEO_Stress_and_Life_Expec tancy_20190901.pdf.

177 **squirted into their nose:** S. Cohen et al., "Sociability and Susceptibility to the Common Cold," *Psychological Science* 14 (5) (2003): 389–95.

178 **is a deadly mix:** Ibid.

179 **boosted immune response:** N. Snyder-Mackler et al., "Social Status Alters Immune Regulation and Response to Infection in Macaques," *Science* 354 (6315) (2016): 1041–45. See also J. Tung et al., "Social Networks Predict Gut Microbiome Composition in Wild Baboons," *eLife* 4 (2015): e05224.

179 **frequently groomed:** Ibid.

Chapter X: Attracting the Incorruptible

181 **opened the door to see who it was:** Brent Hatch, affidavit by police officer in support of complaint, AST Case 10-988830,

17 October 2010. Provided by Kyle Hopkins, journalist at *Anchorage Daily News.*

182 **remove her jeans:** Ibid.

182 **and stealing a car:** Kyle Hopkins, "The Village Where Every Cop Has Been Convicted of Domestic Violence," *Anchorage Daily News*, 18 July 2019.

182 **from being a police officer:** Kyle Hopkins, journalist at *Anchorage Daily News*, phone interview, 16 April 2020.

182 **felony assault and sexual abuse:** Kyle Hopkins, "Cops in One Village Have Been Convicted of 70 Crimes. Here's What They Had to Say about It," *Anchorage Daily News*, 19 July 2019.

183 **"We can't find anybody else":** Hopkins, "Village Where Every Cop Has Been Convicted."

184 *Rebel Ideas:* Matthew Syed, *Rebel Ideas: The Power of Diverse Thinking* (London: Hachette, 2019).

184 **"role model effect":** L. Beaman et al., "Female Leadership Raises Aspirations and Educational Attainment for Girls: A Policy Experiment in India," *Science* 335 (6068) (2012): 582–86.

185 **Christopher Latham Sholes:** Arthur Toye Foulke, *Mr. Typewriter: A Biography of Christopher Latham Sholes* (Boston: Christopher Publishing House, 1961).

185 **school superintendent in Pennsylvania:** Charles Lekberg, "The Tyranny of Qwerty," *Saturday Review of Science* 55 (40) (September 30, 1972): 37–40.

185 **fast enough to jam the machines:** This is slightly contested. See Jimmy Stamp, "Fact or Fiction? The Legend of the QWERTY Keyboard," *Smithsonian Magazine*, 3 May 2013.

186 **Carnegie Mellon University:** A. Fisher and J. Margolis, *Unlocking the Clubhouse: Women in Computing* (Cambridge, MA: MIT Press, 2001).

187 **"Whenever you can, count"**: Martin Brookes, *Extreme Measures: The Dark Visions and Bright Ideas of Francis Galton* (London: Bloomsbury, 2004).

187 **"cross-shaped piece of paper"**: Jim Holt, "Measure for Measure," *New Yorker*, 17 January 2005.

188 **The mean guess:** Kenneth F. Wallis, "Revisiting Francis Galton's Forecasting Competition," *Statistical Science* 29 (3) (2014): 420–24.

188 *Wisdom of Crowds:* J. Surowiecki, *The Wisdom of Crowds* (New York: Doubleday, 2004).

188 **Oxford or Cambridge:** Author's own analysis.

189 **slots of the machine:** See P. J. Rhodes, "Kleroterion," *The Encyclopedia of Ancient History*, 26 October 2012, https://onlinelibrary.wiley.com/doi/abs/10.1002/9781444338386.wbeah04171.

191 **864 participants in Zurich:** J. Berger et al., "How to Prevent Leadership Hubris? Comparing Competitive Selections, Lotteries, and Their Combination," *Leadership Quarterly* 31 (5) (2020): 101388.

192 **"really productive and really helpful"**: Helen King, former assistant commissioner of the London Metropolitan Police, interview, 11 February 2020, London, England.

192 **cocaine in his washing machine:** Max Daly, "The Police Officers Who Sell the Drugs They Seize," Vice News, 23 March 2017.

192 **"corruption cases will come out"**: King, interview.

193 **German federal government:** K. Abbink, "Staff Rotation as an Anti-Corruption Policy: An Experimental Study," *European Journal of Political Economy* 20 (4) (2004): 887–906.

194 **provided real payouts:** C. Bühren, "Staff Rotation as an Anti-Corruption Policy in China and in Germany: An Experi-

mental Comparison," *Jahrbücher für Nationalökonomie und Statistik* 240 (1) (2020): 1–18.

196 **245 teams:** "1991: From Worst to First," This Great Game, https://thisgreatgame.com/1991-baseball-history/.

197 **"extra" wins:** Baseball writer Doug Pappas came up with an initial formula, which has since been added to, challenged, and written about extensively—in particular in response to Michael Lewis, *Moneyball: The Art of Winning an Unfair Game* (New York: W. W. Norton, 2004).

197 **spending far less per extra win:** Author's own analysis, based on data from "1991 MLB Payrolls," Baseball Cube, http://www.thebaseballcube.com/topics/payrolls/byYear .asp?Y=1991.

198 **before Mussolini took power:** David Dudley, "The Problem with Mussolini and His Trains," Bloomberg, 15 November 2016.

198 **ornate train stations:** See Simonetta Falasca-Zamponi, *Fascist Spectacle: The Aesthetics of Power in Mussolini's Italy* (Berkeley, CA: Berkeley University Press, 1997).

199 **O-rings during cold-weather launches:** "Challenger: A Rush to Launch," WJXT, https://www.youtube.com /watch?v=EA3mLCmUD_4.

Chapter XI: The Weight of Responsibility

201 **"two or three hours' sleep":** Lord Robin Butler, former private secretary to five prime ministers and member of the House of Lords, interview, 13 June 2019, London, England.

201 **6.4 megatons:** Kyle Mizokami, "Great Britain's Nuclear Weapons Could Easily Destroy Entire Countries," *National Interest*, 26 August 2017, https://nationalinterest.org/blog/the-buzz/great -britains-nuclear-weapons-could-easily-destroy-entire-22057.

201 **red Colt .45 revolver:** Ben Farmer, "Trident: The Man with the Nuclear Button Who Would Fire Britain's Missiles," *Telegraph*, 21 January 2016.

202 **Letters of Last Resort:** Peter Hennessy, *The Secret State: Preparing for the Worst, 1945–2010* (London: Penguin, 2014).

202 **"ghastly moral problem":** Butler, interview.

203 **"shock to the prime minister":** Ibid.

203 **"lockdown and everything":** Tony Blair, former prime minister of the United Kingdom, interview, 2 October 2020.

203 **"very different things":** Ibid.

204 **"hated them in particular":** Ibid.

205 **"It's humbling":** Cornell William Brooks, former president of the NAACP and professor at Harvard Kennedy School, interview, 3 February 2020, Cambridge, MA.

205 **"crises or difficult situations?":** Kim Campbell, former prime minister of Canada, phone interview, 6 April 2020.

205 **amusingly depressing studies:** J. M. Darley and C. D. Batson, "From Jerusalem to Jericho: A Study of Situational and Dispositional Variables in Helping Behavior," *Journal of Personality and Social Psychology* 27 (1) (1973): 100.

206 **helped the stranger:** Ibid.

207 **Ken Feinberg's phone rings:** See Ross Barkan, "Meet Ken Feinberg, the Master of Disasters," *Observer*, 9 March 2016.

207 **"came to see me personally":** Ken Feinberg, attorney and compensation-fund czar, phone interview, 2 April 2010.

208 **"Mr. Mom":** Ibid.

209 **"I'm sure you'll do the right thing":** Ibid., as told by Feinberg.

209 **you're doomed:** Ibid.

211 **"a true believer":** M. P. Scharf, "The Torture Lawyers," *Duke Journal of Comparative & International Law* 20 (2009): 389.

211 **didn't apply to combatants:** Andrew Cohen, "The Torture Memos: Ten Years Later," *Atlantic,* 6 February 2012.

211 **War Council:** J. C. Alexander, "John Yoo's War Powers," *Law Review and the World. California Law Review* 100 (2) (2012): 331–64.

211 **pouring live insects:** David Cole, "The Torture Memos: The Case against the Lawyers," *New York Review of Books,* 8 October 2009.

212 **"stress about making decisions":** John Yoo, professor at UC-Berkeley law school and former Bush administration lawyer, interview, 28 January 2020, Berkeley, CA.

212 **"costs to each place you stop":** Ibid.

213 **moral philosopher Peter Singer:** Peter Singer, *The Expanding Circle* (Oxford: Clarendon Press, 1981).

214 **psychological distance has four dimensions:** Y. Trope and N. Liberman, "Construal-Level Theory of Psychological Distance," *Psychological Review* 117 (2) (2010): 440.

215 **Ardant du Picq:** Ardant du Picq, *Battle Studies: Ancient and Modern Battle,* Project Gutenberg, https://www.gutenberg.org/files/7294/7294-h/7294-h.htm.

215 ***On Killing:*** David Grossman, *On Killing: The Psychological Cost of Learning to Kill in War and Society* (1996; repr., New York: Back Bay Books, 2009).

215 **twice without firing:** Ibid.

215 **fifty thousand bullets were fired:** N. Sharkey, "Killing Made Easy: From Joysticks to Politics," in *Robot Ethics: The Ethical and Social Implications of Robotics,* ed. Patrick Lin, Keith Abney, and George A. Bekey (Cambridge, MA: MIT Press, 2012), 111–28.

216 **Creech Air Force Base:** James Dao, "Drone Pilots Are Found to Get Stress Disorders Much as Those in Combat Do," *New York Times*, 22 February 2013.

217 **dinner with their kids:** "The US Air Force's Commuter Drone Warriors," BBC News, 8 January 2017.

217 **willing to kill more ladybugs:** A. M. Rutchick et al., "Technologically Facilitated Remoteness Increases Killing Behavior," *Journal of Experimental Social Psychology* 73 (2017): 147–50.

218 **unmoved by the pain of others:** J. Decety, C. Y. Yang, and Y. Cheng, "Physicians Down-Regulate Their Pain Empathy Response: An Event-Related Brain Potential Study," *Neuroimage* 50 (4) (2010): 1676–82.

218 **job stress and burnout:** E. Trifiletti et al., "Patients Are Not Fully Human: A Nurse's Coping Response to Stress," *Journal of Applied Social Psychology* 44 (12) (2014): 768–77.

Chapter XII: Watched

221 **"hot water" ordeals:** P. T. Leeson, "Ordeals," *Journal of Law and Economics* 55 (3) (2012): 691–714.

222 **often a spoon:** Sonia Farid, "Licking Hot Metal Spoons to Expose Lies: Egypt's Oldest Tribal Judicial System," Al Arabiya, 24 September 2018.

222 **cruentation:** R. P. Brittain, "Cruentation: In Legal Medicine and in Literature," *Medical History* 9 (1) (1965): 82–88.

222 ***tangena* tree:** G. L. Robb, "The Ordeal Poisons of Madagascar and Africa," *Botanical Museum Leaflets* (Harvard University) 17 (10) (1957): 265–316.

222 **died *every year*:** See Gwyn Campbell, "The State and Precolonial Demographic History: The Case of Nineteenth Cen-

tury Madagascar," *Journal of African History* 23 (3) (October 1991): 415–45.

222 **asks us to imagine Frithogar:** Leeson, "Ordeals."

223 **newly informed priest:** Ibid.

224 **"wide moral scope":** Ara Norenzayan, *Big Gods: How Religion Transformed Cooperation and Conflict* (Princeton, NJ: Princeton University Press, 2013).

224 **"'Horus of Two Eyes'":** Ibid.

226 **supernatural punishment hypothesis:** See D. Johnson and J. Bering, "Hand of God, Mind of Man: Punishment and Cognition in the Evolution of Cooperation," *Evolutionary Psychology* 4 (1) (2006).

227 **told not to look inside:** J. Piazza, J. M. Bering, and G. Ingram, "Princess Alice Is Watching You: Children's Belief in an Invisible Person Inhibits Cheating," *Journal of Experimental Child Psychology* 109 (3) (2011): 311–20.

227 **overseeing the box:** M. Bateson, D. Nettle, and G. Roberts, "Cues of Being Watched Enhance Cooperation in a Real-World Setting," *Biology Letters* 2 (3) (2006): 412–14.

228 **the effects are overstated:** S. B. Northover et al., "Artificial Surveillance Cues Do Not Increase Generosity: Two Meta-Analyses," *Evolution and Human Behavior* 38 (1) (2017): 144–53.

228 **Researchers at the University of Toronto:** C. B. Zhong, V. K. Bohns, and F. Gino, "Good Lamps Are the Best Police: Darkness Increases Dishonesty and Self-Interested Behavior," *Psychological Science* 21 (3) (2010): 311–14. See also Alice Robb, "Sunglasses Make You Less Generous," *New Republic*, 26 March 2014.

228 **chose the charitable option:** F. Lambarraa and G. Riener, "On the Norms of Charitable Giving in Islam: Two Field Experiments in Morocco," *Journal of Economic Behavior & Organization* 118 (2015): 69–84. See also Norenzayan, *Big Gods*.

230 **Bentham's body:** See C. F. A. Marmoy, "The 'Auto-Icon' of Jeremy Bentham at University College London," *Medical History* 2 (1958): 77–86; and "Fake News: Demystifying Jeremy Bentham," University College London, https://www.ucl.ac.uk/culture/projects/fake-news.

230 **"decidedly unattractive":** "Auto-Icon," University College London, https://www.ucl.ac.uk/bentham-project/who-was-jeremy-bentham/auto-icon.

230 **"invisible omnipresence":** M. Galič, T. Timan, and B. J. Koops, "Bentham, Deleuze and Beyond: An Overview of Surveillance Theories from the Panopticon to Participation," *Philosophy & Technology* 30 (1) (2017): 9–37.

231 **walls separating work spaces:** Maria Konnikova, "The Open Office Trap," *New Yorker*, 7 January 2014.

231 **lower job satisfaction:** M. C. Davis, D. J. Leach, and C. W. Clegg, "The Physical Environment of the Office: Contemporary and Emerging Issues," in *International Review of Industrial and Organizational Psychology* 26, ed. G. P. Hodgkinson and J. K. Ford (Chichester, UK: Wiley, 2011), 193–235.

231 **less social interaction:** Ethan Bernstein and Ben Waber, "The Truth about Open Offices," *Harvard Business Review*, November–December 2019.

232 **buy train tickets:** Louise Matsakis, "How the West Got China's Social Credit System Wrong," *Wired*, 29 July 2019.

232 **$250 billion and $400 billion:** Eugene Soltes, *Why They Do It: Inside the Mind of the White-Collar Criminal* (New York: Public Affairs, 2016).

232 **twenty-five times more costly:** Stephen M. Rosoff, Henry N. Pontell, and Robert Tillman, *Profit without Honor: White-Collar Crime and the Looting of America* (Upper Saddle River, NJ: Prentice Hall, 2004).

232 **without rigorous checks:** C. Michel, "Violent Street Crime versus Harmful White-Collar Crime: A Comparison of Perceived Seriousness and Punitiveness," *Critical Criminology* 24 (1) (2016): 127–43.

233–234 **"jail the bad guys":** Anas Aremeyaw Anas, undercover journalist, interview, 8 October 2018.

234 **soliciting bribes:** "Accused Ghana Judges Shown Bribe Videos," BBC News, 10 September 2015.

234 **Ahmed Hussein-Suale:** "Journalist Who Exposed Football Corruption Shot Dead in Ghana," Agence France-Presse, 17 January 2019.

234 **put a finger to their lips:** Joel Gunter, "Murder in Accra: The Life and Death of Ahmed Hussein-Suale," BBC News, 30 January 2019.

235 **quickly cleaned up their act:** A. Salisbury, "Cutting the Head off the Snake: An Empirical Investigation of Hierarchical Corruption in Burkina Faso," no. 2018-11, Centre for the Study of African Economies (Oxford: University of Oxford, 2018).

236 **right people *seeing*:** R. Reinikka and J. Svensson, "Fighting Corruption to Improve Schooling: Evidence from a Newspaper Campaign in Uganda," *Journal of the European Economic Association* 3 (2–3) (2005): 259–67.

236 **I Paid a Bribe:** See Y. Y. Ang, "Authoritarian Restraints on Online Activism Revisited: Why 'I-Paid-a-Bribe' Worked in India but Failed in China," *Comparative Politics* 47 (1) (2014): 21–40.

236 **failed the clean test:** M. Bertrand et al., "Does Corruption Produce Unsafe Drivers?," no. w12274, National Bureau of Economic Research, 2006.

238 **precincts that aren't monitored:** N. Ichino and M. Schündeln, "Deterring or Displacing Electoral Irregularities? Spill-

over Effects of Observers in a Randomized Field Experiment in Ghana," *Journal of Politics* 74 (1) (2012): 292–307.

238 **routine drugs bust:** This episode is detailed in Charles Campisi, *Blue on Blue: An Insider's Story of Good Cops Catching Bad Cops* (New York: Scribner, 2017).

239 **"more difficult to steal":** Charles Campisi, former head of Internal Affairs at NYPD, phone interview, 17 March 2020.

240 **twelve times more than the reality:** See Campisi, *Blue on Blue.*

241 **randomly entered into a lottery:** Charlie Sorrel, "Swedish Speed-Camera Pays Drivers to Slow Down," *Wired*, 6 December 2010.

Chapter XIII: Waiting for Cincinnatus

243 **"army were blockaded":** Ernest Rhys, ed., *Livy's History of Rome: Book 3* (London: J. M. Dent & Sons, 1905), http://mcadams.posc.mu.edu/txt/ah/Livy/Livy03.html.

243 **"intent on his husbandry":** Ibid.

243 **"resigned on the sixteenth day":** Ibid.

244 **"opposite practices in everything":** Dionysius of Halicarnassus, *Roman Antiquities*, bk. 10, chap. 17.6.

Index

wealth, signaling behavior for, 69–70

weapons use

agricultural revolution and land defense with, 34–35

evolutionary change and, 24–25

need for hierarchy and, 31–33

physical size differences between males and females and, 25

psychological distance in, 215–17

Weber, Max, 226

WEIRD problem, in research, 158–59

Wenseleers, Tom, 115

Western Kentucky University, 13–14

white-collar crime, 218, 232–33

"white guy in a tie" approach, for business credibility, 61–63

Whitehall II Study, 169–70, 175, 176–77

Williams, George Washington, 120

women

challenge of being first woman as Canadian prime minister, 205

height of, in perception of leadership, 78–79

job application evaluation and, 74

percentage as CEOs, 63–65

percentage in elected positions, 65–66

physical size in perceptions of power of, 75–76

police recruitment and, 50–51, 54–55

recruitment approaches for, 186

research grant funding and, 105

sexist perceptions of power and, 74–75

use of ranged weapons and size of, 25

World War II

dirty hands problem in deciphering codes in, 134–35

fighter plane design in, 38–40

Rosenstrasse protest against detention of Jews during, 216

statistical methods in, 37–38

Yap, Andy, 68

Yong, Ed, 92

Yoo, John, 210–13, 215

Zimbardo, Philip, 11–13, 155